How Do I Get My Ex Back?

The most requested inquiry in this Q&A

book on using The Law of Attraction.

Love Live
Holistically

Logo Created by Ryan Downes

First Edition
2025

About the author

Dr. Angela Scott is a seasoned psychologist and dedicated mother of six adult children. With over 30 years of experience in care and more than 20 of those as a practising psychologist, she has worked across a wide spectrum of settings, supporting individuals with mental health challenges, physical disabilities, and behavioural issues. Her work has included supporting young people, homeless women with complex needs, and adults in recovery from drug and alcohol addiction.

Dr. Scott has also provided compassionate counselling for the elderly, including end-of-life patients and their families. Her deep belief is that every person, with the right support, can reach their full potential, achieving optimal health, discovering their purpose, and even turning their passion into a livelihood.

Today, she offers remote Law of Attraction (LOA) life-coaching sessions and a range of personal development courses. Dr. Scott continues to run her private psychological practice, where she provides individual and couples counselling.

Contact: DrScott@loveliveholistically.com

Other books by the author:

What do you do for a living?

Find and Follow your Passion

Spot and Stop the Resident Bully

SELF=YOU

The Exhorted Soul

Lena Body

Love live holistically – A Concept of Self Love

I am Ready to Manifest Journal

Happiness

Contents

Prologue

This book has evolved from the many questions I receive every day, both personally and through social media about the Law of Attraction (LOA). From those inquiries, I decided to compile the most frequently asked questions into a single resource. My hope is that in these pages, you find not only answers but insights that stir something within you, perhaps even awaken a deeper connection to your own inner self.

As you may have guessed, the book is presented in a question-and-answer format. Some questions may appear similar, but each is answered according to its specific context. You may also notice that similar types of questions appear in different chapters; this is intentional. Each question is placed where it aligns most with its dominant theme, which sometimes requires a more in-depth or nuanced response.

Please note that this book does not include success stories of LOA practices. Rather, it focuses on "how-to" inquiries, those seeking understanding, guidance, hope and at times, a renewed sense of faith about the use of the Law of Attraction itself.

The advice I share is based on what has worked for me. Over 30 years ago, I was introduced to a book that changed my life: *The Game of Life and How to Play It* by Florence Scovel Shinn. Since then, I have given away countless copies—in print, as audio cassettes, PDFs, and now through my website loveliveholistically.com/books.php where it is available along with a YouTube reading by WealthCreationLibrary.
The questions shared in this book come from people of many cultures, backgrounds, and beliefs—from all over the world. They are presented as close to their original wording as possible to honour the authenticity of each inquiry.

Disclosure:

To the best of my knowledge, all questions were submitted by adults and are answered with that understanding. All submissions are anonymous and any identifying information has been removed.

One common point of confusion I often see is between the act of manifesting and the use of the Law of Attraction. For example, people might say, "I'm manifesting my ex back," when in reality, they are using LOA techniques to try to manifest their ex back. The confusion lies in the use of the word "manifesting" as both the end goal and the method. Let's clear that up once and for all: We are manifesting all the time. The Law of Attraction is a method, an aid that helps us shape and direct our manifestations. It brings intention, order and structure as well as alignment with the vibration of what we desire, rather than leaving us to attract based on fleeting thoughts or offhand comments (which often happens!).

I truly hope the questions and responses within these pages inspire you, challenge you, comfort you, and encourage you. Some have brought me moments of deep joy and reflection. I trust they will do the same for you.

Introduction

This book consist of questions relating to the Law of Attraction (LOA), a concept that relies on asking and believing one will receive. My answers come from the wealth of knowledge gained through my everyday practice, a practice taken from the books of the Bible, books written by Florence Scovel Shinn, Wallace D. Wattles, Esther and Jerry Hicks, Eckhart Tolle, Wayne Dyer, Louise Hay, Deepak Chopra, Rhonda Byrne to mention a few. My down to earth approach to answering the questions enables the enquirer to question themselves before taking any advice offered, as most answers begin with practical considerations and a very candid look at the wished for item, situation or person.

The questions often come in the form of how can I magically make this or that appear in my life. I sometimes get the feeling that people believe the LOA is a magical wand that once waved with a few incantations (affirmations) spoken out loud or silently, their wish will be granted. They then wonder why they *haven't manifested.* When in fact we are always manifesting, and have manifested our current situation. Trying to get that fact over in a small space can be challenging.

Manifesting is like breathing, we want to breathe, we believe we will breathe and we expect to be able to take another breath, so most of us ensure that we do not do anything that will stop our breath. If we do, we quickly stop and set about bringing our breathing back to a normal resting state (eupnea). Very rarely do we experience a state in which our breath 'is taken away.' These are often times of great manifestations in our lives, for me, it has often been the contentment on the faces of my children or the way my 7 year old Grandson articulates his love for me, or the view of mountains, a live symphony performance, a picture of a log fire burning at night, in a cosy well stocked library, I could go on but I'll be out of breath! Needless to say, I am sometimes asked to set out a written plan for these breath taking eventualities, unfortunately this is requested without the enquirer realising this is something that could be comfortably experienced, if they would only speak it into existence.

Other requests are made although the enquirer does not believe it will work, some don't really want what they have asked for, or know what they would do with what they have asked for. Others do not believe they deserve to receive their wish or out right *know* they will not have their wish granted, as they state, "I never get what I have asked for." And therein lies the issue, many do not believe the concept of what is said, thought or written down, will appear in their life. Just like ensuring we stay in a state of eupnea (normal, unlaboured, and regular at rest breathing,) we are to be mindful of what we say and do as the moulding powers of our behaviour bring about our everyday manifestations.

Everyday requests come in the form of How can I manifest this? or how can I manifest that?
I am often told;
"I've manifested something I didn't want"
"I've noticed that only horrid people seem to get their wishes granted quickly."
Then there is what some call '*big things'* in the form of money, a new house, car, job, better health etc. None of which is big or small to God/the Universe, but is labelled that way by the enquirer, which in turn places a block between them and the wished for item or situation.

I am sometimes asked, "How do I heighten my vibration or get unstuck," which is in essence a state of mind, this can be challenging to explain or direct a person into a state of euphoria, especially when they are feeling 'low.' Some explain the feeling as "everything is falling apart" or as having "negative thoughts." Negative thoughts feature largely in this book, which is not surprising as it is our thoughts that influence the process and outcome of using the LOA.

Given that we have approximately 60,000 thoughts a day, some are likely to be what people call negative. Being able to *catch* those thoughts before they take hold or have us follow them down a rabbit hole of doubt and fear, takes daily practice.

Helping another feel better, get better or just lend a hand, is also featured in this book, in a chapter called "Can I manifest for someone else." Here the inquires range from can I get my husband to stop drinking? To "How do I ensure my daughter marries well" and "How do I stop my teenage son from moving in with someone my age." As you will see, not all good wishes are for *someone else.*

In-order to help or enhance a manifestation along, many people use other esoteric practices and methods. I teach the Law of Attraction but have received questions on the use of crystals, the moon, Angels and Ark Angels, meditation, the 3,6,9 method, water magick, prayer, journal writing etc. All of which I answer to the best of my ability, with little knowledge of what some may call and use as 'Spiritual basics.' You will be surprised at what some people do, find it doesn't work or find 'it's gone wrong,' then ask me what they did wrong! I am happy that people felt comfortable enough to ask me anything, and do just that in a chapter called 'Ask Me Anything.' I have been asked, "Can I manifest something even if it weren't meant for me?" or "Can I manifest more than one thing at a time" to "What is the biggest struggle when trying to manifest?" Also asked is, "When trying to manifest a qualification, do I have to study?" As well as advice on legal cases. Again, I teach LOA and tend to revert to giving practical advice for practical questions, but with the LOA in mind.

This book is full of everyday questions, answered with everyday solutions and the LOA. You will note that the questions range from the mundane to the spectacular, but there is one subject that will always come up as we are social creatures and have a need to interact with others, that is friendships. Whether that is in a platonic relationship or something more. In the chapter "How do I get new friends" we see that need to belong, the need to have more like minded people in their lives and or form lasting friendships. Once that friendship is formed and a bond made, it is sometimes onerous to put back together once it is broken, so it is no surprise that, the most frequently asked question by far is "How do I get my Ex back." As mentioned above, I ask you to question yourself, in order to first find the answer to that question.
Here's a few:
Does s/he want to come back to you?
What is stopping your ex from contacting you?
Have you learnt anything from the break up?

I get many reasons why the ex left, some from people who have been in a long term relationship, some who have had children together. There are others who have just met what they are calling an SP (Special Person) who is not forthcoming. And others who believe they are in a romantic relationship with a person who 'liked' their post on social media! All reach out and ask "How do I get my Ex back?" Some of the stories are sad, and others just need a chat with a good straight talking friend. All the questions are valid as the enquirers wouldn't feel the need to approach me publicly if they had the answers.

I hope you enjoy the questions and the responses that follow, some may make you laugh, others may stir a touch of sadness, but all are designed to prompt reflection, inviting you to look within and consider what you might do or think differently.

Real Questions. Real Talk.

Chapter One

What is The Law of Attraction?

When we think of the word law we may think of a rule that shouldn't be broken as there could be consequences. For me the Law of Attraction (LOA) is just like the law of gravity, what goes up must come down. When a thought is sent up or out and believed, it must appear in your life, whether it is good for you or not.

According to many, positive thoughts lead to positive outcomes and negative thoughts lead to negative outcomes, others believe that these thoughts are energy and like attracts like, so what you focus on will determine what appears in your life.

I believe the LOA is energy that is always always working, as it is listening and watching. Listening for a wish to be sent out or up and watching for you to act on what you believe regarding that wish.

Before we begin I would like to dispel a few misconceptions, you will notice that some of the questions state that they have been manifesting something, someone or a situation, when in fact they have been attempting to use LOA to manifest that someone, something or situation. Many confuse the tool (LOA) with the result the manifestation. The word manifest means 'clear or obvious to the eye or mind' according to the Oxford language, i.e a manifestation is something that appears.

The other misconception is that LOA is only working when attempting to manifest something, someone or a particular situation. As mentioned above LOA is always working as the thoughts that were believed and acted upon, brought that thing, person or situation into your life. More on that later.

So how does this energy work?

You deliberately/consciously or unconsciously Ask, Believe and Act upon your belief, then you must Receive. That's it.

I believe that The Law of Attraction (LOA) is given to us by God as the bible states "Ask, and it shall be given unto you; seek, and ye shall find, knock and it shall be opened unto you" - Matthew 7:7 (KJV). To me, this verse is a clear reflection of the LOA in action. As I believe that God issued the statement, it follows that God is the one who grant the wishes. Do note that we all have free will, and all that we ask for may not benefit us in the long run, so it is important that you ask aright. I will return to that idea later. For the purposes of this book I will use "God/the Universe" to mean God.

The Process

ASK

One has to ask for what they want, but ask aright. Asking for something that you do not believe you will receive, will not bring about your wish. Asking for something you do not believe you deserve will not bring it into your life. When asking for your want, remember to add "by divine right" or words that resonate with you or your spiritual beliefs. By divine right is taken to mean 'by God's will or amicably received'.

This will ensure that what is meant for you, will be received amicably (i.e no one was hurt or deprived in granting this wish, and you will benefit from this want.) Along with asking aright, one has to be aware of what is voiced regarding this wish, I'll dive deeper into that later.

One of the questions I am often asked is:
"Can you ask for more than one thing at a time?"
Absolutely, yes. I always remind people that if I want a new home or another house, I want all the interior and exterior furniture too. I will need the wall and floor coverings, perhaps the bed sheets and pillows or even the bed. The asked for items or wish does not have to be connected as mine was with the house and its contents. The only thing you need to remember is that the process for all your asks are the same. You ask, believe, take action and wait for it to appear in your life.

Another question you will see explored later is:

"Can I ask or manifest for someone else."

You will have to go and have a look how that works, (or more to the point, if) that works!

BELIEVE

One has to believe that their wish will be granted. As you read the questions, you will notice some mention that their wish was not granted, and go on to tell of their process in using LOA and state or proclaim that their wish was granted to a neighbour, friend, relative or work colleague, as they got the exact amount, make of car, promotion or situation that was wished for. The appearance of their wish in some-ones' garage, a friends' financial wind fall and or change in circumstances meant the 'end' of their manifesting process. If only they continued to believe that their wish was still on its way and took the appearance of their wish albeit with someone else, as a sign of things to come. In fact, what they did is halt the manifesting process by stating (remember what you say about your wish is important)

- "My manifestation turned up next door."
- "My friend or relative got my manifestation."
- "I will never get what I want"
- "Other people always get what I want."

They make these statements, sometimes in anger and most of the time believing what they have uttered. Their actions mirror what they believe. Lets do some quick maths. Here's a simple reminder of the process:
Ask + Believe + Act = Receive. In quick succession they have made a new wish as the declarations above become new, self-fulfilling wishes. In effect, they've just *restarted* the cycle, Asking again (without knowing it), and they continue to see their wants being delivered to people around them. Whenever you ask God/the Universe for something, believe you will receive it, regardless of appearances in your life or situation.

ACTION or Act as if

Here you are asked to take action or and 'act as if'. Action is needed as although it is possible, your wish may not just drop into your lap.

It is at this stage or process that you do all you can to bring your wished for item into your life, you must be asking, "Why have I got to do anything; this is the Law of Attraction after all, shouldn't it just appear?" Sure, but most of us, do not believe that strongly! By acting, you stay on task, or in the vibration of the wanted item, person or situation. By taking action you are doing something (positive) towards getting what you want, whether that is thinking (visualizing) about your want or, in the case of wanting a new car, going out and test driving the car you want. Action is always needed. Whilst action is very important, listening and acting upon guided action is also important, being open to inspired action which are those nudges, gut feelings, or quiet hunches that seem to come from nowhere. Are often divine prompts, leading you directly to what you've asked for.

You may get the urge to visit a friend, on the way to your friend you meet someone who is giving away the item you have wished for. Your hunch may be to apply for a post that you have never considered before, you apply, you interview and, there you are, your wish for a better paying job is granted.

In regard to acting as if, you may wonder, "How can I act as if, without having the item, person or situation in my life?" Depending on your want, acting as if may take on different forms, but just as a child who want a particular gift for that special occasion, you imagine your self with your fulfilled wish. Acting as if is not pretending. It's preparing.

- Who would be the first person you tell when it arrives?
- What would your life be like when your wish appears?
- How would I carry myself?

You would also not worry about your current situation, lets say your current situation is debt and you have wished for a sum of money. It can be challenging to 'act as if' a bill is paid when you are looking at the final notice that has been hand delivered, but you should try. Knowing or believing that the bill will be paid or it will be settled. More on that later. Action also involves doing all you can to bring the wished for item, person or situation into your life. If you wished for a new job, what action do you feel you should take? Right, do look for a job, ask friends and family if they know of any openings at their place of work, apply and attend interviews, but you are using the LOA you already know (or believe) that you will find the right job, at the right pay and the right distance from your home. You know this because this is your wish and you believe you will receive what you have asked for.

Action or acting as if, also involves staying in the vibration of your want. Imagine a magnet, Oxford Languages state is a 'a piece of iron or other material which has its component atoms so ordered that the material exhibits properties of magnetism, such as attracting other iron-containing objects or aligning itself in an external magnetic field.' As I have mentioned above, using LOA is using an energy to attract something, someone or situation into your life. By taking positive action or acting as if allows you to align to what or who you want.

RECEIVE

The final process to using LOA is to receive. What do we do just before we receive something? We wait! I have mentioned above why we wait and what to do while waiting for your wish to be granted. Here's a reminder, it keeps you believing and encourage your want into your life by becoming aligned with you. However, one has to be mindful that we are manifesting ALL the time, and it is at this stage that some people become impatient and start the manifesting process all over again by making a new wish, often one cancelling out the previous wish.
Its as easy as saying:

"I never get what I want"

"This LOA stuff doesn't work"

They then act as if, and or believe what they have said is truth and POW one wish cancelled and another is on its way!
While we wait, like the LOA, life continues to happen! During the waiting to receive stage, a few things may occur. As mentioned earlier you may see your wish, driving along and parking up next door, a friend or family member may win or acquired the exact amount of money you have wished for, there could even be that promotion you want, being given to someone who joined your company after you. Its at this stage you may say to yourself, "what is going on?" what comes after that determine whether you halt the manifesting process, or you see what is going on as a sign of things to come. I know, I make it sound so easy!

This stage can have you losing money, getting bills that you thought you had paid, only to surface when you've made a wish for money. My Son got a bill for £465.00 from a transaction that took place 6 years ago (what's that about)? When you ask for something all of that some-things become aligned with you, so you ask for money, you find a penny (don't start believing this is your manifestation, as you asked for much more). Debts (which is money related) begin to appear in your life, a friend ask you for money, you mislay, or lose money...you get the picture. You are to stay the course and remain believing that your wish is on the way. As life still continues to happen.

Another some what strange occurrence during this waiting stage, is something I call the Breakdown Stage, it is when things seem to go belly up. Things like:

- The boiler breaks down.
- The car stops, well just stops.
- Friends leave your life.
- You leave the lives of others.

This is not punishment. This is preparation, a way of God/the Universe ridding you of things people and sometimes places that don't serve your best interest. That boiler breaking down is making room for the latest model. That car that won't start the minute you voice the idea of getting an updated model, (don't say that the car heard you!) I believe it is the Universe moving it on.

4

Be mindful of your thoughts at this stage, you may be wondering, "How can God/the Universe help me, with one wish when I now have several other wishes as the washing machine has now broken down."

Just trust that everything is actually working in your favour and things will work out.
Again, can you see how easy it would be to halt your manifesting process and start a new one?
It's as easy as saying:
"S***, I'm getting the opposite of what I have asked for."

Should you add your belief to that statement, which for all intents and purposes appears to be true as you do have proof, the car won't start and a final notice to pay is right there in your hand. It would be understandable for you to feel that way, but try to stop yourself...You asked, you believe and you should expect to receive what you have made a wish for.

The How, Who and When

Many people wonder how, who and when at this stage in the manifesting process.
It is understandable to be concerned with the:

- How will it come?

- Who will deliver it?

- When will it arrive?

The how is really none of your business, you've asked aright, you believe your wish will be granted or that your want will appear in your life. The who, you may even get it for yourself, you may find it or be given it. The when, Ah, now this is my favourite part. The *when* is what makes the Law of Attraction so exciting for me. It's like watching a story unfold or waiting to see how a psychological mystery movie ends.
As you are now in the waiting stage you may begin to realise that most things in your life are magnified, as you keep a close eye on what comes in, what goes out, who leaves, who you walk away from etc. This enhanced ability to see, hear and feel what is going on around you, is you going within. It's a kind of meditative state, (if done correctly) as you concern yourself with affirmations, visualization, and grounded routines which may become essential tools that help you stay focused and away from any doubt or doubters that may come near.

So here's how you will get your wish using the LOA.
Someone may just give it to you. You may be offered a better paid job enabling you to buy the item you want. You may be led to shop in a different town to the one you live in or frequent, and find the item at a knock down price or on sale. In voicing your want to others when led to do so, (and I do mean *led*, not just randomly telling everyone) you are putting your wish 'out there' for others to get it for you and as mentioned above, they may know someone who knows someone who may be giving that item away or at a price you can afford, so that is where the "who" part gets answered.

It might be a friend.
A stranger.
A colleague.
Or even you, guided to exactly the right opportunity at the right moment.

The when, is whenever it arrives. No one goes to a posh restaurant, order food and continuously ask the chef when is the food going to arrive on the table. They wait, knowing that it will arrive, and that it will be worth the wait. In fact like you, they arrived at the restaurant (deciding to use LOA) they were guided to their seat (maybe you was also shown the way to using the LOA) they ordered (Asked aright) after which they believed they would get what they ordered. Note, not for a split second did the restaurant goers believe they would not get what they ordered. They then sat acting as expected in this posh restaurant (Action and or Act as if) and waited for their meal to arrive. While they are waiting for their food, they may notice that the table beside them had ordered the same meal, on the sight of the same order being delivered to the next table, (being aligned with your want) they do not begin to believe or say that they will not get their food, as their order has gone to someone else, they continue to wait and note how nice the food looked,

in fact they used it as a sign that their meal will be just as nice. Whilst rubber necking the next tables' food one of the restaurant goers accidentally knocks a glass of water over (life situations). They still believe their food will be cooked and brought to their table. (like many people attempting to use LOA, here is another instance when they believe that their wish will not be granted, and may decide to wish for help with their current immediate need, whilst claiming that the previous wish is never going to come, instead of just requesting a dry table cloth!) Whilst back at the restaurant the waiter arrives at the table and in a second, the table cloth is changed, clean dry cutlery is replaced along with glasses which are re-filled with water. After all that, they still wait for their meal, as nothing that had occurred at the tables mean their order has been cancelled. If you stay seated in the belief and trust that what you asked for is being "prepared" just for you, both you and the restaurant goers will receive.

DETACHMENT

This is a little known or unconsciously used process of the LOA that many people utilise to get results very quickly, you will see the effects of detachment in some of the questions. Detachment is not forgetting about your want or not thinking about it. Detachment is not thinking or worrying how, when or why it will happen, a person who has detached know their want will come, they also act 'as if' the wanted situation, person or item has arrived and without a doubt it appears in their life.

Here is an example of detachment for an everyday occurrence, lets say you ask: "I want a good parking space today," you get in your car not thinking about any parking spaces. You do not think about whether there are lots of shoppers out today, you don't worry about having to reverse into a space or whether someone is going to park so close to you that you'll have to climb over the passenger seat in-order to get into the driver seat, when you arrive back at your car. None of that, you just drive to your destination knowing you will get a good parking space, in fact you act as if you will get a good parking space. You arrive at your destination and voilà, there is your 'good' parking space.

Here is using detachment for unwanted situations, you state in anger or annoyance that "I'll never find a good place to park at this shopping mall, as I have never found a good place to park at this mall." You also get in your car, but this time, you know like you know that there will be no good parking spaces, you really don't even have to think of all the ways you will be hindered from having a good parking experience, because you have detached and already have your 'back up'.

In fact you are acting as if you won't find a good parking space, before you even arrive at the mall. On arrival you found that there is no good or any parking spaces.

Both drivers stated or Asked, both Believed and Acted 'as if' and then Detached. One already knew what would happen and the other was open to having their wish granted. In fact they both had their wish granted! Here is a new equation to using the LOA **Ask, Believe, Detach, Action or Act as if = Receive.** The difference with using this formula is results appear quicker! Truly believe you will get what you have asked for, but be open to it or something better, being open is 'letting go' or detaching.

So, you have read the basics of using the Law of Attraction. You now need to be aware of your thoughts, speech and deeds. Why don't you try LOA for yourself? Try the £1 test, Ask for a pound or dollar, whatever your currency is and wait for it to appear, this can turn up in an old purse, a coat pocket, in an ad for a pound off, in your inbox as a voucher, someone may buy you a coffee worth a £. Try it this week.

Now let's go answer some questions.

Real Questions. Real Talk.

Chapter Two

How Do I Get More Money?

We start off with the request of money, many want more of it! However, some do not know how much they want or what they will do with it when it arrives. Some don't really believe they will get it or feel they deserve it. This is a strange thing to say, as one wonders why they would ask for something they don't believe they will get.

Consider this....do you believe that many, if not most people you know, would like a million pounds? Yeah sure they would, then when you delve a little further, you find that they wouldn't know what they would do with a million pounds. Digging further, you find that some believe they will never see a million pounds in their bank account, or own anything worth that much. More investigation shows that the person asking for a million pounds do not believe they deserve the money, let alone know what they would do with it.

How do you support someone with that thought pattern? First you look at what they say or in this instance write down, regarding their want, as many people show or say how they really feel about receiving their want, before they even start the process of using the Law of Attraction (LOA). " I know this is difficult but..." springs to mind. Or "I know I shouldn't ask but..." The first enquirer here, has immediately put a block between themselves and their want. The second doesn't really believe they deserve what they are asking for.

It is important that you Believe, Believe, Believe. Believe in what you have asked for. Meaning: believe what you have asked for is set aside for you (the amount of money, the house, the car, the shoes, the watch etc..) Believe you should have or deserve what you are asking for and Believe it will manifest in your life. Then there is keeping the momentum going. It is surprising how many people wish their wish away by what they say, when they think they are not going to get their wish, as it's taking too long or feel that their wish has been 'given' to someone else. Using the LOA has a few main steps, Ask, Believe, Action and Receive, if at any point and regardless of what is happening in your life, throughout these steps, you faulter, your wish will not be granted, as you make a new wish that begins its way to you.

Enjoy the read, and I hope you learn something about the way you request money using the LOA.

Do you have any advice for me, because have a problem in trying to get money.

Here's how to use the Law of Attraction: All you do is Ask, Believe and you will Receive. There are other processes, but the basics are above. Ask for something you deem 'small'. Believe and wait for it to appear.

The Law of Attraction is always working, you are manifesting all the time, what you manifest is up to you.

Try the £1 test, Ask for a pound or dollar, whatever your currency is and wait for it to appear, this can be in an old purse, a coat pocket, in an ad for a pound off, in your inbox as a voucher, someone may buy you a coffee worth a £. Try it this week.

How do you manifest money? It sounds so greedy, but I have bills I need paid off, I don't want to work forever to pay bills but for fun and exciting things.

Thank you for the question. *"How do you manifest money?"* Ask for it, you know what you want, so ask for it! Stating that *"It sounds so greedy"* immediately adds doubt to your wish for money, doubt and worry about how, when or whether I am worthy will not bring your wish to you.

You need to start your wish strong, It is not greedy, no one wants to look at their future and only see bills and work, You should be mindful of your words, *"I have bills I need paid off,"* saying this, will have you needing to pay off bills, instead state *"my bills will be paid off."* Saying *"I don't want to work forever to pay bills"* will keep you in the state of not wanting to work forever to pay bills. State that I work for *"fun and exciting things."* It will take some time to ensure you believe what you are saying, but if you say it enough times you will get there.

Now prepare for this money, what will you do with it, make lists, where will you go; who will go with you. What will you buy? Ask for what you want and believe it will come, don't worry about how or when it will come, just know it is coming.

How do you attract money?

You ask for it! ensure that you ask for an amount that you believe you will manifest. Then go about your day expecting it.

This money may turn up as an approved loan, money owed to you that you hadn't expected, a raise at work, just be open to how it comes.

Listen for guided instructions, for example you may be guided to apply for that job you had been looking at, or sell that item you have been holding on to.
Perhaps you get the urge to buy a lottery ticket.

Make a list of the the things you will buy when you get the money, on paper, in your notes on your phone or in your mind.

Think about who you will tell first when you get the money you want, where will you go to celebrate, keep your thoughts positive when you think about the money you have asked for.

How do I manifest a large sum of money?

You ask, believe, act and you will receive your *"large sum of money."* However, you need to be able to state/know deep down why you want the item, or situation to appear in your life. Your want can be....

"I want that pair of shoes, because I really like them"

"I want that new house because I'd like to live in that neighbourhood"

"I want a coffee because I fancy a hot beverage, when I get that hot beverage am going to drink it, it will make me feel warm"!

When I get that pair of shoes, I am going to wear it to that event I have been invited to."

So here are some questions for you:
How much is *"a large sum of money?"*
What do you need *"a large sum of money"* for?
What will you do with your *"large sum of money?"*
Who will benefit from your *"large sum of money?"*

Before you can ask for what you deem *"a large sum of money"* you need to know a little about the asked for item and what you intend to do with it, having answered the questions above honestly, you then ask for it, believing you will receive it. Then listen or beware of any guided action you are to take, this can be something like...apply for that job, you have seen advertised, start a business, sell that item you have had in the attic for years...This is God/the universe helping you get that *"large sum of money."*

The job may pay a large sum of money for joining the company, your business may take off the minute you start advertising, that artefact you had forgotten about in your attic, is now worth 'a large sum of money.'

When you have done all you believe you can to bring this money into your life, you wait...While waiting you believe it will come. Take the fact that you found a penny on the ground as a sign your money is coming, in fact take anything that involves money (going out or coming in) as a sign your 'large sum of money' is coming.

What steps we need to take to double our income effortlessly?

Thank you for your question, you both should ask for your incomes to be doubled! The process is always Ask, Believe take Action or act as if and wait to Receive, it is the same for anything you want using the LOA.
As you both already appear to have an income and would like to double that income, I would suggest you both take practical steps regarding your current income.

Ask your boss for a raise, is there overtime you could do (Oh! you asked for effortlessly), so more work may not be something you both considered!
Do you run your own business; is there other products you can sell?

After you have considered what you can practically do to double the income you already have, ask God/the Universe for your income to be doubled effortlessly.

Believe your incomes will be doubled, consider what you both will do with the added income. Start making a list, will you pay off your house, if you have a mortgage; will you both go on more holidays? Know what you will do with the money when it arrives.

Follow any hunch each of you may have and wait believing. Note I have written this reply concerning you both! As you both need to follow the advice given above. One partner can not double the income of another, you should double yours and your partner double theirs.

I am currently facing a financial crisis and require immediate assistance in the form of money. How can I manifest quickly?

Good Afternoon, sorry to hear that you are *"facing a financial crisis."* In order to manifest quickly, you have to ensure that you do not state, utter or think situations that you don't want.

Anything said after I AM is a wish and is happening or will happen. We also should not demand our wants, i.e *"require immediate assistance."* If your situation is dire, you need to do what you can do, to help yourself, for example ask friends or family to help.

When using the Law of Attraction one has to be willing to trust that any or every situation will work out in their favour and not claim to have the solution to it. Did you consider the idea that your financial *"crisis"* can be averted? Instead we often decide we know how to correct the issue ourselves, which is understandable as right now, you feel that you have *"a financial crisis."*

As mentioned above you have to be willing or open to have your situation come to an amicable end. Let me explain. Lets say you feel that £20,000 will alleviate the *"financial crisis"* you believe you are in. You can ask for £20,000 or you could ask for your financial issue to be solved, leaving it to God/the Universe to solve the issue in your favour. It would seem you would rather have the £20,000 to sort the issue yourself.

This is why it is important to ask aright, is there a possibility that you get the £20,000 and have a more dire situation that warrants you to pay out the money you received or more to solve it?

Before attempting to use the Law of Attraction one has to take all practical steps before asking, believing and trusting that the situation will be resolved. Listen and take guided action, knowing that your situation will be solved.

Dr Scott
I am really sorry I am sending you again a query, however I am unable to phrase my wants to universe. I mean I want to end my debt and lead a lavish life which requires wealth or money now how do I phrase my words?

Example : Should I say "Thank you almighty I want to end my debts and live a lavish lifestyle" or I want money in-order to do this?
Please could you guide me through this toughest block ahead.

Thank you for the question.
You should say what *feels* comfortable and real to you.

Saying *"Thank you almighty I want to end my debts and live a lavish lifestyle,"* keeps you open, meaning you do not put any restriction on God/the Universe who will send what is best for you, thus sending you an end to your debts and the ability to live a lavish lifestyle.

Being thankful that your debts have ended and you are living a grand lavish life, is also great, but you really have to believe this and act 'As If' you are living this way. It is all about really believing and feeling what you say or ask for until it becomes true to you.
Whereas if you say I want a certain amount of money, you could see this money come in only to have to pay that amount out!

I understand that you are finding this part of the process challenging, however one has to ensure they do not speak lack or put stumbling blocks on the LOA process from the start.

Stating that this is the *"toughest block ahead,"* starts the whole process off with a struggle. Be-aware of anything you say regarding your want, as you are aware that words have moulding powers, otherwise you wouldn't be here asking me how to phrase an affirmation!

How do I attract a lottery win?

Do you believe that you will win the lottery?

I don't know.

Then you will not win/attract a lottery win. Start by considering what you do know about what you want.
How much do you call a lottery win?
What will you do with the money?
Will it be enough money to retire?
Do you want enough to buy a house?
Do you want enough to give to grown up kids?
Do you want enough to give to elderly parents or give to charity?

Many feel that 'a lot of money' will allow them to live the life of their dreams, and many do, because they had a dream before they got the money. What's your dream? When you have taken the time to think seriously about what you want, then you are able to tailor your manifestation to the life you would like to live, it will then come into your life harmoniously and stay there. Here's the basics again. Ask, (know what you want and why) Believe, Act (you must do something to get this lottery win, this could even mean just buying a lottery ticket if you are guided to do so) Receive - be willing to receive the money you want from the many different sources God/the Universe has to deliver your want to you.

Do you think lottery winners always think they will win.
I do not believe that all lottery winners know they are going to win,

although we all hope we will win, as we wouldn't spend money on the ticket knowing we will not win. I know quiet a few lottery winners who was given guided instructions (a hunch) to go and buy a lottery

ticket or scratch off and won big. I believe some people have a strong sense that they will win big.

Here's another question? If they are desperate for money, do they need to feel okay with being poor or do they need to feel rich despite it to win?

When asking for anything, being desperate will get you more of *'being desperate.'* Remember what you think about or desperate about will come about. If you are okay with being poor then you're okay with being poor, you are not desperate for anything you're okay.

We may need to distinguish what you call *'poor.'* I take it you mean living without a lottery jackpot win! Most of the time when we want something, we are with out that something, we may be grateful for what we have but would like more or other things.

The need or want for more makes us by definition, not okay with our current situation and or items that we possess. There has to be some feelings or urge for that something more, that urge impedes us from feeling okay, so one does not *'need to feel okay with'* their current situation in-order to win or have a wish granted.

The second part of your question *"do they need to feel rich despite it to win?"* It can be challenging to 'feel' rich when you have never been rich, but because you want to be rich, you will have an idea of what that may feel like. Visualizing what your life will be like when you get that big win, will help here, as you begin to live in the vibration of what you want.

So one can not be desperate when asking for something, if you're happy with your current situation, you'll stay in that situation, However if you are happy with your situation but want more, you can get that too by Asking, Believing and visualizing a big win will get you closer to your want, and of course buying (Action) a lottery ticket!

Hi, I'm very unlucky when it comes to money currently in tones of debt and want to get better hold of money. I find it hard to bring up my vibration sometimes & I've loads of crystals I just can't connect.

Thank you for the question. Sorry you feel you are *"very unlucky when it comes to money."* It is important that we are mindful of what we say and how we feel when saying it. We are all mega manifestors, you have managed to manifest being *"very unlucky when it comes to money,"* because that is what you believe, so it has no choice but to show up in your life. That is actually how the LOA works...You Ask (or say a thing) You Believe (a saying) and so You Receive it Simple! I understand that speaking positively about something that we feel is negative in our lives, as it can be challenging to believe it. But what we can do is re-word that negative aspect of our lives, in such a way, that we believe it.

For example:
"I have been unlucky when it comes to money, but things are going to change."
Find ways to make it believable to you. *"Currently in tons of debt"*

is not true, do you know how much a 'tonne' weights? An actual Tonne! I know its just a 'saying' but that 'saying' may be keeping you in a lot of debt! Remember what we think and say, we attract.

Change that narrative to something like 'I will become debt free' even if you add 'someday' to the end of that sentence, it will be a true statement of your current situation.

"Wanting to get a better hold of money" has you 'wanting' it and never 'getting'! It also implies that money goes, slips or runs away from you! Although this may be how you see things now, it is really important that we think about what we say at all times, this may take some doing, but what we say directs our lives, then we wonder why things are not working the way we would like.
You state:
"I find it hard to bring up my vibration."

I totally understand, being in debt (at the moment) isn't something that makes you want to jump and dance about, but deciding to do something about it, may have you feeling better about it. On a practical note, do what you can to address what debt you have (see professional debt organisations) find ways to earn more money...But above ALL of that BELIEVE that you will become debt free.

So I asked the universe for my business to hit a million pound. But I struggle massively trying to imagine myself having that or myself living with that. I try really hard but I find it hard to be on the same wave length as what I want.

So find a number that you are comfortable with, half a million; one hundred thousand?
Find a number that resonates on the *"same wave length as what [you] want,"* not a number you have picked out of thin air.

Then do the work:
How will you attempt to generate this money, if you sell a product.
Will you be able to produce the items that warrants the amount of money you want?
What do you need the money for?
Who will benefit from this money; You, your family, the business?
How much will you plough back into the business?
What will you buy or pay for first?

Before you ask to generate a million pounds (or the amount you feel comfortable with), you need to know a little about the asked for item and what you intend to do for and or with it. Having answered the questions above honestly, you then ask for it, believing you will receive it, you then listen or beware of any guided action you are to take. Then you wait.

Hi, how to stay in the vibration of asking for money when there is so much lack around my area?

Hi, thank you for your question. You stay in the mood of the money.

You are asking for money or gain, do not focus on lack. When someone starts to speak lack, change the subject, if you live in an area that appears less rich than you'd like, go to a corner of a park that looks lush and green.

What ever you do (going to work, going shopping) act 'AS IF'. Dress as if you have the money you want, visit stores, window shop or do it virtually.

Start making your list of things you will buy when you get the money you want. Amazon has a wish list facility! Other stores have the same.

You may not be able to change the area you live in, but you can control or steer your thoughts towards the money you want. You can also create a space in your home, that feels lush or abundant.

Take a small bathroom, you can make that into a space that makes you feel abundant every-time you walk in there. Or perhaps a small corner of your bedroom, think of an area where you live or in your home that allows you to block out the lack you believe you have around you and spend time there.

Staying in a certain vibration is like becoming a child again, remember when you use to make believe, you was a singer, doctor, astronaut! You conjured up the audience, the patients and the moon and would most likely visit it at least once a day.

Getting or staying in the vibration is doing just that, picture yourself with what you want and how it will make you feel, as an adult we may need prompts like the lush park area or that abundant looking bathroom, do what you can to keep the image alive, but most importantly, keep believing your want will come.

I have a 6 yr old who is always wanting stuff. How do I phrase we don't have the money without repeatedly saying that. I'm at the point that I feel like I'm making it so because I have to tell him we don't have this or that so many times throughout the day.

Thank you for the question, it can be challenging when you have children that want, want want and you are unable to provide some of the things they have asked for.
You could say:

"We can not buy that right now"
"That is not something we are going to buy right now"
"We won't be buying that right now"
"'We will be able to get that soon"

Your 6 year old will want to know, when you'll be able to buy it. Maybe during the winter holidays, maybe during the spring or summer holidays. Find words that are positive, find practical things you can do around the asking and saying we will get that soon! Start a wish list with your 6year old, show him the amazon wish list and add his wants to it, discuss which one he wants first, you may find that he begins to ask for some-things to be removed from the wish list.

By actively 'doing' something (Action) towards your childs' want you are showing God/the universe that you expect to be able to buy these items. I'd actually put them in my basket on different sites. Ask, believing you will be able to buy some of your 6 year olds wants and the item or the money to buy them will appear.

Say I ask for $500, then a day later, I will make a sale for $50 or I read the local paper that is someone in my town who won $500. It never quite works for me. And it's not because of my belief that it won't work as I've tried with an open heart for ages.

Thank you for the question. Two things may be happening here: Just before a manifestation, things may seem to go wrong or what I call the 'Breakdown stage'.

When everything seem to go belly up! It is at this stage many people halt their manifestations, by proclaiming that *"It never quite works for me,"* or begin to voice their frustrations causing the whole process to begin again.

The voiced frustration is a wish (Ask) the frustration is believed, then they detach from the situation (part of the process most do not use, or use it unconsciously). Then unwanted situations will appear, and so much quicker than other wishes.

The other thing that is happening is PROOF has just showed up that your manifestation is on it's way... a situation I call 'a penny instead of a pound.' When a penny shows up after I have asked for money, I take it as a sign money is coming! Voicing destain or annoyance, *"It never quite works for me"* is voicing a wish that your manifestation hasn't come or will not come, but $50 has turned up instead, is stating that you believe and accept that you got a penny instead of a pound and the end of that wish, which re-starts the process with a new wish.

Many people will find out that the person down the street, received the exact amount they had been wishing for, or their colleague got the job, car or house they wanted, you for instance read *"about someone else in your town who won $500!"* again proof that your $500 was on its way. How did you take that news? for me, its proof my manifestation is on its way...Why? Because news of $500 has entered my ear shot or eye sight, funny how its the exact amount I wished for! Its a sign. As your wish for $500 has not yet appeared in your life, remain expectant and it will come.

Response From Enquirer

Thank you Angela for your kind reply! So if the $50 keeps turning up, it's a sign.... But what if it never steps up to the next level?! Are you saying if I stay positive, it definitely will? It hasn't yet and I've tried for years?

I don't know your situation, but I hope you haven't been trying to manifest $500 *"for years"*! Getting to the next level, I don't know what that is for you, but here's what I would do. I would start today insisting that that *"next level"* is on its way and prepare for it in any way I can, if it is more productivity in my business I would:
Seek out people in the same business and get some advice, this can be from youtube.
If I have a physical store, make the place look more appealing to passers-by.

Your 'level up' could be a promotion at work, you should:
Prepare for it.
Do what you can.
Always knowing and beliving that you will get what you have asked for.

If it is a large sum of money:
Prepare for it, in your mind.
How much do you want?
Who would you tell first?
What will you buy with it?
Who will benefit from you getting this money?
Believe that it will come, do not write or say anything that is not positive about getting it, know what you have asked for will come.

I'm diving deep into the world of manifesting and changing my belief system around everything, but especially money and finances. My husband and I have children and have always struggled financially. I've been making a lot of progress and am seeing things change and shift, however, my husband doesn't think the same.
He often says things like "we don't have the money" "we can't do that, we don't have money" "we are never going to have money" etc. He is VERY pessimistic and doesn't want to change his thoughts around money. We don't have money? Well we don't have money, end of conversation."
So my question is, can I still get abundance and financial freedom for me and my family, even if my husband has limited beliefs and is constantly sharing them with me? I try to ignore it and just continue with my beliefs but of course that's difficult when your other half thinks completely opposite of you (especially because he's the one that makes the money).
I feel like there is one last blockage before getting to my final destination, could it be him? How can I break through that blockage myself?

Thank you for sharing this with us and asking the question. It is great to know that you are "*diving deep into the world of manifesting and changing belief system[s] around everything, [ ] especially money and finances.*" This is a great start. The next step to manifesting anything is 'saying it', you will change the way you think about money, because you have said it and believe in the change you are attempting to make.

Having to hear "*we don't have the money,*" "*we can't do that, we don't have money,*" "*we are never going to have money*" or "*Well, we don't have money, end of conversation,*" can be challenging when attempting to change the life you have been living for some years.

However, just wanting, believing it will change will change it. Note that we have covered the first two basic steps to manifesting, that is: Ask and Believe. In order to Receive, one has to do some work, in your case there are at least two things you can consider.

Firstly - Every time your husband makes a statement that is not productive to encouraging money into your lives, make a counter statement, this can be an affirmation that resonates with you, or simply say "at the moment."

This can be said out loud, under your breath or in your mind. "at the moment" ends your husbands' statement, he may not know that but you do, you're the believer.

As humans, we tend to look for proof, that what we believe is the way things are going to be.

Many look to their parents and note that their life wasn't so great, so it follows that the life they are currently living may not be too great, and they add, their future may not be destine for anything good either! (Not sure why people think or speak damnation over their future, but they do)!

The same could be said of the life your husband is living at the moment, if things are challenging regarding money, we tend to think it will stay that way, especially if you are the only person bringing in the money.

Think about it, you work 12 hour shifts, you feel that there isn't anything else you can do with the rest of the time you have left in a day. You too would proclaim that *"we are never going to have money,"*

because you just can't see this changing and the proof comes in the form of the money you bring in and the bills it has to payout. Let's give him some proof that things does not have to remain the way it is, as we look at the second thing you could consider.

Secondly - I understand that you are not working, but there are many things you can do to bring some money into your home....I will not go into it here, but you could find online work that you could do when the children are at school or in bed. Even if its enough to pay for the childrens' treats on the weekend, you will begin to take some of the financial burden off your husband, he in turn will begin to see that *"we are never going to have money"* isn't true, as we now have money for the childrens' treats. In attempting to make some money will also show God/the Universe that you want more!

While trying to find a way of generating some more money into your household, start thinking of how happy the children will be when you state, we are going out for ice-cream or whatever event that is not the norm at the moment. Think of how you will feel when you say to your husband 'I've got this' as he goes to pay for something he normally pays for. I do not know your situation or whether an online job will be possible for you, but I do know you have access to the internet, as you're here now! There are also things you could do within your neighbourhood, go have a look...The mere fact that you begin to look for ways of making more money will bring money making ways your way.

You ask: *"I feel like there is one last blockage before getting to my final destination, could it be him? How can I break through that blockage myself?"* You have already broken through whatever block you had, the hard part was believing that you deserve more, and that it is possible to get more. Just getting people there, is challenging enough.
Your husband is not a block, he is doing what he feels he can do.
So if he isn't a block and you're not a block, all that is left is to do something about your current situation while believing whatever you try will yield more money.

I'm struggling with time frames at the moment and maybe I'm not clear enough because of my time frames. I'm very busy manifesting a certain amount of money, i know how I'm receiving it and what I'm doing with it. I'm currently needing a car while I'm waiting for the money, any car will do. Should I start concentrating more on the temporary car rather than the money? Can you manifest more than 1 thing at a time?

Thank you for the question, You should ask, then leave it to God/the universe to bring it to you. There is no need to "*concentrate*" on any of your wants. Ask for what you want and make space for it. You state that you know how you will receive a 'certain amount of money'. Although you are open to receiving a "*any car will do*" vehicle! Do you realize that a brand new car could be in your future, you sell the car (for money) and you buy a used or cheaper brand new car, so now you have both the money and the car?

Why limit yourself to something that you class as "temporary" and why would you drive something that is temporary? The word temporary, to you may mean, until I can get a better car. As I have mentioned to others we have to be aware of what we say regarding our wants. I believe that the word temporary and car shouldn't be used in the same sentence, for me it conjures up a car that is likely to break down, while I'm at a stop sign or on the motor way.

There is nothing overly positive about the word temporary in-regard to a vehicle that will hold your life and the life of others, maybe I am too deep, but that's just the way I see it. Perhaps you feel that as you have asked for money and you know it is on its way, you do not deserve a 'permanent' car or you deserve a lesser gift or wish to be granted. God/the Universe has unlimited funds and cars!

Ask for what you want, do not find comfort in the fact you think you know where part of your want is coming from, God/the universe may have bigger better plans for you! After asking, believe you will receive.

You state that you know what you intend to do with the money, that's great.

Now start preparing for the money and get ready for that car, buy a car scent to put in the car when it arrives, clear out your garage if you have one, tell friends and family that you are looking for a car. Look in the ads for cars, you could even test drive the type of car you want. (although I'm not sure they will be legally allowed to sell temporary ones)!

If I want a new home I want everything that goes with that new home, as my old furniture may look out of place....I want new beds, a new sofa, maybe rugs...perhaps new window treatments...see where i'm going with this? You can ask for as many things as you believe you will receive...and that's just it, you ask, no need to concentrate on one thing or the other, you need and want both so ask for both believing you deserve both.

Hi Angela I am a 41 year old Male. Recently due to crisis I lost my money and was in debt. Currently I have applied for a bank loan to get me back on track but the approval is pending for long. Could you manifest or guide me the process where I could get the loan amount ASAP. Would be very grateful to you. Thanks

I am sorry to hear that you feel you lost money.
Take a deep breath, you'll get the money back. Your money is not lost, it will find you.

Stop thinking about a LOAN amount but think about the AMOUNT you want.
Thinking that YOU LOST something sends a message to God/the Universe that you may lose anything that is given to you.

You did not lose the money (Unless you bet on a horse and it lost, and even then...The horse lost NOT YOU). Money is suppose to come into your hands and go out of your hands. You can not lose anything that is meant for you. OK with that said, here are some questions for you:

How much do you need?
What do you need the money for?
What will you do with the money?
Who will benefit from the money?

Before you can ask for anything, you need to know a little about the asked for item and what you intend to do with it.

Having answered the questions above honestly, you then ask for it, believing you will receive it, you should listen or beware of any guided action you are to take, this can be something like, applying for a loan(as you have done) it could be that you are to apply for that job you have seen advertised, start a business, sell that item you have had put away for years...This is God/the universe helping you get that money.

The job may pay the money you need, for joining the company, your business may take off the minute you start advertising, that artefact you had forgotten about is now worth the money you want.

When you have done all you believe you can to bring this money into your life, you wait...While waiting you believe it will come. Take the fact that you found a penny on the ground as a sign your money is coming, in fact take anything that involves money (going out or coming in) as a sign your money is coming.

Can someone help me. money has been stolen from me twice by someone i know. how can i have attracted it? How can i prevent this from happening again? how can i get this money back?

Hi, So sorry to read that you have had money stolen from you twice, by someone you know. On a practical note, do you think you may be too trusting? It may be wise to ensure that your bank card or whatever you store money in, is placed in a safe place when you have visitors to your home. If the theft has occurred via your bank details, ensure you have passwords that are only known to you and be aware of your surroundings when entering your pin or password.

In regard to using the Law of Attraction, what are your thoughts on keeping or losing money? As I do not know the actual circumstances that you 'lost' money I can only give you assumptions.

A person that hoards money will have the mindset that it may be taken from them, or they may never have and keep enough...Money will be stolen or taken from them, in one way or another.

A person that don't really care whether they keep the money they have, and spends it recklessly...Money will leave their possession recklessly (ie stolen or what is bought may be of no or ill use).

A person who values their money and ensure that it is safe and well spent, may also have money stolen from them, but they know it will return, via the bank, the company who took the money (this can happen when a company charges twice, innocent mistake.) or the same amount given back to them in a surprising way! Know that you will receive the stolen money back, and keep what you have safe.

Whenever I think about money, it comes in the way of debt and loan. Now it has become huge amount of debt. Why is it happening this way. Is there any solution to change it?

Thank you for the question. Here's the thing, if you ask for money, all manner of bills will turn up, debts that you had forgotten about lands in your mail box. You find that you are not able to make as much money as you normally make. Anything to do with money starts appearing in your life. You have aligned with money, money you owe, money that you could generate in the form of loans, you may even find that people you know are asking to loan money from you.

At this stage you wonder what is going on or ask *"Why is it happening this way."* As mentioned above, you have aligned with anything to do with money in your life. You are to 'keep the faith' and realise that as your wish hasn't yet materialised, it is still on its way.

This can be frustrating as you feel you have completed the steps and the opposite appears to be happening. It is these frustrations that cause many to halt their manifesting process and make a new wish.

Remember it is what we believe that brings our manifestations into our reality. If you start off by believing *"Whenever I think about money, it comes in the way of debt and loans,"* what do you think your reality will be, whenever you think or ask for money? If you get to the stage where a debt appears after asking for money, you end the manifestation process for that wish, as you believe (and wrote down) *"my manifestation has come in the form of debt."* Here you resigned yourself to the fact that you are not going to get your wish, and that was the end of the manifesting process. If you found a penny after asking for money, would you believe your wish was granted? I hope not, as I believe you would have asked for much more. Finding a penny or any money related issue that surfaces, should be used as a sign that your manifestation is on the way.

As mentioned to many in this forum, 'keep the faith' or keep believing your manifestation is on the way, know that this is just another stage of manifesting, know that regardless of what is happening you have asked, believed so it must come.

Hi, I'm new to this and I realized I manifested and I got soooo excited! I wanted to make donuts for my kids; I went online and searched for recipes and realized that due to the time needed for proofing, it was too late to start. So I said okay maybe I'll make them tomorrow morning. And the next morning I remembered about the donuts, but was feeling a bit lazy. But I still wanted them. So again i said, maybe later. But guess what. 2 hours later, my in laws dropped by, with some snacks, and in there was 2 donuts. Not 16 like what I wanted to make, but just enough for my girls. One each for them. And i thought to myself, I think i just manifested that! And I know, the universe is just giving me a glimpse, showing me how it's done.
That I can do the same thing to stuff no matter how big or small, and it will grant it for me. It cements my belief in LOA.

I'm wondering, I want to manifest an x amount of money because I want to use it for ABC. Should I just manifest the x, because with the x I can do the ABC, or the ABC, because it would mean I have manifested the x, or both?
Also, I'm a housewife. So when I think of the x amount, I'm visualizing my husband getting it and then he passes it to me (because he always passes me most of his money for me to handle like paying the bills and stuff). Does it work that way? Cuz it's like i'm manifesting for him but I can only manifest for myself right.

Hi, Thank you for the question. You have just described how you wanted doughnuts for your daughters, being a housewife, or having your husband bring you what you wanted, did not enter your head when you thought of manifesting the doughnuts. They turned up accompanied by your in laws! That is how the Law of Attraction works, you ask for what you want, believing it will arrive and you get on with your day! You also displayed 'detachment' which is a vital component of manifesting, and one which most people find challenging to do.

You asked, believed and (detached) that is, you did not worry, or think of how you would get the doughnuts, you carried on with your day to day activities. When asking for anything that would benefit others, we just ask, when asking for anything that will be purely for ourselves, we just ask. We do not add how, who or when to the equation,

just ask, believing that God/the Universe knows how to produce and bring the wish to materialise in our lives.

What's the Hardest Part about Manifesting Abundance into your life?

Thank you for your question, it seems a little strange to me, as people do not normally ask what makes Law of Attraction not work, they tend to want to know what works and how to make it happen quickly. I will answer your question, but there are a few things that would need to be established, in order to answer your question.

What do you class as *"Abundance?"* Depending on the part of the world you live in may determine what you class as 'Abundance'! Let me assume some answers to the questions I have posed for you. To answer the *"Hardest part about manifesting"* bit of your question. There are no hard parts, you Ask, Believe, Act and Receive...Simple as that. The *"hard part"* for you may not be 'hard' for another person, as what is believed is personal to the individual, it is this belief that determines whether a wish becomes a reality.

Here's how you conjure up 'hard.' You start off believing there must be a *"hardest part about manifesting abundance into your life."* You don't ASK aright, you don't really BELIEVE you'll get or deserve what you have asked for, with those two actions down, you don't take ACTION or ACT as if you are going to RECEIVE what you have asked for.

As you are manifesting all the time, and with thoughts of hard and easy, what do you think will appear in your life?

Let me be presumptuous in answering that question, what will appear in your life is.....doubt and MISBELIEF that you can manifest abundance in your life, your ACTIONS will bring you to this forum, and other avenues to ASK *"What's the hardest part about manifesting abundance into your life?"* With those three steps taken, what do you believe you will RECEIVE? There is nothing wrong with gaining knowledge about using the Law of Attraction, however, when you learn that your thoughts, speech and actions have moulding powers, one is careful to ensure they do not put a halt on anything they actually want in their life.

To recap, there are no 'hard parts' to manifesting what you want, we are manifesting all the time, so we need to be aware of our thoughts, speech, what we write down, and actions. We are taking those three steps mentioned above ALL the time! We determine whether an asked for item, situation or person enters our life. Start today...ask for something you believe is small/easy and see if it turns up, don't worry about when, why, or where it will come from, just believe it will appear.

End of Questions

Well, that was asking for money, did you learn something about your requests for money? It is important to ask for what you want believing that you will receive it. For me, what ever wish I ask for I believe comes from God, so I would not limit the how, who or what is going to present it to me. I remain open, knowing that God has bigger better plans for me. I once asked for 'some money' as I had a celebration coming up. I didn't even have enough to get to the venue, let alone buy something to wear or give a gift. I was expected at this large celebration and wanted to attend.

People would call and ask me if I was attending, I would say, 'yes, I am hoping to be there,' It wasn't a lie I was hoping God would send me the money to be able to attend. During the waiting time, I did everything I could to earn more money, I cut back on certain things in the hope that God would see that I was trying to help myself. I knew that something would turn up and I will get what I asked for, do note I was also open to not getting or going to this event, as I believe that God knows best and if I didn't get to attend, it would be in my favour. One week before the event I got a £4,000 cheque, far more than I needed. If I had insisted on a certain amount i.e just enough to buy an outfit, a gift and travel I may not have received that £4,000.

Equally important is ensuring that when you think or speak about your want, you do it with positivity. When using the LOA one has to consider the practical things first. No use asking for water when you have a hole in your bucket, mend the bucket first then ask for the water, be open to the fact that your water may come in the form of rain. In regard to money note that it also can come to you in many forms, it doesn't have to be in your bank account, although we'd prefer it that way! If you frequent charity shops, you may find an item that is worth much more than you paid for it. Items in your own home may be worth more than you think. Don't be afraid to ask for a raise, when you want extra money. If you need money to buy something, listen for guided instructions, that item you want could be found on the day you get a hunch to visit a different town. Do remember you do not have to ask for one thing at a time, once you believe your wish will be granted, you will receive what you have asked for.
In the next chapter we will look at getting a new or better job, still money related, but a new job as we will see, can bring out your vulnerability, your neediness and frustrations as you seek what may not be seeking you.

Real Questions. Real Talk.

Chapter Three

How Do I Get A Better Job?

Wanting a job, house, new shoes, it doesn't matter what you want, the process is the same. Ask, Believe, Act and you will Receive.

It can be challenging not to focus on that job with that company at that pay, when this is what we naturally do when we are job seeking, the 'I want that job from that company' is even stronger after you have interviewed i.e interacted face to face with someone from that company. But one has to be aware of becoming too focussed on a particular post when using the LOA. Even at this stage in your job search journey.

It is possible that the interview that went so well, and warranted a next day follow up call from the company to tell you just that, may not be the job God/the Universe has chosen for you, as while they are on the phone, they mention that they still have to see some other candidates and will let you know at the end of the week. This can put you in a tail spin, as you focus solely on that job, not noticing the other posts that has landed in your inbox, nor do you remember the notice board that you said you would check out.

At this stage regardless what the person on the end of the phone said to you, you have not signed a contract, so you are not bound to them or them to you. Be open to the possibilities that the best job for you will come, with all the benefits you envisage for yourself.

But what if you are just hoping to get to the stage where you can interview? Here you prepare, you prepare your home, as you intend to leave it for at least eight hours everyday, prepare yourself, do you have interview clothes, could your hair do with a cut or styling, if you have children, do you have an idea who could take them to and from school, if you are seeking an in office type job....There is lots of things you can do to prepare, in doing this you are telling God/the Universe that this is what you want and showing the world around you that you mean business.

As you have prepared, don't lose hope when the job offers don't come straight away, they will come if you keep believing.

I am manifesting my writing career. I'm applying for at least 8/10 jobs a day. I feel good about some of the companies hiring. Anything else I need to do to manifest?

Thank you for the question. You should not be applying for ten jobs a day. When you ask for something, and take action, as you have done, you should wait for a response. When you was a child and went into a sweet shop, although you may have wanted ALL the sweets in the shop, you SELECTED one or two....Ten applications a day, sounds like you are not being selective and willing to take anyone of them that respond, or you don't believe that you'll get the job that you really want so, 'i'll just apply to them all'. Another consideration, why are you applying to companies that you do not feel good about?

Do you know that you could apply to ONE job and get it? (I know you don't). Another thought, instead of applying to job ads, why don't you select the company you want to work for, and email them! Tell them what you have to offer and arrange a meeting. (Do you believe that would work)?

Here's what else you can do, 'Act as if', decide that you will get the job you want, ensure you have the qualifications for the jobs you are applying for. Start acting as if you already have the job you want...Set the alarm to wake you up at the time you would need to be up, to attend this job, have lunch at the time you think you would be having lunch at this job. Get a hair cut, window shop or buy an outfit for the job you will get. Start preparing your household for being out 8-10 hours a day, get familiar with the train/bus or busy times on the road....get the picture? Ready yourself for what you want. Stop throwing things in the air hoping something will stick, be intentional.

I need tips on manifesting a better job. I know I know it seems like I've asked about this before but with the way things are in the world where college degrees don't seem to matter any-more and there's more rejection than acceptance, it's a little discouraging. Please help me.

Hi, always good to hear from you. Sure, I can give you tips on manifesting a better job. When attempting to manifest anything, one has to be careful and very deliberate about what we think, say, write and believe. Have a look at your statement above and see where you could be manifesting things you don't want. I'll help you, you state that *"with the way things are in the world where college degrees don't seem to matter any-more."* This is obviously in your world. The world you think of, self talk about, write about and believe. A brain surgeon needs a degree, my line of work as a psychologist needs a degree and they very much 'matter'.

I understand that you may feel this way regarding your line of work, and perhaps use those thoughts as a defence mechanism because you may not be getting the type of Job you want, or as a way of 'blaming' the industry because you are not being called in for an interview for the type of job you want.

But as mentioned above you must be deliberate about what you say especially when annoyed! You go on to declare *"there's more rejection than acceptance."* Let's recap your wishes to God/the Universe, *"my degree doesn't matter any-more and there is more rejection than acceptance."* It's no wonder you feel 'discouraged',' if you don't want it don't say it.

So you want a better job, do what you can to secure the job you want. While job searching, believe that you will find the right job, paying the right salary, at the right distance from where you live. Also believe that you are the best person for the job, that your degree will be appreciated and know that the job you are seeking is seeking you. Only apply for posts you genuinely want.

Start living 'As If'. if you are currently unemployed, get up at the time this new job would start, what time would you lunch in your new job? Get clothes ready for this new job, take 'work clothes' to the dry cleaners, clean shoes, maybe you need to buy a few items.

Do whatever you need to do to get ready for this new post. One has to keep thinking and speaking positively on their life to ensure one does not keep repeating life events they don't want.

Hello! I am new here, my english is not very good. I need help from you. How can I have a good job for me? Thank you.

Hi, I believe you are asking 'How you can get a good job'? If that is your question, you ask, look and apply for your ideal job, it is as simple as that.

To manifest your ideal job, you look, knowing you will find it, you apply knowing that you will get called for an interview, you attend the interview knowing that you will either get the job, or the interview was practice for the other interview you will go on.
Tell people you trust that you are looking for your ideal job, somebody may know somebody who is looking for someone just like you! Contact companies you would like to work for, it only takes an email!

Be open to receiving your ideal job from anywhere. A friend may tell you of an opening at their place of work, your ideal job may pop up in your email box if you have join any job-sites. Do not be too rigid on anything regarding this job. Be practical of course, it should be the type of job you want and at the pay you want, but things like 'I must have an hour and half lunch break, or it must be walking distance from my home', should not be on your want list for this job. After you have applied for your ideal job, get ready for it! Having Asked, Believe and taken action, start acting 'AS IF'. Start preparing, go shopping (window, virtually or actual) what would you wear to work everyday?

Pick out some items from your wardrobe and get them dry-cleaned, ready for your new job. Get that hair cut or style, how would you do your make up (if you wear makeup) what time would you get up in the mornings to attend this job? Start getting up at that time, what time would you have lunch if you was in this job? Start eating lunch at this time. All the above is to make your mind and body know that this is the new you, it also 'shows' God/the universe that this is what you want to do and God/the universe will conspire to make it so.

How can loa give me a job? I've seen multiple different types jobs I can do that pay 6 figures.

Thank you for the question.
Please note, as I mentioned before, applying for multiple jobs of different types, may come across as if you are throwing different things in the air and hoping something will stick! Is it the 6 figures you want or the job? As all the jobs you state you have applied for pay 6 figures? Concentrate on one type of job and go after that, if you just want the 6 figures in your bank account and really believe you will get 6 figures, then you need to concentrate on manifesting that. I have also mentioned that one can request more than one item or situation at a time, one just have to believe they will get it. As your want is a job (at the moment it would appear that you want any job in that particular field, just as long as it pays 6 figures) you should narrow it down.

For example, if you are an artist, what type of art would you like to do:

Painting, Abstract Expressionism, Art Deco, Art Nouveau, Avant-garde or Baroque? Sculpturing, Craving, Kinetic art, Modelling or Cast sculpture?

If it's music will it be:
Rock, Pop, Jazz or R&B? Pick one and request that job with the remuneration package that you would like.

I write, but will not just apply for any writing job because it pays 6 figures! In narrowing down your want you are not restricting God/the Universe, you are just making your request clear.

One has to ask aright, you could be offered a 6 figure job, doing something you morally dislike or in a country that is not safe for you! Would you consider the job? After-all it does pay 6 figures? Start making a list of your wants from a particular job, note down how far you are willing to travel, what benefits would you like. Then look at your qualifications and experience. So you have looked at what they can offer and what you can offer in return. Start start applying, knowing that the right job will appear with the right pay.

What are the steps in manifestation.. I am off work due to injury partner has been looking for a job.. I been thinking all positive thoughts but a lot is going on I want to heal I want to have some cash flow..

Thank you for your question. Sorry to read that you are off work due to an injury and that your partner is out of work. Healing should be your first concern. I understand that both healing and getting cash flow is important. Also challenging is attempting to think positive through it all. You asked for the steps in manifesting, you have made the first one, by enquiring, as it shows that you already believe that you can heal, attract cash flow and remain positive. You just need to ASK. It is important that we take practical steps before attempting to use the LOA. Alert friends and family to the fact that you are injured and ask for help. Seek out and ask local organisations for help. Being injured and needing cash-flow may be in their remit to help and provide you with the necessities while you heal and your partner finds work.

Ask God/the Universe for healing and cash-flow, believing you will receive it. Listen for any guided instruction i.e a hunch to do anything or go anywhere as this may be where your want materialise.

Encourage your partner to keep seeking employment, this will help with moral support and eventually bring in cash-flow. Although it may be challenging, but start making lists of what you will do and the places you will go when you are well. Maybe that will be back to work, a holiday, visits to friends and or family. While you wait for healing and cash-flow make a list, mental or otherwise of what you would like to do with the cash-flow after you have paid your bills and bought the necessities.

Doing something, anything regarding your want is action taken. This action allows us to feel less hopeless and boost morale in the pursuit of getting on with our lives and another step in the manifesting process of using the LOA.

Taking action will also ensure you stay on task, that of believing you will receive what you have asked for. Just like the process of healing, one takes the recommended action of the doctor, believing they will get better, your actions of believing, keeping in a positive mood and encouraging others in your case your partner, shows God/the Universe that you are attempting to help yourself and your household to heal and bring in the needed cash-flow. I wish you well.

Hi I'm feeling so low at the moment, third time I've not got the job I wanted or manifested. Can you give me some advice or suggestions how to get out this bad head space and back into manifesting what I want please! Really do with some support.

Sorry you feel the way you do. I understand that when you want a certain something and then it seems to be here only to slip away, one can become disheartened.

It is at times like these I say 'Everything is working in my favour,' If you have asked for a particular job, you will get it or something better. You have Asked, Believed, took action (went to an interview) you will Receive the best position for you. Whether it is at your chosen place or somewhere else. I get it, you done everything you should do and it appears not to be working! It is working, although you can't see it...One of those jobs you interviewed for may still call you or better yet, there is a better position out there with your name on it.

While you wait get ready, get ready for that new position, de-clutter that cupboard as you won't have time for spring cleaning when you get your new job, prepare outfits for that new job, throw out or give away clothes that don't fit the working person you are becoming. Prepare a list of lunches you'll carry to work, prepare a list of dinners you can cook and freeze or meals you can easily cook when you arrive home from that new job you'll get. Get ready for that new job in any way you know how, it will come if you keep believing it will arrive.

Can I get some help manifesting? I had an interview this morning and I should know about the job by Thursday. What can I do before then to get that offer letter??

Thank you for your question. To answer your question quickly...Trust that you will get the right answer for your career! That may be *"that offer letter."* Have you considered the fact that there may be a better job, paying better wages, giving better benefits? No, just *"that offer letter."* eh! In order to manifest what is best or good for you, one has to be open to what God/the Universe deems is best for you. I totally understand that when we take the time to seek out and attend a job interview we hope the outcome is favourable.

However, one has to be open and not stress, worry or cross fingers for exact outcomes. It comes across as if it is limiting God/the Universe. Yes you want that company to send you an offer letter, after all, you did the LOA work, you wanted a job or a better job, you believed you would get an interview, you attended and they appeared to like you, now you are in their waiting room! Waiting for them to decide your fate. Grant you its a place you don't mind being, however, when using the LOA one should become almost blasé, in their attitude towards what they have asked for. This helps you to 'act as if' and detach.
At this point ideally, you should expect the offer letter to arrive before Thursday.

At this point you should see the offer letter as a foregone conclusion! I know this is not how you feel, as you wouldn't be here.

At this point you should be clearing your schedule to accommodate this job or you could be carrying on with your life knowing that the next few days will bring you the right job at the right pay.

You should be open to what God/the Universe sends you whilst remembering that everything, everything is working in your favour and that could mean no offer letter from this company. Not sure how that sits with you, but that is how you get the best job for you, paying the best rate at the right time. Nothing should be dictating your fate! Not an offer letter, not anything.

Hello, I want to seek some guidance because I'm feeling quite disheartened. I've been working towards manifesting my dream job at a specific place. Things seemed to be falling into place initially; I heard a lot about this new place, they even began construction nearby, and I was invited for an interview.
However, things took a turn, and it's been a few months since I've heard anything from them. I followed up, it would seem that they read my message without replying. I'm at a loss for what this means. I found myself in tears yesterday, as I truly believed I belonged there. Now, I'm unsure whether to continue manifesting or to let go. Any advice would be greatly appreciated. Thank you.

Sorry you feel the way you do. I understand that when you want a certain something and then it seems to be slipping away, one can become disheartened. It is at times like these I say 'Everything is working in my favour.' With that attitude in mind, if you have asked for a particular job, you will get it or something better.

Never pin your hopes on one thing, one person, situation or particular job position! That job may appear to be your everything as you found yourself "*in tears.*"

Do you realise that God/the Universe knows what's best for you? And as you have Asked, Believed, taken Action (went to an interview) you will Receive the best position for you. Whether it is at your chosen place or somewhere else. I get it, it's the 'somewhere else' that is causing the tears, isn't it?

Try not to be too concerned with the 'somewhere or something else' because it will all work in your favour if you will let it. I understand that you may not be able to see that right now, because you have pinned your hopes on this particular place of work, if you would stop for a second and take a breath, you would realise that all you have done is applied for a post and was invited for an interview! That's it.
Now you are:
"*At a loss*"
"*In tears*"
"*Feeling quite disheartened*"
"*Believing you truly belong in this company*"
"*Unsure whether to continue manifesting or to let go*"

Truly believe you will get what you have asked for, but be open to it or something better, being open is 'letting go' or detaching.

The tears were caused by the 'holding on' so tightly and finding or feeling that it was slipping out of your grasp, detach and wait for your manifestation to come to you.

Hi, I am in a little confusion here. I want to earn well and have financial stability. The job I'm in is a contract job which is very uncertain. If they make me a permanent employee I would stay in the same job and make money. I am continuously manifesting this. But the employer is not giving us any hope and they might end our contract anytime. Now I'm confused on what to focus on. Should I manifest the same job with more salary and trust it will happen and universe will show a way or should I consider any other similar opportunities with the salary I expect. A lot of information on manifestation is confusing me. They say just think of ONE thing and never doubt it then it will align.

Thank you for the question. Sorry you feel confused. You have a few questions and I will attempt to answer each. You state that *"I want to earn well and have financial stability."* That is it, nothing more nothing less. Imagine if you just focussed on what you really want and nothing else?

Earning well comes with more than one thing:

It comes with being healthy enough to be able to 'earn', it may come with ensuring you have someone to take the kids to school, if you have to be at work at a certain time, earning well may have you dressed a certain way, which cost money and time, that's another thing. Earning well may mean staying over night at a hotel a few nights a week that too, is another thing that may be involved in earning well.

"....financial stability."

You also want *"....financial stability."* Money in the bank, perhaps at the end of eaning well, that again is another thing. In just asking or saying *"I want to earn well and have financial stability."* is asking for more than one thing. But it is the way I would go, that's it., whether it involved or included more than one thing, I would just ask, it would not be my concern if my want was five or ten fold. I would not concern myself with how all these 'things' are going to come together to give me my want. (This act is called detachment, when you leave the who, how and when to God/the Universe). If you asked for what you actually want, there would be no confusion, no waiting for a person (employer) to decide your fate. There would be no wondering whether you should go there or stay here. There would be no staying up at nights knowing someone, yes a person has your next life decision in their hands. Take that power from them and own it, after all it is yours. Decide what you want and ask for it.

"The job I'm in is a contract job which is very uncertain."

You are freelance it would seem, so you are free to take or leave work, yet you are not acting or feeling FREE. The reason for this is, you have given your earning power away to a person or company to decide at will, whether you stay or go! At the beginning of this sentence I stated that you are free to take or leave work as your role as a Freelancer dictates, you have decided to wish for the confinement ushered out by this one employer when you state:

"If they make me a permanent employee I would stay in the same job and make money. I am continuously manifesting this." This may not be the employer who will enable you *"to earn well and have financial stability."*

But it seems this is your belief, as you are *"continuously manifesting this."* In fact, *"the employer is not giving [you] any hope and they might end [your] contract anytime."* Why wait for that moment? You are FREE, you are a Freelancer, take back your power and demand an answer from the employer or begin looking for something else, better yet ask God/the Universe to enable you *"to earn well and have financial stability."* Be open to what comes.

"I'm confused on what to focus on."

You go on to state that *"Now I'm confused on what to focus on."* Focus on you and Free yourself, be a you, that is able to do what they want to do...your job title tells you that!

Ask for what you ultimately want, believing you will receive it.

"A lot of information on manifestation is confusing me."

Unfortunately, your confusion continues as you deliberate on what to do, when you had the answer at the beginning of this question, ask *"to earn well and have financial stability,"* see this is as your ONE thing. I'll leave you with your own words *"never doubt it then it will align."*

Thank you for accepting my membership. I am trying to manifest getting accepted in a job I applied for in another country. I am not sure where to start . Appreciate your guiding tips. Thanks.

Thank you for the question. Firstly I would like to say, well done you. You are very brave to want to work in another country. This type of manifesting takes time, strong belief and practice. In order to manifest any job, whether in your current country or another, you need to get ready for that new job. Get your note pad out, you're gonna make some lists.

Your list:
Start buying or putting together the type of clothes you will be wearing in this new job.
Get clothes dry cleaned, buy some new ones.
Prepare 7 days worth of outfits.
Get your hair cut, styled or coloured the way you will be wearing it for this new job.

As you will be moving:
De-clutter where you live now.
Give or throw away items you will not have use for.
Will you be leaving your current furniture and belongings in situ or do you have to find storage for them?

Whatever the situation, get that sorted whether in your mind or by finding out where and when you can use the storage facility.

I trust you have sorted out any visa needed for this new post! Just get ready for your new life and work in a new country, by doing this you are forcing the subconscious to believe this is happening and it will conspire to make it a reality.

Hey girlie, I was just wondering if anyone had any ideas or tips on how I can manifest me being a realtor this year thank you.

Thank you for the question, we can manifest most anything. In-order to 'be a realtor' you need to ask, believe that you will be a realtor, take action, that could be, study and take any realtor exams or certificate, get the licence needed to be a realtor, but I am sure you know this. Having Asked, Believe and taken Action, start acting 'AS IF'. Start applying for realtor posts, or do you intend to open your own business? Regardless whether you decide to work for yourself or a company, start preparing:

Go shopping (window, virtually or actual) for clothes you would wear for work.
Pick out some items from your wardrobe and get them dry-cleaned.
How would you wear your hair? Get that hair cut or style.

How would you do your make up (if you wear makeup).
What time would you get up in the mornings to attend this job? Start your day at that time.
What time would you lunch if you was in this job?

Start eating lunch at this time.
Attend open house viewings act as if you was the realtor (not sure how you are gonna pull that one off, but try, it would be fun!)

All the above is to make your mind and body know that this is the new you, it also 'shows' God/the universe that this is what you want to do and God/the universe will conspire to make it so.

Good day all. I'm a real estate agent and would like to manifest selling a house a month. Please advise.

Thank you for the question. We can manifest most anything. Although we shouldn't limit God/the Universe, we should ensure we don't limit ourselves. You state that you "*would like to manifest selling a house a month."* I would change that to 'at least one house a month'. That way you don't limit your manifestation.

Find affirmations that you can use while getting ready for your day at work, something that will get you in the mood of 'I am going to have a great day, I will sell a house today'. I am not sure what your company does when a sale has been made, whatever they do, picture yourself daily being the person who 'made a sale'.
What does that feel like?
Think what you would do with the bonus if your company gives a bonus, who would be the first person you phone and tell you made a sale?
Get in the mood of 'it has already happened'.

When meeting prospective buyers, picture them celebrating, as they have just bought a house from you.

Ask for what you want, believe it will come, set about doing what you can do to bring your want into reality (the affirmations, the right mood, the visualising) and wait for it to appear.

How do I go about manifesting a promotion at work? I feel like I work so incredibly hard and I'm so deserving of a promotion but the opportunity just doesn't seem to come my way. I have already tried visualising techniques am I doing something wrong?

Thank you for the question. We can manifest most anything, however we sometimes need to work on a practical level. I do not know your situation but here are some practical tips. Have you asked your manager for a promotion; If not, why not? It would appear that you know your worth, when you say "*I work so incredibly hard and I'm so deserving of a promotion.*" I am unsure of what 'opportunity' you mean when you say it "*just doesn't seem to come my way.*"

Is it to come to you or should you take it! Working '*so incredibly hard*' is a good way to get promoted, but if the people in the position who can give you the promotion doesn't see you or know that you are looking for a promotion, you won't get it.

Many business owners will be happy to keep things as they are, especially if the people "*work incredibly hard*" without asking for anything other than their current pay!

On another note and a little story. I was once offered a role of Deputy Manager from a person I had worked with in the past, when I arrived to begin the role, a woman who had been there for five years and assumed she would definitely progress or get the promotion to Deputy Manager, felt very put out, (and other things too, i'm sure) needless to say she wasn't best happy! In fact the Manager had no intention of promoting her.

Set some boundaries, don't assume they know you want a promotion, or that you are in line for a promotion, ask for it. If the answer is no, set new boundaries like how long do you intend to be overlooked, when will you look for a company that will appreciate you and know your worth.

You may be surprised to know that the experience you have gained from this job can be transferred to a better paying post elsewhere! Now, I am not telling you to leave your job, I am alerting you to the fact that you are feeling under valued and you should be in a place that you are valued.

As for manifesting a promotion in your current job, yes you can do it....believe that an opportunity will come your way, stop voicing anything negative around getting this promotion, set a realistic time limit on when you will get the promotion offer. But be open as this promotion may come from a different department in your current job, it may come from a whole different company.

Ask God/the Universe for what you want, believing it will come and be open to receiving it, wherever it comes from.

What does it mean if i want a job then others get the job i wanted. Others search for a job and get it, when i search i don't get a job. It was strange that many times when

i wished for something then others seem to get it. I noticed that when a friend want something I would like, they get it and I get something that isn't as good, but less or nothing at all. How can I fix this problem?

As mentioned above to others, nobody can get your wish (stop saying that) and others can not stop you getting your wish, unless you allow it! Stating that someone got your wish, stops the manifesting process or YOUR wish coming into your life. What you have done is made another wish. "*Somebody else got my wish*" so God/the Universe set about granting that wish, the wish is to see others with what you want.

This is how you did it.
You noticed that a friend was looking for a job and you then helped them, by watching for it to materialise, you believed that they would get a job and probably acted as if they already had the job they were seeking. You said it, Asked ('I bet they get the job'), you then Believed (helped along by using self-deprecating words, "*I won't get a job but they will*") You may have even ACTED in a certain way, knowing that they will get the job, you may have become a little jealous or stand offish towards them. (We are here to tell the truth)! The only thing to happen now, is for your wish to come true....Receive...They got the job. Seek and you will find....If you sit there watching and waiting for others to get what you want, what do you think will happen?

Remember what you think about you bring about.
(Don't get this confused with the idea that you made the wish for them, they have had to have that same wish or want for themselves). Other people wishing or wanting and getting the same job you want, has nothing to do with your manifestation, they wished, they believed and they got their wish (with a little help from you!).

You looking at them enjoying their wish has nothing to do with you getting yours, you have made what they received about you, and not in a good way...As mentioned to others above, you should be jumping up and down stating 'mine is coming'.

Again you should only be attributing other peoples wishes to you in a good way! You 'didn't get' has nothing to do with their wish for themselves. You need to stop looking at others as if they have the power to grant or not grant you your wish, only God/the Universe grant wishes.

The time spent noticing others, could be spent working on you. If you want something then do the work. The work is to Ask Believing you will Receive. Not ask, look at others to see what they are receiving. Keep your focus on yourself that is, in a state of waiting for your want to come into your life.

Once a wish is made, start preparing for it, regardless of what is happening around you. Say affirmations that keep you believing your wish is on the way. If you ask for something that shows up in your eye sight, i.e someone else receive what you want, take it as a sign that you are aligned with your want and it is making its way to you. A wish is granted when it arrives, as you can see it can be halted by what you say, believe and do.

How do I manifest a job for someone?

You can't! You can only wish others well in their endeavours. The person you want to "*manifest a job for*" may have told you that they would like a job, or to change jobs. You may have noticed that this person has been looking for a job. All are actions of someone who would like a new job. The person wanting the job, has to see the manifesting process through of their own volition.

Here are some of the activities they may wish to do to manifest a new job for themselves:

They need to Ask for a new job.
Believe that they will get a new job.
They would also need to take constructive action, job search.
Buy or dry clean the interview clothes.
Research the type of job or company they would like to work for.
Know what salary they would like to achieve.

This person could also:
Act as if they already have the job they want, by perhaps getting up at the time they would need to be up in-order to get ready for this new job, they could lunch at the time they believe they would have a lunch break at this job.
They could map out the route to and from the place they would like to work and the cost of travel.

These are just a few things they could do to secure a new job. Note I said they could or should do. You can not do these things for this person.

With all the good intentions you have for this person you can only wish them well, and perhaps encourage them in their endeavours.

I am new to this, I wanna manifest a rap career

What are you doing in order to manifest a rap career?

Response From Enquirer

listening to music to get inspiration to write lyrics, and manifesting through angel numbers.

Ask for what you want, be specific, but realistic. Seek out companies that may want to see your lyrics, be pro active and believe you will get what you have asked for.

Response From Enquirer

Realistic how? I can rap but not that good, well compared to successful rappers. But I really have passion and ambition for music especially writing, I just want to manifest something I'm already in alignment with.

Realistic to mean doing or asking for what you feel is achievable. You should follow your passion and the rest will fall into place, as mentioned above, it is important that you take action, by beginning to write and seeking out companies who may be interested in your work.

After some time the enquirer returned and stated

I can't learn this new skill of rapping.

Maybe rapping isn't your natural strength. There's so much a person can do that comes naturally, and there's also a great deal that can be learnt with time, practice, and guidance. From your many questions in this forum, it's clear you're passionate about becoming a rapper. But it's also clear that you're currently finding this *"new skill of rapping"* or writing lyrics challenging.

You appear determined to be 'a good' rapper without seeking out a teacher or someone to guide you. The Law of Attraction won't just 'make' you a good rapper. One of the processes of using the Law of Attraction, is being open to other avenues of getting what you want.

If rapping isn't coming naturally, perhaps it's time to consider other ways to be in the music industry. For example, with training and development, you might become a strong lyricist for other performers. I've mentioned this before, and it's worth revisiting. You don't have to abandon your dream, just be open to evolving it. Success often comes when we stop forcing and start flowing.

You may have to be open to being in this industry as something other than a rapper, but I have also mentioned that too.

End of Questions

We looked at the questions posed by job seekers, do note that when we decide to seek employment or a better paying post, we are in need. Most do not intentionally leave a job that they feel happy or comfortable in. So be kind to yourself while you seek that new position. Seeking new employment is an intimate endeavour as you tend to open yourself up to scrutiny whilst you bear all your qualities along with your qualifications and experience to someone who most likely is a complete stranger.

Deciding what you want, would seem a foregone conclusion, not so. It is good to know what you want and go after that, however, should you not find what you are looking for within the time frame you have set yourself, may have you throwing anything in the air hoping any company that is paying the amount you want will interview you. It is important at any stage of seeking a job that you be mindful of what you say around the job you want, as this will have a bearing on the outcome of securing the job you want whilst using the LOA.

Stating that the degree you took four years or more to gain '*doesn't matter any-more*' will have the potential employer feeling the same.

Prepare for the job you want, be specific when seeking that job and note that everything is working in your favour, whether you get the interview, job or promotion. No one company should hold you ransom, although you are in need, you are offering your expertise, qualities, your man or woman power to enhance their productivity.

You should have the attitude that the company you approach is in need and you are offering to help, after all that is exactly what is happening here, they are paying for your service! If they take you up on what you have to offer, great. If they do not, note that you will get its equivalent or better. Happy Job search.

Real Questions. Real Talk.

Chapter Four

How Do I Get A New Home?

What is the first thing that springs to mind when you think of moving? We can conjure up the mess of decluttering the old house, while mentioning "I never knew I had so much rubbish."To thoughts of the mess of living out of boxes in the new house.
Let's do the pro's and con's of 'why are you thinking of moving?'
Here's some con's:
I can't stand the neighbours.
It costs too much to live here.
It's too small.
I have to leave here!

Now the pro's:
I'm moving because I've got a new job.
I've outgrown this home and want something bigger.
I can afford to live in a better neighbourhood.

We could go into the pro's and con's of the cost of moving, or what the new neighbours might be like or how nice the new landlord will be, or whether there will be any nasty surprises with the house you will secure and buy. I have said all that to say, moving or getting a new place to live, a place you can call home can be daunting. We are aware that one should attempt to stay in a high vibration (good mood) in order to help your manifestation along. Whatever the reason for your move, you should stay positive.

As you have seen it is easy to become overwhelmed with this want. Wanting a new place to live is not like wanting a new bag, pair of shoes or even more money, and although we are to leave the how and when to God/the Universe, there are a few things we have to put in place before we ask for a new home.

One needs to have an idea of where the new home should be, how many bedrooms, should it have stairs, a lift or both. Should there be a garage or parking spaces; does it need to be near good schools, is public transport important? The distance to work may also be a factor. We set off attempting to manifest with all and more of the above questions in mind. It is only after we have the basic needs of a new home set in our minds can we move forward with the actual wish. We then move on to the practical steps.

No use attempting to manifest a 2 million pound town house, when your practical budget is a 1 million pound 2 bedroom semi. Ok, so the practical steps would be to get your finances in order, as whether you are buying or renting, you will still need to show some income. Be realistic as this will help you stay on task and believing you will manifest your new home. To recap: You know where, and the size of the property needed. You have the means (or near enough) to achieve what you want. Armed with this knowledge you Ask, Believing you will achieve your goal.

While you wait continue with the practical steps, get yourself an Estate agent (Realtor), ask them to send you details of properties in your price range, go on viewings, you can do this virtually too.

Tell trusted friends and family members that you are thinking of moving, as they may know someone who has just the right property for you.

After taking those important steps, your thoughts should be how do I decorate my new home. Make lists, picture or visualise living in your new home.

Where will you eat breakfast, in-front of that large window in the kitchen or on the balcony in summer. How cosy will it be in the evenings? Think of your bedroom, will you have a TV in there or not. Whilst you prepare yourself for living in your new home, declutter your present home, keeping items that are of use now and the ones you will be taking with you to your new home. On your shopping trips, buy something for your new home only to be opened and used when you move.
With all you should do and continue to do while you wait, the most important aspect of this wish is to believe you will find the right home, at the right price and at the right time.

Now the disclaimer: You can have no money with no idea where you want to live, but you decide that you want to leave your current home for another. You take the practical steps i.e you declutter giving or throwing away what is not needed and you make a wish, believing that God/the Universe will accommodate and furnish you with your ideal home. Then you wait, picturing yourself in the perfect home for you. This could also work! But because most of us are not such great believers the many steps mentioned in the main body of this introduction will certainly get you in the waiting to receive stage. Happy house hunting.

Hi I'm new to this forum.
Has any of you actually manifested successfully something you have always wanted? I've been trying to manifest my dream home (impossible to get on property ladder in UK as it's so expensive,) but I try, I vision myself in the home how the kitchen looks etc but as I think I will need a lottery win to make it possible, could that be blocking me? I visualise said lottery win, I actually believe and have a feeling I will win 1.2 million.. but it hasn't happened yet.

Welcome, to answer your first question "*Have any of you actually manifested successfully something you have always wanted.*" Yes, the sex of my children I have three boys and three girls,(none of which are twins) houses, cars, jobs, the ability to sell the books I've written, my professional status, this forum which started with two people! I could go on, but it would bore you. Doubt will halt your manifestations, that is any doubt!

You start your question with doubt, as you have come to a 'LOA Manifesting Forum' asking if anyone "*has actually manifested successfully something [they] have always wanted?*" You then state that you have been trying to "*manifest [a] dream home*" but you quickly stick doubt in the sentence right beside it, by stating "*impossible to get on property ladder in uk as it's so expensive.*" I personally only owned houses in the UK!

You go on to say that "*I try, I vision myself in the home how the kitchen looks etc but as I think I will need a lottery win to make it possible.*" You not only doubt you will get the house and pay cash for it or it is given to you, you add how it should come to you! Why can't you have the dream house and the 1.2 million pounds you have been visualising? (You can't see that happening, can you?)

When attempting to use the LOA, one should be aware of what is said regarding the want, if you start off disbelieving it will work, then what you will receive is 'more disbelief it will work.'

When using the Law of Attraction, we Ask, Believe, take action and leave the rest to God/the Universe.

When wishing for a new home, one should, as you have done, visualise every detail of the home, take action, go view some, virtually or in person. Get on the mailing list of Estate agents, start getting your current home emptied of the things you are not using, and will not be taking with you to your new home, buy a picture or something small to be displayed in your new home, get the picture? Start acting as if you have this new home, don't worry about how it will come, just know that it will come.

Dear Angela,
Could I please ask the best way to do this? I was manifesting a house move for my husband and me back to a coastal area. My husband is ill and I want him to continue to have the best medical care that he is receiving at the moment. But...... I cannot bear the thought of living in our present city and certainly not without him should the worst happen. What would be the best way to continue manifesting our house move without confusing the Universe?

Sorry to hear that your husband is ill. You are unable to 'confuse' the Universe, remember what is granted is what is believed. If you have asked for a house move and continue to do all you can do to ensure this happens, it will happen (if you believe it). If you ask for the best medical care for your husband, like he is receiving at the moment (and believe it), he will receive the best medical care for him, whether you both move or not.

There is never any confusion for the universe, it only works and deliver what you believe and feel.

Note from the Enquirer

Hi Angela, Thank you so very much. You have put my mind at rest and I love your 'I am ready to manifest Journal.' Best Wishes.

Hi, I'm new to this forum. I am so ready to move out of this apartment and into my dream home any ideas on how to manifest my forever home?

Thank you for the question. Just ask for your dream/forever home! Start today, get a scrap book and start making list, things you want for each area of the house, yes every area.... (you need to know the size of the house you want, how many bedrooms, how many bathrooms, the colour of each room etc..That's the fun bit.

Ensure you have your finances in the best order you can get it. Get a realtor (in the UK an Estate agent) to send you listings in the area and price range you want (be realistic). No need requesting £10million houses if you do not believe you will receive this price home.

Go on viewings for the type of houses you want to live in, if you do not qualify to view these houses YET, view them virtually, go to open houses, do what you can to be in the area you want to live. Shop in that area, take the long way to and from work, in-order to BE in the area you want to live.....In doing this you are sending a message to God/the universe that 'this is where I want to live,' the message is also going to your subconscious, they will conspire to make it so.

Start moving! Yes, start de-cluttering where you live now, (after all you are moving aren't you?) throw or give away items that you will not be taking to your forever home, buy a little or large item that will be unwrapped and used when you get your forever home.
But more than anything else, believe that you will get your forever home soon.

I would like to manifest a Residential Park Home. Any tips/ideas would be greatly appreciated. Thank you

Thank you for the question. The advice is the same as manifesting any home. After you have asked for the home, do the practical stuff i.e. get your finances in place, ask a realtor for the area to send you available Park homes.

Then the fun stuff starts, go on viewings for the type of Park home you want, this can be in person or virtually. Do what you can to be in the area you want the Park Home.

Do more research on the area you wish to live, find out what activities take place in the area. Find out where the nearest supermarket is, school, if you need it. Where will you go out to eat or have a drink...Invest your time in the area you want to live. If your Park Home is a 'permanent buy' and you would like to live there.

Start moving! Yes, start de-cluttering where you live now, throw or give away items that you will not be taking to your Park home, buy a little or large item that will be unwrapped and used when you get your new home. But more than anything else, believe that you will get your new home soon.

Hi all, I am manifesting a house move. Should I start sorting and clearing out cupboards to help me move quicker?

Thank you for the question... yes, you're absolutely right, it's time to start moving!
You may already be doing some of these things, but here's what I would suggest:

Start today.
Get a scrapbook or notebook and begin making lists. Write down everything you want for each area of your new home... yes, every area. Think about the size of the house, the number of bedrooms and bathrooms, and even the colour schemes for each room. That's the fun part!

Get your finances in the best shape possible.
Make sure you're in a strong financial position. This will make the process smoother and less stressful.

Connect with a professional.
Reach out to a realtor (or, in the UK, an estate agent) and ask them to send you listings in your desired area and price range. Be realistic, don't request £10 million homes unless you truly believe that's within your reach.

Start going to viewings.
Even if you're not quite ready to buy, go and see the types of homes you'd like to live in. Doing this helps you build faith and clarity around what you want. Trust that the right home for you and your family is out there.

Do the practical things, and the emotional ones.

Declutter as much as possible. it does *"help [you] move quicker,"* practically and spiritually. It sends a message to God/the Universe: *"I'm ready to leave this house."* It also signals to your subconscious that change is coming and everything will begin to align to support that.

Most importantly, believe.
Have faith that your new home is coming. Keep your vision clear, your spirit hopeful, and take action as if the move is already happening.

Dear Angela,
I am loving your Forum and want to manifest a move. During March I have manifested parking spaces, daily. I also manifested a black, grey and white feather. That took 2 weeks. I also manifested seeing a robin. That took 3 weeks. Any advice for manifesting my house move would be greatly appreciated. Many thanks.

Thank you for loving this forum.
I am so pleased you have manifested all that you have had appear in your life, please share it with us, it helps others to see that it is more possible than impossible.

You have proven that the LOA works and works for specific things. No reason why you can't manifest a house move. With the practical things done i.e an Estate Agent on board, finances sorted, the where, how big and type (terraced, semi or detached) all set in your mind, you should start visualising yourself in your new area.

Where would you go to shop?
Where would the kids go to school, if you have kids?
Where would you walk the dogs, if you have dogs?
If you go to the pub, church, Spiritual organisation, which one would you become a regular?
If you want work in the new area, where would you work?
What company in that area will you work for?
Find out as much as possible about where you want to move to, then get packing!

Start by de-cluttering where you live now, throw or give away items that you will not be taking to the new house whilst picturing yourself and your family in the new home.
You know how many bed and bathrooms you want, decorate them in your mind.
Then move on to the other rooms and areas of the house.
Make wish lists, many online companies have them, start filling in you new home buys wish list.

You could even add some items to 'cart' ready to purchase when you have been given the keys of your new home. But most importantly is believing that you will move soon.

I need tips on manifesting a new place to live I know it seems like I've asked about this before. Right now things are a little discouraging. Please help me.

Hi, always good to hear from you. Sure, we can give you tips on manifesting a new place. I take it you mean a new 'place' to live. What are your thoughts around securing a new place to live? Well whatever your thoughts, this is what is happening now! Let's change that.

Start by doing what you can to secure a new place to live, this will help to encourage you and the move.

Get a real estate agent to send you properties available in the area you want to live in.

Make a list:
Where do you want to live?
Consider the size of the property.
How many bedrooms.
How many bathrooms.
Does it need to be close to public transport.
Do you need off street parking.
Know how much you are willing to pay.

Start viewing properties you would like to live in, even if you can't afford it right now..(Do be realistic though). Believe you will find the right property for you,

Start buying small items you will need in a new home:
New bedding
Cutlery.
Cushions.
Mats etc.

Tell selective friends and family that you are looking for a new place to live, somebody always know somebody, who know someone, who may be able to help.

Start de-cluttering your old home, in doing this you are showing that you mean business, you are ready to move.

Ask for the home you want, believing you will receive it. When you have done everything in your power to secure a new home, then you wait believing the right property will be open to you.

One has to keep thinking and speaking positively on their life to ensure one does not keep repeating life events they don't want.

What affirmations can you use to manifest a dream home?

Thank you for the question.
I don't have specific affirmations to help you manifest your dream home, but I encourage you to find affirmations that truly resonate with you. They should feel natural and believable.

Personally, I'm more of an action person when it comes to manifesting.

Here's what I'd suggest:

Start packing.
Yes—start now. Pack away things you don't use often but want to take to your new home. Throw out or donate anything that you do not use.

Start decluttering.
Start with that cupboard under the stairs, that will take a full day!
Then tackle the kitchen drawers. Go room by room until only the essentials you use daily are left visible. This tells your subconscious and God/the Universe: "I'm getting ready to go."

Know where you want to live? Go there.
Visit your new area often. If it's nearby, drive or walk there regularly. Shop there. Take the long way home just to pass through the neighborhood. Take in the area, it makes it real.

Create a visual wish list.
Start a scrapbook or make an Amazon wish list filled with things you'd love for your new home. This isn't just about shopping, it's about preparing. Emotionally, mentally, spiritually. You're already moving in.

In doing all of this, you're slowly leaving your old home and starting to 'live'—even if only virtually—in your new one.

And when you do move? Come back and tell us how it went.
Better yet, let us know when you're throwing that house-warming party (do people still do that?)

I am working on learning to manifest. Right now the only thing I desire is stability, I will be homeless after November, so trying to manifest approval for a safe place to rent for me and my small children. Right now I am writing it down, doing gratitude journaling, is there anything else I should be doing?

Wishing you and your children a safe home.

On a practical note ensure you contact all the relevant organisations and agencies in your area who may be able to help.

Do all you can to secure a safe place for you and your children whilst believing that you will find your new home.

Be very aware of your speech in regards to getting a new home. "*I will be homeless after November*" is not what you want for you or your children. In changing the way you speak, will keep you in the expecting or believing mode as opposed to the vibration of an unwanted situation.

After you have done everything you can to secure a new home,
Start packing:
Give or throw away anything you will not be taking with you to your new home.

Make a wish list:
Whether you can afford what you put on this list or not!
List what you would like for each room.

If you know the area you may be approved to live in,
Visit that area, to get familiar with the amenities:
The shops.
The parks.
The schools etc.....

If you currently live too far from your new expected area, go on google maps and virtually visit the area. In doing this you are showing God/the Universe that you are ready to move, you are also stating that you have mentally left the old and ready to step into your new home and life with your children.

Hello! I'm trying to sell my house, I was wondering what is the best way to go about this please.

Thank you for the question.
Start by speaking, thinking (and writing) in the past tense. *"I'm trying to sell my house"* will have you always *"trying to sell"* your house. Make statements you would *like* about your house, for example say, 'My house will be sold soon' or 'I am in the process of selling my house.'

Ask, then believe you have sold your house. Begin acting as if you have a buyer! What would you be doing now?
I would start packing, throw or give away items that you do not want and will not be taking to your new home.
Get the house ready to leave it.
De-clutter and clean, you will be surprised how long it takes, and the amount of items you own that needs to be packed when you start clearing it all out.
A buyer could turn up tomorrow and would like a quick purchase, are you ready?

What are your plans after the house is sold? Start concentrating on that.
Will you be moving in with family?
Are you moving abroad?
Have you bought or buying a new property?

Think of your life in your new home: what will it feel like?

if you have kids, will they be moving schools?

Will the commute to work be longer, shorter, will be start working remotely.

Fill your mind with your new home:
Are there items you could place on a wish list to buy for the new home?

In visualising your life in your new home, takes you out of your old home, spiritually or consciously, laying the path for God/the Universe to join your body and mind in the place you really want to be.

Hello everyone, I live near the Indian Ocean. I want to settle in Eastern Europe or in the United Arab Emirates. How do I attract this with LOA

Thank you for the question, just Ask for what you want, and start the practical stuff. I am sure you have thought this through.

But here are my thoughts. If you do not know anyone personally in these countries who can give you advice.

Start by getting your documents in order.
What would you need in-order to travel and live there.
What type of visa would you need.
Are you intending to work in the country you decide to live in; If so, what documents will be needed?

Before we even consider working abroad, what about where you will live?
Use your waiting time to work out where you will live if you are not being accommodated by someone you know.

Are you familiar with the languages spoken in these countries?
What about your finances, what if you can not find work before your finances become low, or is this not a factor?

You also need to bare in mind leaving your present country before you settle in another,
Do you need to end a tenancy?
What about furniture and or belongings that you will not be taking with you when you leave?

Do make sure you do your research whilst believing that you will get to the country of your choice. Beware of your intuition at this time, if it doesn't feel right it isn't right.

The advice I have given you may seem a little different from others, as your situation is a little different from others, many want to move up or down the country they reside in, you would like to leave the country you live in, to start a new life in a different country that may speak a different language from your own.

The 'work' you need to put in to aid your manifestation is also a little different, it has basically been to get the 'practical' things done. Having Asked, you Believe you will be leaving your home country to another because you are taking Action, in that you are doing the research and getting documents ready to leave.

You are also 'Acting as if' because you are considering how you will get to and where you will live, in the new country. Plus with all this 'doing' you do not have time to doubt that you will manifest your want, with all this doing you know that you are getting closer to your destination. Keep believing you will live in the right country for you and reach there at the right time.

Hope this is allowed on this forum
I'm homeless and living in a care centre. I have applied for loads of homes since March, I'm not having any luck and I manifest them each time and have even bought wallpaper for one that was guaranteed to be mine but it all fell through. There's 2 homes left now and I think should I give up or keep manifesting. I'm so drained with it all. Thank you for reading.

Thank you for sharing this with us. So sorry to hear about your situation.
You are a strong person, and I feel privileged that you felt comfortable to share your experiences with us. Keep going you have come this far, you are almost there, you got to the stage where you felt you wanted to buy wallpaper.

Take the homes that you lost as a sign that they weren't meant to be and that you will be offered something better. In my recent course, I call this the 'Breakdown stage'.

When everything seem to go belly up! It is at this stage many people halt their manifestations, by feeling that their manifestation is a failure, often thinking and asking themselves *"should I give up?"* and feeling somewhat *"drained with it all,"* this causes the whole process to begin again, which is often unwanted, but voiced (Asked for) situations.

For me, I welcome the 'belly up' stage when I have asked for something, because it tells me my manifestations are on the way. This stage is also a time of 'clearing out,' that is people, places and things. Have you ever wondered why your life came together after a certain someone left your life? Or when you moved to a different address, town or country? It works with things too...The house you wanted fell through, only to find out that that house had mould and the one you are now offered is larger, cheaper and up the road from the school you want to send your kids...This is just an example, but you get the gist.

The aim while attempting to manifest is to continue to show God/the Universe that you still want what you have asked for and continue to believe its on the way.

As you have done all you can do, start making lists of what you want for your new home. Put things in your online basket. Decide on your colour scheme..busy yourself the best you can, on preparing to move and you will, if you keep believing. Stay as strong as you are...Your home is on its way.

Hi, all I'm currently in a situation where I'm living where I have picked up that the person next door to me is having mental health issues and it has started to make me feel unsafe in my own environment. Did I manifest this? I lived here for 3 years without a problem this person had no issues. I have now considered leaving my home over this. Does the universe sometimes push you in different directions because you might meet someone you meant to meet else where?

Thank you for the question. First and foremost, I need to advise, please ensure you are safe, do alert any organisation in your local area who may be able to help. Talking about help, it is imperative that you seek help and or advice on behalf of the person you feel is having mental health issues. You may feel unsafe, they may be feeling the same way too!

Your question I believe is: *"Does the universe sometimes push you in different directions because you might meet someone you meant to meet else where?"* Sure it does, if you have ASKED, BELIEVED you must RECEIVE and this may mean a house, area or country move.

The reason why you are pushed to consider the house move, could also be as a result of you asking for something. If you have asked to meet someone and you are open to what God/the Universe has in store for you, you maybe sent to where ever that person is. God/the Universe will also give you the means to get there.

Being open the way you are, is called detachment. It is a little known or unconsciously used term or process in manifesting. Detachment is the act of letting go or detaching from the outcome of the want. Here one does not worry about the Who, Why or When the wished for item or situation will appear. Using Detachment in any attempt to manifest, will bring the wished for item or situation to you quickly.

If you have a hunch to move, then you should start the process of a move, while you sort through all this entails, believe that you will find the right home at the right price...and anything else that you may be seeking along the way.

Okay. How to manifest these things... I'm always working on being the best version of myself. I've got obstacles that seem to constantly prevent me from fully being the highest version of myself. I have people who block me from growing into being the person I want to be. I am working on manifesting prosperity in abundance so that I can have my own home.

Thank you for the question.
When attempting to use the LOA one has to be aware of what they say. I understand that you are working on yourself and feel that there are challenges along the way.
I will break your speech down and assist you moving forward.
You state, *"I'm always working on being the best version of myself"*. This is great, nothing wrong there. Then you state *"I've got obstacles that seem to constantly prevent me from fully being the highest version of myself. I have people who block me from growing into being the person I want to be."* I understand that this is how you feel, but it can be rephrased.

The reason we are careful with what we say, is because we are making wishes every-time we use the word 'I'. Any words used after 'I or I am' is a wish. What comes after I or I am is happening, has already happened or will happen. So based on what you have said, what do you think will continue to happen, let me remind you: *"I've got obstacles that seem to constantly prevent me from fully being the highest version of myself. I have people who block me from growing into being the person I want to be."* Rephrasing the way you feel right now, to: I may be finding it challenging at the moment, but I know I will grow into being the person I want to be.

Have a look at every word used after 'I' in my sentence. I know that you may not speak the way I do, but try and say, think and or write down the way you would like things to be, what you should aim for is to speak in the future tense.

Here are some examples of speaking about what is happening now. You have the flu and a friend asks you 'How are you?' Remember you have the flu, you reply with the present and the future:

'I am hoping to get over this flu soon.'

Your car has broken down, when asked about your broken down car, you reply:

'It will get fixed as soon as I can get it to the garage.'

Whatever the issue always add your preferred outcome.

Right, with the way you speak taken care of, we can address the other questions you appear to have, that is 'obstacles and people.' As I do not know what your 'obstacles' are, I am unable to fully advise you on them, however if you call them challenges, instead of something you have to 'jump, blast, or tunnel' through, you may find them less of an 'obstacle' and more of a manageable task. Can you see the difference in words used?

You state that you have "people who block [you] from growing" Are you aware this is impossible! I get it, you may have people around you that are not like minded or want different things to what you want for yourself, your situation may be different as I am only assuming, once you are 'safe', you may be able to overcome whatever "blocks" these people have put in your way, by concentrating on your goal, that is "working on manifesting prosperity in abundance so that [you] can have [your] own home."

I am unsure what you are doing to manifest "prosperity in abundance" but the mere fact that you are working on it will keep you busy, as you focus on this goal and what you say going forward.

End of Questions

Getting a new home, somewhere to live that you can feel safe, and or grow a family, to leaving your country to live abroad can be challenging as we have seen. From wanting to sell a home, rent or buy a home, one thing is clear, one needs to Ask, Believing they will Receive.

With moving house, as mentioned above, the practical Action taken is slightly different from wanting a new job or more money as there are many processes that need to be addressed when wanting to move house.

In some ways having something to focus on keeps you busy and in the vibration of 'I want to move house' as you are working towards a common goal.

There may be challenges along the way, setbacks, delays, or even deals falling through but once you are determined to move, you find that you follow the road until you get to your goal or should I say the front door of your new home. It is harder to fall into the trap of doubt and believing that a house will not sell, as houses are sold every day. I sold a house in the mist of the COVID pandemic, it can be done.

Having things 'fall through' doesn't mean you will never find a new home as there are many houses for sale or rent, and you know that you will find one that is right for you.

The aim as with any wish, is to continue to believe whilst doing all you can to have your want manifest in your life.

Real Questions. Real Talk.

Chapter Five

How Do I Get Better Health?

Most people who are aware of the LOA may not use it for a cold, flu or even a broken bone, as they know or believe that they will heal in due time, they may say, 'if I keep warm or take this medication and rest, I will get better.' Note they say or declare that they will get better. They take action (medication or rest) and within a set time frame, they may begin to feel better. If this is not the case they may seek the advice of a health professional. Still believing that they will get the remedy to their ailment.

What is the difference between asking for the flu to leave your body and asking for Cancer to return to its dormant state in your body? I will leave that unanswered for you to consider, while you read the questions asked by some who want a healthier life for themselves or for others.

Is it possible to train your body by manifesting?
I'm losing weight by saying daily, I feel it, I think it, I say it.

You have answered your own question. However, it is your mind that you train, your body will always follow suit. It is always the mind that we instruct...Try it now, tell a limb to move...did it move? Your mind had to get the information in-order to tell that limb to move. Once the mind has the information, everything else will follow suit..Losing weight using the LOA is telling yourself (the mind) or proclaiming that you are losing weight, it is the mind that keeps the momentum going, it is the mind that tells you that you are losing weight.

We see the opposite of this in people who have body dysmorphia disorder, no matter what the mirror is showing, (their body) they (the mind) believe they look different.

You have a great affirmation and it will work for you. Just as ANY positive affirmation will work, one has only to believe what they say, take action, exercise, eat healthier etc and they will lose weight.

Hi, I comfort eat every now and again... Any tips? I know it's related to past stuff and I'm working on that and being kinder to myself.

There is nothing wrong with a bit of comfort eating, you have acknowledged that your body needs comfort and you have obliged. What is important is what you think of yourself after you have eaten it? 'Yum that was nice' or 'I wish I didn't eat that.' Can you see how that snack that you had can be a comfort or a hindrance in your eating habits?
If it is related to your pass, you may need to look at the pass issue, which has come up to be healed or placed somewhere safe in your list of experiences.

When people state that they comfort eat, it is often voiced in a derogatory manner, as if food should not be used to give comfort. Just a note here, if your mother use to cook you chicken or any other type of soup as a child when you was ill, you may yearn that soup as an adult when you are sick. Your mothers' soup did not have healing powers, it was the fact that you, as a child, felt cared for and a bowl of soup may have been easy to digest! Why then as an adult we feel that eating something when feeling a little low is not allowed?

Everything in moderation springs to mind here.

On cold winter Saturday afternoons, after I have cleaned the house, as my mother did when I was a child, I like to have a big pot of steaming soup on the stove, so when I am finished cleaning I can curl up and enjoy the soup. It brings me comfort, as I smell the soup and see the clean house.

Comfort eating is what you attribute it to and how you feel after you've eaten it.
If your eating food instead of something else, like talking or attempting to fill a void, then as mentioned above you may need to address that issue.

In regard to using the LOA what would you like to know. Could your question be, how can I stop comfort eating as I am not being kind to myself when I do? Or do you want to use the LOA to address your past issues? I will assume you would like an answer to both questions.

First and foremost one should take practical steps before attempting to use the LOA. If you are doing anything that you believe is 'not being kind to yourself' then you should address why you have the urge to be unkind to yourself, could it be for instant gratification, could it be a habit. Habits are grown, they are not given the title of habit if they are once or twice indulgences.

Consider what drove you to indulge in the first place. Only when these and a few other questions are answered, should you embark on using LOA to stop a craving for comfort foods as they may be being used to mask bigger issues. The practical steps, I suggest is to seek a medical professional who may be able to answer the questions above.

I'm manifesting i will feel happy and will be healthy, instead of thinking I am sick of feeling sick and unhappy at this time.

Sorry you're feeling unhappy right now—but please know this: you will feel better.
Take just 30 seconds to think about a time when you felt genuinely happy.
  • Where were you?
  • Was the sun shining, or were you cozy indoors with a hot drink?
  • Were you alone, or surrounded by people you love?

Happy memories can bring a little happiness back into the present.
Even briefly. Try it. Let those feelings rise again, even if just for a moment.

Simply saying:

"I will feel happy," begins to open the door to happier thoughts.
Saying, *"I will be healthy,"* brings with it a sense of hope and forward movement.

But remember:

Before using the LOA, always take practical steps.
If you're unwell, please seek professional medical advice. Do what needs to be done in the physical world first, your wellbeing comes first.

Then, having done what you can, ask in faith believing that you will become happy and healthy.

And in truth, you've already started the process by saying:

> *"I will be happy."*
> *"I will be healthy."*

Keep going. Keep believing in the life you want—because you already know what that looks like, and just as importantly, you know what you *don't* want.

You're moving in the right direction.

My life has been turned upside down after a car accident and now I medically can't drive because of it. I feel isolated at times, my camper van and freedom was my life, now I feel like a caged hen at times and thinking of how life was, doesn't always help me. The life I had planned was just beginning. Things will get better with making huge huge adjustments, especially being on my own.

Sorry to read that you was in a *"car accident and medically can't drive because of it."* Being unable to move freely because of ill health can be frustrating. Know that this time in your life, is for a season. The fact that you know that *"things will get better"* is certainly a step in the right direction and two steps closer to your goal. You voiced it and believe it, what you now do towards getting better is the action needed to see your goal come to fruition.

I understand that *"thinking of how life was, doesn't always help"* as you have also stated that you may have to make *"huge huge [adjustments]"* to your life in the future. You are looking to the future with the belief that *"things will get better."* And they will, if you continue to remain optimistic and note that you need the time to be still and rest (not always easy). Feeling *"like a caged hen at times,"* can also be frustrating, when you want to get on with your life.

If I am unwell, I sit on the sofa (as I can't be at my desk and in-front of a screen), while there I think of ALL the things I could be doing, but can't.
ALL the things that should have been done, but I couldn't do, until I come to the realisation that maybe, just maybe, God wants me to rest right now.
Plus the fact that I will be better at what I do, when I am able to get back to it.

Do what you can do from where you are, make lists if you can. Decide on what changes you are going to make, what help you may need and the organisations that are available in your area to offer some assistance. You do not need to do things alone as there are groups and charities that may be able to help. Keep as busy as your health will allow, knowing that you will get where you want to be, if that is your path to take.

Hi, I watched the secret years ago. I knew it was true.
I have been really ill with depression and stomach issues. I want to heal myself. I often manage to manifest small things. So I know it works. I just struggle to manifest big things and find all the negative thoughts take over. Any tips please.

Welcome, thank you for your question. Firstly I must advise that you seek medical professional help as you claim to *"have been ill with depression and stomach issues."* It is always important to take practical steps before embarking on the use of the LOA.

When one is unwell, it can be challenging to concentrate on what you want, as fighting through the pain of ill health is a process all of its own.

The mere fact that you think, voice and in this case write down that you *"want to heal"* is the first step in the LOA process, you proclaim that you believe and have proven that *"it works,"* yet another step towards receiving what you have asked for.

We can manifest most anything, and you know that healing yourself is possible. However, we often put blocks in our way when we call our wants big or small.

Attempting to heal yourself is no different from manifesting what you may call a small thing. You asked, believed took action and it appeared! Simple.

We often think or believe things are hard to manifest the bigger the want, and smaller things are easy. The reason for this, is if we could possibly get it, make it happen, get the money or the money to buy the item ourselves, we consider it easy or small. When the item, person or situation is beyond our reach, we believe it is hard or big. Note, the process has not changed, it remains the same. Ask, Believe, take Action and Receive.

Stating that a want is big is inadvertently adding doubt to the process of using the LOA, it lengthens the waiting time, as one would need to take time to get into a state of complete belief, knowing without a doubt, any doubt, that the want is achievable and is on its way. We are often unconsciously willing to wait, as we have put that want, in the category of big so will take some time. Wants appear when they should, that could be instantly if you believe. Adding a time frame to the process can prolong its arrival, and giving you time to halt the process all together.

As mentioned above, giving a want a title of big or small may determine the length of time your want takes to arrive. During that waiting time, we give doubt and *"negative thoughts,"* an 'in'. The minute you get what you call *"negative thoughts,"* acknowledge it and dispel it with an affirmation that resonates with you. For example, state out loud or silently 'I'm going to get better, watch this space' or 'I will be better soon.' By using an affirmation about the future, allows you to stay in the expectant state, wanting, waiting and affirming that your want is on it's way. Remain believing that you will get what you have asked for as you know *"it works."*

My Dad has health issues. How can I help him, improve his health, without him having to do anything. He doesn't believe healing is available to him. I believe he can though.

Sorry to hear that your Dad is unwell and feels that he *"doesn't believe healing is available to him."* We all wish well for our loved ones, even if they don't wish it for themselves.

I have mentioned this in regard to parents, who want the best for their children however, when the child becomes a teenager and want something else, no amount of wishing, affirmation or manifesting is going to turn that teenager into what has been wished for him or her.

You can manifest most anything, however it is important that the person you are attempting to manifest for, believes it will work.

I tend to encourage people to take practical steps before embarking on the use of the LOA, your practical step is to ensure that your Dad is seeking advice of the medical profession.

If a person believes a certain way, you can only wish them well and hope that they see themselves the way you see them. Your Dad would need to ask, believe and act in-order for your will to be acknowledged.

Consider a game of tag of war, you are pulling one way and your Dad who has more belief in his illness than you have in his getting well on his side, who do you believe will win? Your Dad has free will and may have chosen the power of sickness over the will to get well. I am sorry if it appears this way, and it is for this reason we are unable to manifest for anyone who has free will to control their mind, body or life.

My dear I didn't know how manifesting actually works thanks for explaining through this forum. I'm on my trauma healing journey and so it's really hard for me to be on a high vibration. I just discovered that I have soul fragmentation. This explains why I have been feeling empty for years. So manifesting is impossible for me at the moment.

Sorry to hear that you have experience trauma, but pleased to know that you are on a journey of healing.

I understand that you may feel that it is *"hard to be on a high vibration."* I totally get it, one can not jump up and down when life is happening. I get it, however you can try remembering when things were good and you felt better than you do now....Any time a low vibration thought comes your way start thinking of when things was good, it happened for you before so it can definitely happen again.

You mention that you *"just discovered that you have soul fragmentation"* I do not know what this is, but if it has any negative connotation, I personally would not attribute it to me, my life or to any reason to explain why life happened! Attempt to take control of how you feel (I know this can be difficult at times). Remember the good times.

The Law of Attraction is always always working, you are manifesting all the time, what you manifest is down to you.

Use affirmations that resonate with you when you are feeling low or when negative thoughts return. Some thoughts return to be healed and as you are on your healing journey I take it you are being supported by a medical professional who would be able to guide you.

You state that *"manifesting is impossible for me at the moment."* As the LOA is working

ALL the time and you are manifesting ALL the time, it is impossible not to manifest! In fact you have manifested the feeling of *"manifesting is impossible for [you] at the moment."* Remember what we say, do and write down is often what we believe. Sounds like two of the LOA steps to manifestation to me! What do you think will come after Asking (or voicing) Believing what you have said, and in this instance, Acting 'as if' what has been said (or written down) is true? The only step left is to Receive...and there you have it. *"manifesting is impossible for [you] at the moment."*

You can change that! Believe it or not. Lets manifest something this week, try the £1 test, Ask for a pound or dollar, whatever your currency is and wait for it to appear, this can be in an old purse, a coat pocket, in an ad for a pound off, in your inbox as a voucher, someone may buy you a coffee worth a £. Only you can change the way you feel, regardless of how you feel right now, that also means getting back on that high vibration whether it takes a while or not, but you'll get there because you want to.

I am struggling with moving on with my life and never seem to have enough energy.

Sorry to read that you are struggling. As I am unaware of where you are in your life as opposed to where you believe you should be, I am unable to advise on the direction you should be aiming or what may be hindering your energy levels.

As this forum is about the use of LOA I can suggest that although you feel the way you do, it is imperative that you re-word, revoice and re-write your statements about yourself. By adding 'but hope to feel better soon' puts the fate of your life on a upward trajectory. As what we say tend to be what we believe and act upon, which inevitably lead to experiencing those voiced situations into our lives.

After some time we may wonder when we will 'feel better.' I suggest that you start today, yep feel better today! Decide today that you are going to change the struggle you mentioned above into a challenge. A change of wording will help you 'see' your issue differently.

Now that you have a challenge instead of a 'struggle' you can set about finding ways to alleviating your energy levels. My practical suggestion is to consult a medical professional regarding how you feel and the fact that you "never *seem to have enough energy."* Do change the "never" to 'sometimes' as you may have enough energy to go to the kitchen, bathroom, and bedroom! You may have enough energy to feed, clothe and wash yourself. You certainly have enough energy to read and write in this forum!

So armed with a change of wording, a trip to see your local medical professional and a challenge instead of a struggle you may be on your way to 'feeling better'.

How to help my son to heal from Tourette?

Thank you for your question. As parents we want the best for our children, and make wishes everyday when we say I love you, be safe, eat up, wear a coat, its cold outside etc. We work out the life we would want for our children in our minds, which are all wishes.

When using the Law of Attraction, one has to be practical, it is important to seek medical help and advice as mental health treatments can help manage the symptoms of Tourette.

As with every question asking me for advice to help someone else using The Law of Attraction, the answer is the same.

The person you would like to 'change' also has to have the need want or wish to change. I do not know the age of your son, but he would need to put that wish out there, he would need to believe he would be 'healed' from Tourette syndrome, while working with a health care professional, for your wish of healing your son from Tourette to manifest.

Can you manifest cancer to go away?

You can manifest better health, whatever the diagnoses.

I want to know about loa about hair regrowth. Please enlighten me about this.

Thank you for your question. You can manifest most anything. First and foremost, you must believe that you will have hair regrowth.

Seek out any professional who may be able to help. Find a mantra that feels true to you, then say or think it every-time you see or think of your hair.

For example:
'My hair is growing everyday'
'My hair is going to be lush'
'My hair is beautifully long'.

You have to find what resonates with you. Now, in private or public, act as if you have the hair growth that you want, this may take some creative thinking!

What would you wear if you had longer hair.
Would you wear something that showed your neck line.
What colours would you choose to wear if you had longer hair.
Would you apply your make up (if you wear make up) differently if you had longer hair?
Believing and acting 'as if' will get you there.

End of Questions

How do you help someone feel or get better, what you may call 'well, better or in good health' may not be the same for the person you are wishing it for. For this reason, it can be challenging to help others 'get better'. To help yourself get better, will depend on what you say and believe about your illness.

All use of LOA starts with taking practical action, in the case of health, one would need to seek professional medical advice.

In doing this you increase the ability to 'get better' as you would have sought or Asked for help, you may Believe what you have been directed to do. You then take the Action prescribed, thus leading to your recovery.

The LOA is the same process, we Ask or voice what we would like to appear in our lives, in this case its better health, so we state that we would like to feel better or use everyday language by stating, when asked, 'how are you?' you proclaim..' I have or had (whatever the ailment) ...I am hoping to get or be better soon,' the more you say this, the more your belief will grow.

Once you Believe what is voiced often, you may begin to Act as if you are getting better, you may do a little more today, than you did yesterday, as you are getting better!

From reading the questions and answers above, it would appear that all you have to do is change the way you speak and that you can't help others to get better.

This couldn't be further from the truth, Yes we all need to be aware of what we say at all times, as the LOA is always working, however, it is what is believed regarding the illness that gets the wanted or unwanted outcome. Saying, believing and acting will always get you results, using the LOA correctly will always get you the positive results you want.

Chapter Six

How Do I Stop Negative Thoughts (Part One)

What can be said about negative thoughts..
It is not surprising there are many questions relating to negative thoughts, whilst attempting to use the Law of Attraction (LOA), as ones' thoughts are paramount to manifesting what is wished.

Using ones thoughts appears in every step of the process:
Asking, which can be achieved by saying it aloud, quietly or silently (in the mind). Knowing that you need a certain amount of money to pay a bill, may not be voiced to anyone, but silently wished or Asked for in-order to pay the bill. One uses the mind to continuously Believe that the money will arrive on time to pay the bill.

In taking Action one may make calls to the company that the money is owed or attempt to get a loan, whilst taking any action, ones thoughts are important.

A note here, one should bare in mind the saying 'what you think about you bring about.' This is important at all times, but especially when attempting to manifest a particular thing, person or situation.

Having a positive attitude or mindset throughout life is conducive to less stress, having a positive attitude or mindset during the process of manifesting keeps one in the expectant stage and on task to Receive.

Should the ability to stay in a positive mindset while using the LOA be compromised, one may find that their wish takes longer to arrive. There is also a possibility that many may halt the process altogether and herald in a new wish, often something they don't want.

Negativity is often sensed within a person, but there is also environmental negativity that is voiced or displayed, as mentioned above, one should be ever mindful of their own thoughts when using the LOA as it can delay manifestations or facilitate the end of the current wish or process. In the questions below we will see the challenges people face when negativity creeps into the process of using the LOA.

Any ideas on visualizing, when there are a lot of naysayers trying to make you negative?? And you don't have a lot of time.

Thank you for your question. No-one can "make you negative." When that person or persons say something you feel is less than positive, say an affirmation that counteracts what they have said.

Find an affirmation that resonates with you and say it loudly, under your breath or in your mind. For example, I answered a question recently in which the partner would always say, 'we don't have any money' or 'we just can't afford that.' I suggested that the other person finish their sentence with... "at the moment," which is a more positive statement. In doing this it stops you feeling that their not so positive words haven't landed in your environment or your space.

You could also use this time to commence your visualizing, begin with your wish fulfilled! What will it feel like, where will you be when you get the news that your wish has come true.
Will it be at your front door as you open the post.
Will it be while you are steering at the computer screen.
Perhaps you will get a call while out shopping.

You can use their naysaying as a cue to begin your pleasant visualizing journey. Your aim here is to not let anything that is not positive encroach on the mindset you are trying to build and maintain.

Ideally you should attempt to put some distance between you and the person or persons who are trying to convert you into a 'naysayer.' If this is not possible, know that what they say is not what you believe.

Your time is precious and should be spent wisely, limit the amount of time you are around these people. I understand this can be challenging if you live or work along side the naysayers, do what you can do to occupy your mind with a positive melody or affirmation when your environment becomes less than positive.

What are some smaller tests I can do to strengthen my belief in the law? I'm definitely seeing the link between manifesting bad thoughts but not enough positive.

Thank you for your question...This is an easy one. Just remember how you manifested in the past, think of how you felt when you received what you had wished for.

You can also try it out again....Ask for something you would consider 'small'. Let me help you here, ask to see a 'paint brush', now this can not be one you have in your garage or one you own. The paint brush may show up on a TV advert, a bill board, a sticker, you may even hear someone talking about a paint brush as you stand in line!....As soon as you see or hear about the paint brush, you'll know that you still 'have it'.

Then start making your list of things you want and attempt to manifest them one by one or in multiples. In regard to 'not enough positive' thoughts, create them, they belong to you as they come through you. Insist that only positive thoughts live here. This may seem like a silly game, but it works.

Every-time you have a thought that is not so positive or perhaps thoughts of doubt, acknowledge it and dispel it.

Find affirmations that resonate or are true to you, say or sing them until the negative thought goes away. This will take some practice as your negative thoughts may be use to hanging around until you are convinced that what is being said is true.

Hopefully you will get to a stage when the minute you get a negative thought you begin to hum and the thought goes away.

Just a few questions. So like attracts like so positive thoughts and feelings attract more positive feelings and higher vibrational frequency. And negative thoughts and emotions attract negative feelings and lower vibrational frequency.
So trying to have more positive mindset. What emotions would I replace with anger, resentment and failure? Every time I feel them I want to swap those thoughts/change feelings into positive thoughts and feelings. Love your thoughts. Thanks

Thank you for the question. You are right like attracts like...Thank goodness that while using LOA you do not manifest what you think about straight away, one would need to ruminate on the thing or situation in-order to bring it into reality.

According to research, we have about 60,000 thoughts per day, so you can't help feeling *"anger, resentment or failure."* However, it is what we do when these thoughts appear. I would acknowledge that I feel anger, resentment or failure, (after a rant) I deal with the feelings individually. What is making me feel the way I do, what lesson am I to learn from this experience.

This can be challenging, but I then say "everything is working in my favour." If everything is working in my favour, there has got to be a good outcome to the feelings I am experiencing. I also know that after things appear to be going wrong, (i.e. I feel angry, resentful or there appears to be a failure in something attempted) my manifestation will arrive shortly.

In my recent course, I call this the 'Breakdown stage'. When everything seem to go belly up! It is at this stage many people halt their manifestations, by becoming *angry, resentful* or feeling the manifestation is a *failure.* You can and should *"swap those thoughts [ ] into positive thoughts"* say them out loud or silently until the unwanted thoughts go away, practice makes perfect here. The more you "swap" them the less you will get. Note I did not say they won't return, as mixed up in those 60,000 thoughts we have each day, some will be unwanted. Again its how we deal with them that counts, not that they had appeared.

The aim while attempting to manifest is to continue to believe, by finding affirmations that resonate with or are true to you. Say or sing them to show God/the Universe that you still want what you have asked for, and continue to believe its on the way regardless of appearances or any thoughts that make you feel otherwise.

Someone I "think I know" has intentionally hurt me to the point that I now wish her a bad karma because I feel so betrayed and disappointed. It makes me think of all possible bad karma happens to her. I tried to forgive but it's very hard. I know the anger within me ruins my life but why is this happening to me, I never did anything wrong to her but she is just jealous. What should I do? What am I attracting? Why has she manifested to hurt me and make me suffer?? How does all this work? Please I need advice. Thanks.

Thank you for sharing this with us.
I am sorry you are experiencing this type of treatment. Firstly, ensure you are safe, please contact any local organisation that may be able to help.

I understand that when we get hurt, it can be an instant response to hurt back, and that it can be challenging to forgive when we are still feeling the pain the other person has caused.

It can be difficult to be positive when there is a lot of negativity around us, but try. It is important, if you can, to distance yourself from this person. As I have mentioned to others.

On a practical note and this goes for EVERYBODY in your life...If anyone dis's you, you distance your self from them. That is Dis-respect, Dis-honours or you have Dis-trust for that person...distance yourself from them. We often allow people in our lives to treat us crudely because they hold a title, Mum, Dad, Husband, Sister, Brother, 'Friend', Boss even Child! If someone who we have not given a title, was to 'dis' us, we would instinctively know what to say and do. You need to tell this person (if you can) how she is making you feel, and ask her to stop. I believe this person knows how they make you feel! You may need to alert or confide in someone close to you about what is going on.

I do not know your living situation, but would suggest if possible, to distance yourself from her. No amount of manifesting is likely to change the situation if you do not change what you will allow in your life. Find ways to ensure you are not in this persons' presence.

Ask God/the Universe to bring this episode in your life to a amicable end. When you know you have done all you can to avoid this person, you wait.

You should not ask for any bad thing to happen to this person, as it is not your responsibility of dishing out karma to anyone, it also keeps negativity around you as you carry them in your thoughts. Be aware that what we think about, we bring into our lives, that is for ourselves and those around us.

You asked *"what am I attracting?"* You are attracting all that you are wishing for her! If you spend time thinking about all the bad things you would like to appear, albeit to someone else, it will appear, but maybe to you! Be careful what you wish for springs to mind here.

"Why has she manifested to hurt me and make me suffer??"
I can not answer, why she has manifested the ability to make you suffer, however you can manifest the end of this suffering by doing practical things and ensuring that your thoughts are positive as often as possible.

The next question below was left by someone who had seen the conversation above and had some questions of their own.

I'm following this post and thank you for this answer but what if " that person" is someone you can't distance yourself from, not immediately anyway, life circumstances sometimes cause us to have to be around people we don't want to be around and it's extremely challenging to not walk around all day thinking ugly negative thoughts about them because of the way they treat you?

I am sorry if you are going through this type of treatment.

Do try to keep yourself safe and note that there are emergency organisations available should you feel you need them.
It is important that I mentioned not being in that persons' presence, as much as you can.

One has to think on a practical level, in that they make plans to distance themselves from this person. There are local organisations that may help you to do this when you can. I totally understand not being able to get away and having to walk on 'egg shells' as not to instigate further ill treatment.

We are human and the feelings of fight (in which we can't) or flight (in which we can't immediately do) kicks in, so we internalize these feelings in *"ugly negative thoughts about them because of the way they treat you."*

Use this thought time, as best as you can, to start making plans, plans to leave, seek help to leave, confide in someone you trust. This can be challenging thinking of leaving a person you love, but note that that person is also an adult and has chosen to be a total ****
towards you.

"That person" has made a conscious effort to treat you the way they do.
"That person" has lost respect for you and your well being.
"That person" may be treating you as property instead of the human being you are.
"That person" may believe that they have a right to behave the way they do.
"That person" is ill treating (abusing) you.

If you are thinking and planning of ways to remove yourself, you may find that you have less time to think up negative things regarding the other person.

Think about YOU and any children you may have, and ways you can live a stress less life. No one should have to walk on egg shells or find themselves trying desperately not to have negative thoughts about something that is happening to them. Do reach out for help as it appears that *"that person"* need some too!

I am in a situation in which I am trying to get away. I am also trying as much as possible to practice self control with my words & thoughts but some days it's impossible and I feel like I'm creating A LOT of negativity & manifesting bad stuff to happen.

Thank you for sharing this with us. I am unsure of your situation, but if your circumstance is around a domestic issue, do ensure you are safe, contact any local organisation that may be able to assist you to *"get away."* These organisations are non judgemental and are there to help.

I understand that you will do anything within your power not to instigate any ill treatment as you mention *"I am trying much as possible to practice self control."* You state that *"some days it's impossible and I feel like I'm creating A LOT of negativity."*

Although you are aware what you think about, say and do can cause negativity, remember that you are human with emotions, give yourself some slack.

The best of us may jump up and down and shout expletives should we accidentally hold something hot, then we learn or ensure we are more careful next time.

You feel that you are *"creating A LOT of negativity,"* so occupy your thoughts, the best you can, to getting away from the situation you are in.

Make a list of people and or organisations that may be able to help.
Think about your immediate needs, and what you will take with you.
Consider any documents you may need etc..

Find affirmations (not always easy at times), to recite when ever you feel that you are about to *"create negativity."* A mind that is busy trying to arrange a better situation for themselves has less room to create negativity. Try to be mindful of what you say, again this can be challenging, it really is better to say nothing, than to utter words that you may regret or have you feeling that you are *"manifesting bad stuff to happen."* If this is what you believe, you need to try and change what you do and say.

Dwell on thoughts of the future, in which things are as you would like them, and take action towards a better time in your life.

My mom has lot of anger issues and keeps insulting me. I try a lot to write affirmations that she should have awakening that she is hurting me, and that we should be able to set healthy boundaries. But whenever I do this, I find my mom more agitated and angry.

Thank you for sharing this with us, I am sorry you are experiencing this in your life now.
I can't go on without saying that you need to send your mother love, I know this may sound strange but try! As humans, we tend to act how we feel, maybe your mother isn't feeling love, happiness or contentment.

One would need to find out what is causing her to project insults and hurt unto others. I can't help thinking, what would happen to the insults and hurt she has inside her, if there was no one to hurl it at! (but that's just my thoughts).

I do not know what may have caused your mother to behave the way she does, if you have sought advice from a medical professional and found that your mother is of sound mind, then you need to take practical action which goes for EVERYBODY in your life...If anyone dis's you, you distance your self from them. That is Dis-respect, Dis-honours or you have Dis-trust for that person...distance yourself from them.

We often allow people in our lives to treat us crudely because they hold a title, Mom, Dad, Husband, Sister, Brother, Boss even Child! If someone who we have not given a title, was to 'dis' us, we would instinctively know what to say and do.

You need to tell your Mother how she is making you feel, and ask her not to continue to insult or hurt you.

I do not know your living situation, but would suggest if possible, to distance yourself from her.

It is not your job to 'fix' her, she is on her own journey and although you would like her to be a different type of Mother, she is how she is! What you can do is decide what YOU will put up with! And how YOU can make YOUR life better.

We have autonomy (In most cases) of our actions, things get very challenging when we try to 'make' others do certain things or be a certain way. If your Mother has chosen to be this way, You should choose not to accept it.

I am trying to manifest everyday. I try and have gratitude for the good in my life, I forgive the past, I repeat manifestations over and over, look for signs. But I am going through the biggest heartbreak I've ever went through in my life and I am struggling. I don't want to feel this way any-more. How can I feel what I'm trying to manifest while still feeling heartbreak?

Thank you for sharing this with us. Sorry you are experiencing a heartbreak and struggling, as many of us have.

This is something that you are going through and will emerge out the other end. The operative word here is *going through*, it will come to an end, when you have cried all the tears that belong to that heartbreak, when you have replayed all the good and bad times. When you have repeated the incident to yourself, friends and or family 100 times.

The fact that you are saying *"I don't want to feel this way any-more"* means you are progressing, however you also state that you are struggling, I do not know your situation and your struggling can look very different from what I call struggling.

I would advise that you tell a friend or family member how you feel. You may be inclined to consult your GP if you feel your struggling is encroaching on your daily routine.

To answer your question of *"How can I feel what I'm trying to manifest while still feeling heartbreak?"* You can't, right now! You need to be in the right frame of mind to manifest a change or a want in your life.

When using the LOA we concentrate on what we want in the form of visualisations, we say affirmations regarding the want, we occupy our minds with what we want, the colour, the size, the amount, the area, the style etc.. and then some may even 'Act as if' they already have the want. We take action, in the form of house and or car viewings, we gather documents, get our finances together etc...Can you see yourself being able to do any of the above, right now? Perhaps not, the reason for that is because you are going through a heartbreak. It is down time, it is time to focus on you and get through this heartbreak.

You need self care, your mind body and perhaps Soul has been through trauma for which you need to heal. This is why it can be challenging for those who are ill and attempting to 'feel better' when the illness is pain, they are feeling the pain whilst attempting to wish it away.

Practical steps are always called for, before embarking on trying to manifest. Self care and nurture is needed and for as long as it takes, before you are able to fully immerse yourself in trying to manifest anything other than feeling better, not struggling and getting through this heartbreak.

Hello, it's my mind which is full of negative thoughts and fears and I have been trying to write and manifest the same things for years but I am unable to do it...I fear so many bad things and I am in a cycle of negative thoughts...I feel I get sucked into all the time. I am going through so many problems and I want to experience life which is stable and secure free of fears and negative experiences. How do I do it. Plz guide me. Thank you

Thank you for sharing and the question. Everything in our body can be controlled by its owner! That includes our mind, grant you, we have approximately 60,000 thoughts a day! How do we control our mind? When what you call a negative thought arrives, you acknowledge it and replace it with an affirmation or saying.
Here's a few:

'I do not accept that thought.'
'I don't believe that will happen.'
'Everything is working in my favour.'

Find an affirmation or saying that resonates with you and repeat it every-time what you call a negative thought enters your mind. Note, I am implying that you are to 'say' the affirmation, you should use your voice! What we say, think and in this instance write down, we bring more into our lives. Do you know that everything we say after "I" is happening, has happened or about to happen in our lives? Re-read your question above and see where you have brought *"negative thoughts, fear, constant trying, being sucked into a cycle, so many bad things and so many problems,"* into your life.

("I" have been trying to write and manifest the same things for years but "I" am unable to do it..."I" fear so many bad things and "I" am in a cycle of negative thoughts..."I" feel "I" get sucked into all the time. "I" am going through so many problems)

Regardless of what is appearing in your life right now, DECIDE TODAY that things are going to change. TODAY you will start to *"experience life which is stable and secure free of fears and negative experiences,"* those are your words, not mine. TODAY begin to believe these words you have written, and re-write your life, re-think your life, take control of your thoughts, repeat what you want for your life and STOP repeating what you don't want.

Hi, someone said that if you want something good to manifest in your life but subconsciously you are expecting and prepared for negative outcome,
The result is you'll get the things what you EXPECT and PREPARED for.
Is this true?

Yes, this is very true.
What you think about you bring about. This is why we suggest that you stay in high vibration or try to align to the situation or item you have wished for...For example, if you have asked for a brand new shiny car, what vibration do you think the brand new shiny car will be on?

It will not be on a vibration of lack, untrusting, unbelieving or undeserving.

It would most likely be on the vibration of, 'I'm going to get a brand new shiny car' or 'I deserve this brand new shiny car.' Having that attitude ensures that you naturally complete a few other processes connected to manifesting what you want. You begin to 'Act As If' You wished for item is here or about to arrive....That brand new shiny car we spoke about, will need a clean garage to sleep in at nights, so you begin to make space for your wished for item. You also know, like you know, that regardless of what is happening in your life at the time of making your wish, your manifestation is still on the way. (Known as Detachment).

So as you rightly said, what you prepare for and expect is what you get.

Hi, I have friends who think they're going to die or get cancer everyday but they never do. If it was true, many things in this world will go wrong because everyday people are thinking bad every minute.

Thank you for your comment.
I am sorry to hear that you *"have friends who think they're going to die or get cancer everyday,"* and the fact that you are expecting them *"to die or get cancer but they never do!"* To be in a life that has you thinking those things must be torment!

To that I say everyone is on their own journey, and perhaps, this is why it may be assumed, that as many everyday people are thinking bad things, every minute of every day, it follows that many things in this world will go wrong.

This is a fact and way of life for many people, however, there are many more who know that although things go wrong, people get cancer and expire, there is a reason they are here and want to make this life, their life and the life of all around them a nicer, more pleasant or better place to be. This may be the reason you joined this forum, here you will notice that some members have had horrid things happen to them and are trying to understand why this has happened, as well as how to feel better.

Others are trying to get to a nicer, more pleasant or better mindset than some of your *'friends.'* Some members are here to be around 'like minded' people, that is people, who have a nicer, more pleasant or better outlook than others! and know that to think doom and gloom will only bring about situations and people who only think, talk about or expect doom and gloom.

You have the free will and ability (I assume) to distance yourself from the people you call *'friends,'* that constantly wish death upon themselves. It would seem that being around these *friends*, have managed to give you a gloomy outlook on life too.

Did you know it is easier to spread doom and gloom than to spread happiness and light? Just turn on a news channel and see how many views each type of report receive! If doom and gloom is contagious, why would you be in its line of fire? I do not know your living situation or whether you have to care for your 'friends,' but just as a nurse, can not cry or take on the ailment every-time they see a sick or dying patient, you too can ensure you do not carry your friends' 'illness' around with you.

As mentioned above you have free will and you should use it, to ensure you do not 'catch' what your friends are attempting to spread.

Hi, can you help me to be positive no matter what. I am sure I can be positive.

Hi, thank you for the question.

You ask *"can you help me to be positive no matter what."* For me to help you be positive or use 'equanimity' it will take coaching or mentoring. I can not profess to have a 1,2,3 step program to being *"positive no matter what."* However, you could start by proclaiming 'Everything is working in my favour,' regardless what has happened.

The boiler breaks down you say 'Everything is working in my favour.'

You are late for a meeting you say 'Everything is working in my favour.'

You get a raise, you shout 'Everything is working in my favour.'

In doing this you remain positive as you know and believe that 'Everything is working in your favour.' So to answer your question, yes you can be positive no matter what, you just have to choose to be.

As we are everyday people, we have everyday issues and challenges to over come. In-order to remain *"positive no matter what,"* takes training and perhaps practice everyday. Think about the people you may have read about or those around you who remain positive no matter what.

Let me start with Socrates, I understand that this is not the space for a lesson in philosophy, but Socrates believed that one could and should remain positive regardless of what is happening to them, so much so that even when taking his dying breath he was 'up beat' and teaching others to be. Socrates lived and died thinking positive, in fact he died teaching it!

Lets get a little more practical. Think of members of the armed forces, those on the front lines, no matter what is happening, going to happen or has happened, they have had to think *"positive no matter what."*

Lets bring this closer to home. Consider our Police officers, who turn up at horrid crime scenes. They have to appear positive, for their safety and for those around them.

A little closer now, Doctors and Nurses all have to appear positive regardless of the diagnoses they have to deliver! Now think of a caring parent whose child has fallen from the climbing frame and landed awkwardly on their arm! How positive do you think that parent needs to be, in-order not to send that child into shock, and get them to the doctors and nurses I've mentioned above?

All these people have had training to think *"positive no matter what."* So failing a life time habit, field, university or on the job parent training. I would state 'Everything is working in my favour.' I feel it keeps me positive and knowing that regardless of what is happening, it is happening for a reason or to teach me something and it will be in my favour.

End of Part One

On that positive note I will leave the rest of the 'Negative Thoughts' for part two, and go on to show how some harness that negativity to manifest quickly, some times even instantly!

Real Questions. Real Talk.

Chapter Seven

Why Does Anger = Manifest Quickly?

Have you ever said something in anger or frustration and see it materialise quickly in your life? We do it when we don't want to go to the mall on a Saturday afternoon and state, "there will not be any good parking spaces and the lines are going to be long." You arrive at the mall and there are no good parking spaces and the lines are long, in fact you may join a line that has an issue with the checkout machine, only to have to join the end of another long line!

Note there will be someone, leaving their house at the same time you leave for the mall, they will be heading to the same mall, but have a different attitude than you....See that car that just pulled into a spot right by the entrance? They might have just been lucky, or maybe they left their house saying. "I've got to go to the mall, I hope I get a great parking space again, and the lines aren't too long." Annoyance build in you as you spot that person around the store, and again being served at the till as you arrive at the end of the long line, that seem to just appear out of nowhere.

I can only imagine the atmosphere in your car as you drive home or when you eventually get home, as you're bound to have met a lot of shoppers on the road, at the traffic lights and pedestrians causing you to stop at every crossing. All contributing to your frustrations of having to go to the mall on a Saturday afternoon, your trip to and from the mall, may not have been a good one.

This isn't a lesson in mindset, but you could take a minute to consider what you think about, you bring about. If you think a thing with emotion, say a thing with emotion, believe what you have just uttered, then begin to act as if the believed event or situation has happened, it will happen and happen very quickly.

These are the steps or process of using the Law of Attraction (LOA). The process is exactly the same for wanted situations, but we tend not to have the passion, vigour or heightened emotion we have when angry, annoyed or frustrated. Below you will see evidence of this.

Why do devious people seem to attract more quickly/easily?

Thank you for the question. I am unsure what or whom you class as devious, but I will attempt to answer your question. It is always important to add a practical eye over a situation when attempting to use the LOA, with that in mind I assume you mean someone who appears to be cruel, uncaring, unfriendly, perhaps a person who has gained wealth by underhanded dealings.

Regardless of your idea of devious, if they have used the LOA, they followed the steps of manifesting! They asked, they believed it will happen, then they detached, meaning they didn't think about how, when or why it will happen, they just knew it would come, they stayed in the vibration of the believed situation, they may have also acted 'as if' the wanted situation had arrived and without a doubt it appeared in their life.

To recap they ASKED, BELIEVED, DETACHED and ACTED 'AS IF' all in a short space of time and POW, here comes their manifestation. You may also notice that that person, is never in want as they may believe that lack is not their natural habitat, so they stay in the vibration of gain as opposed to lack and need.

We may wonder why some people maintain their wealth while others do not. Many wealthy people 'believe' that they should be wealthy and remain wealthy, even if they become bankrupt, as they get up and make the wealth again because they do not except being in need or want.

I do not know if this is the case with the person you call devious, however once you ask, believe and take action you will receive. Now, there is a saying that goes something like this, " be careful what you wish for."

Note I teach, asking aright, that is to mean, when you ask God/the Universe for something, ensure you add words to the effect of 'by divine right,' in adding this to the end of your wish, you are asking God/the Universe to amicably grant your wish, you are asking for your wish to arrive without causing any ill to anyone or causing anyone to go without, and that the wish is beneficial to you and anyone you choose to partake in your gain.

If this person appears to gain using 'devious' methods or they intend to use what they have gained in a devious way, the gain will not be sustainable, and Karma, is perhaps the answer for another question!

Usually the things that manifest instantly are things I don't care about much or things out of anger. Why is this??

Thank you for the question. Simply, you followed the steps of manifesting! You asked, or said something in anger, you believed it will happen, then you DETACHED, meaning you didn't think about how, when or if it will happen, You knew it would come, you stayed angry or frustrated (i.e you got into the vibration of the believed situation) you also acted 'as if' the unwanted situation had arrived and without a doubt it appeared in your life.

To recap You ASKED, BELIEVED, DETACHED and ACTED 'AS IF.' The law dictates that it must come.

In order to do this for wanted situations you use the same steps, however, because it is something you want, you may hold on to the how is this going to work, who will give this to me, and will it really come. Can you see the difference?

Here are some differences.
Many of us ask, but what we ask for may not be realistic, meaning we don't believe we will get it or deserve it, we then go on with the steps not really believing we will get the wished for item or situation, we do not detach, as we are constantly thinking about the how, when, or why the wished for item or situation will arrive, and stay in that vibration or mood, there is no acting 'as if' because the wish was not believed in the first place. You do not get your wished for item or situation.

To attract wanted items or situations quickly, you Ask, Believe, Detach and Act 'as if'. As mentioned above, this is easier said than done as life goes on while we wait for our manifestations.

One has to ensure they stay in the mood or vibration of what they have asked for regardless of what is happening in their lives.

Many asked for situations or items are thwarted in the 'waiting stage', and a new wish begins the process of making its way to you, that new wish may have been made in anger, believed in anger and expected in anger, you even find that you act as if the situation or item has already arrived. All done in quick succession whilst staying in the angry vibration, and thus we are back where this question started..Manifesting quickly when angry.

My response to the above question elicited a further question.

Thank you. It is frustrating because of how hard it is to be detached from something you want very badly.

I totally agree, it can be challenging to detach when you really want something....Here's what I do. As I can't help but think of the wanted item or situation. I ensure I add to my thoughts of my wish, 'this will work out in my favour,' 'this will work out in my favour.' Every-time I think of the wish I have made. I remember that it is God/the Universe who has my wish in hand and it will come when it comes, as everything is working in my favour. I also know that if I do not get my wish, I will get something better, as everything, every wish I put out there will be granted in my favour.

Another tip to help you detach, is to get ready for what you have asked for, If it is money to pay a bill, start making a list of what you need to buy or pay for with what you have left, if its an item, prepare for the item, if I have asked for something many may class as small, I make space for it in my house....A new pair of shoes springs to mind...I make space for it on the shelf it will reside when it gets here. If it is something people may consider big, I'd clear out that garage, in-order to park it in, or get rid of that large wardrobe...You get the picture...In preparing for the wished for item, one detaches from the who, how and when.

The other thing to consider is your wanting something *"very badly."* I get it, and I have been there myself, when you think you have the only solution to a particular problem and nothing, yes nothing else in the world will solve this problem, but what you have decided is the only and ultimate solution. That sentence sounded dramatic didn't it? It is the wanting or needing it *"very badly"* that hinders the detachment!

When using the LOA, most people are in want or even need, but for quick results, one must detach quickly. Quickly understanding that the want or need is no longer their personal responsibility to provide the solution, will allow detachment to set in quickly. This doesn't stop the need for the item or situation, however by saying an affirmation every-time the thought of the want comes up, one is occupying their mind with other things than how desperately they want a solution.

This brings us back to what I stated in the beginning of this response, my affirmation of 'everything is working in my favour.' Find an affirmation that resonates with you and when in situations of wanting something *"very badly"* say it silently or out loud. You will be surprised how quickly you let go and let God/the Universe get you the right solution at the right time.

Hi everyone ... is it just me or is it actually the right process that whenever i think of something negatively it manifests easily than when i think of it positively.
Eg: if i want something... if i visualise this thing with my imagination ... my thoughts and my feelings it never happens to me but when i visualise myself not having that thing and feel sad about it, it instantly manifests I get proof that the thing will not be mine... so now my mind only thinks of negative visualization. But people often say if you think positively and imagine it .. it manifests ...Need help ... need someone to clarify this to me please.

To clarify simply, you had followed the steps of manifesting! You Asked, or said something in anger, you Believed it will happen, then you DETACHED, meaning you didn't think about how, when or why it will happen, you just knew or believed, you wouldn't get what you asked for, you then stayed angry or frustrated (i.e you got into the vibration of the believed situation) you also acted 'as if' the unwanted situation had arrived and without a doubt it appears in your life.

To recap You ASKED, BELIEVED, DETACHED and ACTED 'AS IF.' You may have completed the steps within an hour or even five minutes, your wish will begin to make its way to you as soon as you complete the steps sincerely.

In order to do this for wanted situations you use the same steps, I would add that while you wait, you use affirmations to keep you believing or on task. Doubt that your wish is on the way will stagnate or halt your wish all together.

Here's what happens: Many of us ask, but what we ask for may not be realistic, meaning we don't believe we will get it or deserve it, we then go on with the steps not really believing we will get the wished for item or situation, we do not detach, as we are constantly thinking about the how, when, or why the wished for item or situation will arrive, and stay in that vibration or mood. There is no acting 'as if' because the wish was not believed in the first place. There you have it, well there you don't have it!...You do not get your wished for item or situation.

To attract wanted items or situations quickly, you Ask, Believe, Detach and Act 'as if'. Now this is easier said than done as life goes on while we wait for our manifestations. One has to ensure they stay in the mood or vibration of what they have asked for regardless of what is happening in our lives.

Many wishes are halted in the 'waiting stage', and a new wish begins the process of making its way to you, that new wish is often the opposite of what you have asked for. For-example, the new wish is: "I am not going to get what I asked for," this is 'wished for' in anger or frustration.

Can you see the vicious cycle?
And we are back where we started at the beginning of this question!

How come most people become successful because they hit rock bottom or went through some kind of tragedy. When others who aren't going through anything but have difficulty trying to get somewhere in life takes them longer than people who have it worse than us?

Thank you for the question. These *"most people"* you speak of, become successful despite the fact that they *"hit rock bottom or went through some kind of tragedy,"* and not because of it.

Consider this, if *"rock bottom"* is your gauge or barometer, then these *"most people"* have no where to go, other than up.

If the *"most people"* who have had a tragedy have two options then they can either hit rock bottom and go up or they can bypass rock bottom and go up. In the up, I mean be successful.

One could attempt to decipher what you class as successful, but I assume everyone here has the same understanding of it to mean, financially comfortable and as you say *"get somewhere in life."*

The rock bottom people have less to loose and all to gain, by getting *"somewhere in life,"* as according to you they are at rock bottom. Maybe where they were in life was their incentive.

The others you mentioned who *"aren't going through anything"* may have a safety net, a save roof over their head, food to eat, and or a loving family. Perhaps they didn't have much of a drive to succeed, as they don't or didn't have a rock bottom as a starting block, but a nice soft cosy life or bed to get up from!

The common denominator here are the people, not what they did or didn't go through.
I have mentioned the above to make you aware that it is the person that has the need or want to *"get somewhere in life"* and it is the magnitude of the want or need that propels the person to get up and start the process of becoming successful.

The person who has the comforts of home life may have the same zeal to succeed as the person who has hit rock bottom or endured a tragedy. Both may start off on the same journey of success and one achieve their goal of success (whatever success is for them) sooner than the other. How long did it take them to achieve their goal? If you are unable to answer this question, you may never know if the people who started at rock bottom or those who have had a tragedy took less time than the ones who hadn't been through anything.

Okay, enough said. Let's get to the LOA answer part of this response. Let us assume that you are right and a person who went through some kind of tragedy gets somewhere in life quicker than the people who *"aren't going through anything."*

What would they have had to do to achieve this, using the LOA. Not to dispel your myth, but they both would have done the same thing.

That is Asked Believed, Detached, they took Action or Acted 'as if' and then they received.

What motivates the two or three sets of people you have mentioned in your question, to start and complete the LOA process, has nothing to do with where they started in life.

The LOA is the same for everyone, all the time. The LOA works with your belief. Maybe as mentioned above, the people who are at rock bottom have nothing to lose, so start the LOA process with no doubt that it would work, as it had to work for them.

Where as the people who have the comforts of home, have a safety net. They may start their process with thoughts of, 'If this doesn't work and I can't pay the rent or mortgage, a member of my family will pay it for me, or I'll be able to borrow some money from somewhere'.
The rock bottom person may only have his or her belief to fall back on, with no one else to put their trust in, they wholeheartedly believe that the LOA will work for them. (remember they have nothing to loose, and all to gain). They also know in their heart that if they do not get what they have asked for they will get its equivalent or something better. Getting nothing leaves them where we found them, rock bottom.

The people who *"aren't going through anything,"* on the other hand have lots to loose if this LOA process does not work. They may lose face, the money they have been given a hunch to spend, their time, as they have doubt, they may feel that it would be wasted if they do not get what they have wished for, they may loose sleep as they spend their nights worrying about how or if their wish will come true and ultimately knowing or like yourself, believe that *"most people become successful because they hit rock bottom or went through some kind of tragedy."* They may also believe, If their wish does come, it will take some time.

See the difference?

Now I am not suggesting that this is what happens in your *"most people"* cases, but to show that this is a possibility. I am here to tell you that, should both sets of people follow the LOA process unwavering they will all achieve their goals.

Why is it that attracting something bad is easier than attracting something good?

Great Question. The simple answer, you followed the steps of manifesting! You asked, or said something in anger, you believed it will happen, then you DETACHED, meaning you didn't think about how, when or why it will happen, you then stay angry or frustrated (i.e you get into the vibration of the believed situation) you also act 'as if' the unwanted situation has arrived and without a doubt it appears in your life.

To recap You ASKED, BELIEVED, DETACHED and ACTED 'AS IF' all in a short space of time, and without a doubt, your manifestation appears in your life.

In order to do this for wanted situations you use the same steps, however many of us ask, but what we ask for may not be realistic, meaning we don't believe we will get or deserve it, we then go on with the steps not really believing we will get the wished for item or situation, we do not detach, as we are constantly thinking about the how, when, or why the wished for item or situation will arrive. You stay in that vibration or mood, there is no acting 'as if' because the wish was not believed in the first place. There you have it, well there you don't have it!...You do not get your wished for item or situation.

To attract wanted items or situations quickly, you Ask, Believe, Detach and Act 'as if'. Now this is easier said than done as life goes on while we wait for our manifestations.

One has to ensure they stay in the mood or vibration of what they have asked for regardless of what is happening in our lives.

Many asked for situations or items are thwarted in the 'waiting stage', and a new wish begins the process of making its way to you.

Response From Enquirer

Still don't understand. Lots of times it feels like everything is working out then something bad happens.

As mentioned above life goes on while we wait for our manifestations. One has to ensure they stay in the mood or vibration of what they have asked for regardless of what is happening in our lives.

Many asked for situations or items are thwarted in the 'waiting stage'.. During the waiting stage and just before the manifestation is due to arrive, a few things may happen, one of which is what I call the 'Breakdown stage'. When everything seem to go belly up! It is at this stage many people halt their manifestations, by feeling that their manifestation is a failure, and proclaiming that 'i'm never going to get'..what they have asked for, along with thoughts of giving up, this causes the whole process to begin again.

This stage is also a time of 'clearing out,' that is people, places and things. Have you ever wondered why your life came together after a certain someone left your life? Or when you moved to a different address, town or country? It works with things too...The boiler broke down...Circumstances ensue you get the best one on the market, the car windshields develop a crack, it works out that you get all new windshields (front and back) with the side windows all fitted for free!

One is to 'keep the faith' and continue to believe that what they have wished for will come regardless of what is happening. Just because you are attempting to manifest something, does not stop life from happening. It is the new life situations that throw you off task, you shouldn't let it, you should see it as a sign that what you have asked for is on the way. See the new life situation as God/the Universe moving or shifting things in your life in-order to allow what you have asked for to come in.

I understand this is easier said than done, when the boiler has broken and an unexpected bill has just landed on your door step with a pay in 14 days or else attached to it. Stay the course, keep believing that your wish will arrive.

Regarding the boiler and the unexpected bill, you'll find that easier to deal with as you understand how the LOA works, you Ask, Believe, Detach, take Action and wait for your wish to manifest, regardless of what is happening around you.

End of Questions

We may see anger all around us, whether big out bursts or the smaller acts of anger as someone gets cut off at the lights. We may see it on the news, documentaries or films. The angry person tends to get what they want, like a child they may learn (sooner or later) that anger has its consequences.

Using the LOA may appear to act the same way. When someone is angry they may unconsciously make a wish, which may come true in minutes. The reason we see this is because they followed the LOA steps fully and without doubt, in fact they were unwavering in their belief of what they wished or asked for, they just knew it.

We have seen in all the scenarios given above, in the form of questions, that most of the characters gained something, often something they didn't want. With others receiving success having hit rock bottom or being devious in their ways. But they all had one thing in common, they all believed. This belief was voiced, acted upon and then showed up in their lives or could be seen by onlookers.

Whether you wish something in anger or not the LOA process remains the same, that of Ask, Believe, Detach, take Action and wait to Receive.

Chapter Eight

How Can I Stop Feeling Stuck?

Many people ask me to help them to get unstuck and start manifesting again. As we know you are never stuck and you never stopped manifesting, in fact if you feel this way, you have manifested feeling stuck and unable to manifest!

Once the mindset shifts so will the situation. (What we think about, we bring about). Perhaps their questions should be how can I get out of this rut, this mindset or way of thinking. This can be challenging when feeling in a rut, low, depressed or physically ill. Change the way you think or speak about yourself.

Here is one way of remaining stuck. Ask or voice something wanted or in this case unwanted. "I am unable to manifest any-more, I am stuck." Believe - You believe the way you feel as you have physical evidence that you are 'low, in a rut, or down.' You Act as if you are 'low, in a rut, or down,' with shoulders bent and perhaps the need to stay away from others.

The outcome can only be..... lets say it together...You are in a rut, low, down, stuck and feel unable to manifest. Changing what you say about yourself will evidently change your belief, which may lead to a change in behaviour (the way you act), and the outcome.

See if you would be able to answer the questions below.

How do I reconnect with the universe and start to manifest again?
I've been through a rough year and I have lost connection with my highest frequency. It has been hard staying positive and be able to manifest as I usually did. Thank you for helping.

Thank you for the question. It can be challenging to raise your vibration when you feel 'low' or *"had a rough year."* You have not *"lost connection with [your] highest frequency."* It's still within you!

I understand that it can be challenging to be or stay positive when all around appears to be the opposite of what you want in your life. You have acknowledged that you have been low and now ready to *"reconnect with the universe and manifest again."*

Do you realise that you was never unconnected? We are manifesting all the time, yes, all the time, even when feeling low. It is at this time, and regardless of appearances voicing what is wanted as opposed to what is not wanted should be our affirmations, for example saying or thinking, things will get better or better yet, state 'things are working in my favour.' As you are always connected, the universe has no choice but to bring about what you think about.

Just like when feeling low, we stay in that space longer than we would like, causing more thoughts to become things, and bring unsolicited people and situations into our lives.

Attempt it today...Set about trying to change the situation, if you can't change your current situation, as it is out of your hands, find a cupboard to tidy or re-arrange, clear out the garage or spare room, do something to occupy your mind.

Thinking about a cleared or clean space in your home is better than thinking about what you believe your life looks like now. If you are physically unable to clean or clear out a cupboard, room or garage. Use the people you speak to in-order to bring about a change to your circumstances. When asked 'how are you today?' speak your future into existence by saying what you hope will happen.

'I am feeling better.'
'I hope to get or feel better soon.'
'I'm getting there, slowly but surely.' or perhaps
' I am on the mend.'

Use your own words, words that feel real or resonate with you. The more you speak or think about a brighter future the closer you will be drawn to it.

I came to a point, where I can't manifest anything. It's like nothing works out for me any-more.

So sorry you feel this way.
When attempting to manifest anything, one has to be careful and very deliberate about what we think, say, write and believe. Have a look at your statement above and see where you could be manifesting things you don't want.

I'll help you, you state:

 "I came to a point, where I can't manifest anything. It's like nothing works out for me any-more."

This is obviously your world. The world you think of, self talk about, write about and believe. Do note that we are manifesting ALL THE TIME, so if you believe you *"can't manifest anything,"* you won't manifest anything. If you feel that *"nothing works out for [you] any-more."* Nothing will work out for you...Simple.

You said it, you believe it, you expect it so it MUST appear in your life...Why do you believe it is any different to manifest what you actually want?

I understand that when life happens it is challenging to see what you want, when what you don't want is showing up. It is at this point in your manifesting journey that you stop, take a breath and decide...yes decide what you want...Go into detail of what you want...If its an item...know the colour, the size, it's weight, its shape.

If it is a particular situation...How would you feel when this situation appears in your life...Would it benefit other members of your family; how do you think they will feel when things change for the better.

How will you all celebrate its arrival in your life?

Change the narrative of your life TODAY, decide that how things appear in your life is not what you want and that things are going to change.

Then set about trying to change things.

If it is the case that you are unable to do anything to change the situation, know that all you have to do is wait, while you wait find a cupboard to clear out...encourage a friend or family member to allow you to get started on their cluttered spare room.

Get some old paint out and touch up the scuffs around your home...Do something to occupy your mind because sitting in the belief of nothing working out for you, isn't working out for you!

How can you get past manifesting basic or less than basic things. I can't seem to get past a certain point in my manifestations. I can manifest food or money for one bill but I can't seem to do more. And even if I seem to get close it falls through. I'm assuming my growing up with a poverty mindset has a lot to do with it. Any advice/opinions?

Thank you for the question.
Mindset does have a lot to do with how and what we manifest. Manifesting what we call small is exactly the same as manifesting something we call big! We Ask, Believe, take Action and it turns up.

We tend to put barriers in the way when we believe or class something as big or difficult. You agree that you can manifest something less than basic, that is proof that you can do it, even with what you call a *"poverty mindset."* A few things can be happening here.

Firstly, you may not believe you deserve what you have asked for!

Secondly, you begin to classify wants in "less than basic" or the "food and money for one bill" category. Where does £1,000 fit in? Perhaps in the *"get close, [..] falls through"* category!

Thirdly, there is a stage during the manifesting process that I call the 'Breakdown stage.' Here life situations may get in the way of our manifesting mindset, as the boiler has broken down we now feel that the £100 we had asked for is insignificant compared to the £297.36 quoted by the plumber to fix the boiler.

It is here that we give up on the waiting expectantly for the £100 and voice or make a new wish, believing that 'My manifestation is not coming, now I need more money.' You have Asked (or voiced) and Believe that statement, your Actions are those of somebody who needs more money and have been let down as 'your manifestation is not coming, now you need more money,' shows up as your new situation! What follows, is your belief that *"even if I seem to get close it falls through,"* this belief acts as proof that when manifesting things always *"falls through."*

The 'Breakdown stage' is also a time of 'clearing out,' that is people, places and things.

Have you ever wondered why your life came together after a big shake up, someone left, you left, something in your life changed in a big way. Hence that broken boiler mentioned above.

If you continue to believe through these stages, circumstances (life situations) will ensure you get the best boiler on the market, if the car stopped working, your continued belief will see you get the car you've always wanted.

One is to 'keep the faith' or keep believing the manifestation is on the way, regardless of what is happening, you have asked, believed so it must come.

I feel like I'm failing with manifesting. Any advice? I want to manifest good things in my life, open new doors and move ahead and feel excited about my future.

Thank you for your question.
I am sorry you feel like you are *"failing with manifesting."* Did you know that you can not fail to manifest, as we are always always manifesting. Right now you are manifesting *"failing with manifesting."*!

We have to be aware of what we say when attempting to use LOA. You go on to say that you *"want to manifest good things in my life, open new doors, and move ahead and feel excited about my future,"* and you will, if you keep repeating that.

You have Asked, now Believe that you are manifesting what you want, not what you do not want. Take Action towards what you want, know that new doors are opening for you. Only you can feel excited about your future. This can not be done if you feel or say that you are *"failing with manifesting."*

Try it today, say what you want, believe you will receive it, regardless of your current circumstances, take whatever practical steps you need to take, this could even be saying an affirmation that resonates with you, whenever you feel like you are *"failing."* Listen for guided instructions, these are hunches one may get to go somewhere or do something.

For example. You would like a particular outfit for a special event. You have seen the outfit, perhaps in a magazine, or as you pass a high end store, you are sure you saw a famous person wearing something like it on the red carpet! All that to say, you really want this outfit. The high end store, you feel, is not in your budget, but you want it. You have Asked for the outfit, you Believe you will get it, you just don't know how!

You are trying to save towards it (Action) then you are on your travels around the stores, just window shopping, but you feel guided to go to the next town and have a look. You have no intention of buying a substitute but you'll have a look. In the next town, you come across a small store or boutique that is closing down and today is the last day....Everything must go! Do you get where I am going with this scenario? There at the back of the store is the outfit....with Everything must Go in the back of your mind, you suggest a price to the store owner, they accept and you get your wanted outfit.

In this scenario the wish was voiced whether out loud or just in the mind of the person who wanted the outfit (Asked). They Believed they would get it as they took practical steps (saving), and may have also used an affirmation or two (Action), when they too felt like they wouldn't get their outfit, as the special event was drawing near.

They also followed the guided instruction that appeared as a hunch, to go to another town, just to see what they had to offer. And there their wish was granted, as they made the store owner an offer they couldn't, wouldn't, well they, didn't refuse.

End of Questions

All the enquirers above stated that they felt stuck as they either couldn't connect with the Universe or manifest. One enquirer claimed that they could only manifest the basics.

At times we may feel that things are not going as we would like. This is why it is important that we remain aware of what we say, as we are constantly making wishes, even if we don't believe we are.

Stating that 'I can't manifest' is two wishes in one, cementing the wish. The first is the use of 'I' as mentioned to other enquirers, anything said after 'I' has happened, is happening or will happen, if the statement does not end with a future hope. The second part of cementing this wish is the statement it self, 'I can't manifest.'

We are always manifesting because we are always making wishes with our utterances, if we change our narrative to future tense, we may feel to move, take action, even if it is small steps towards changing our current situation, which will inevitably lead to things happening to help us along the way.

Once you see movement, you will realise that your current situation is not stagnant but fluid, a transient experience with you at the wheel. As soon as you notice that you are the driver, you may decide to get unstuck, the minute you decide, you will be off.

Let us return to the thoughts that keep many people stuck in situations they would rather not be in, we will return to Negative Thoughts.

Real Questions. Real Talk.

Chapter Nine

How Do I Stop Negative Thoughts (Part Two)

What method are you using to manifest your dreams, if you manifest bad stuff when you are thinking positively and when you are waiting for a positive outcome, but you manifest bad stuff?

What's in the back of your mind when you attempted to manifest? What ever that is, is the wish you make!

Response From Enquirer

I thought about stuff, about what I could manifest, but it sounded unrealistic because when I think its a too big a dream (although we can manifest anything) then in my mind I have doubts, that's why I didn't try to manifest dreams that are too big. I think that is why I didn't manifest the stuff I thought of because it was not realistic to manifest.
I thought about it, I was happy, and took action to search for what is needed. Then I thought that the situation will turn out positive, but the opposite manifested. I don't want to be negative. What can I do differently?

Try and change the way you 'self talk', using words like *"unrealistic," "too big dream"* and *"in my mind are doubts,"* will not get your wish granted. I would never use the words *"Unrealistic" "Too big"* or *"Doubt"* in the same train of thought as my wish. Only positive words will be used around anything I want to manifest.

You have even taken to writing these not so positive words down, in regard to a wish you have! No more negative thoughts, sayings and writings when you think about what you want to manifest in your life.

If you think something is *"too big"* for you, it will be too big to come into your life, you have no space for it to enter, its too big. Maybe you don't believe you deserve it! That will also stop it coming. Ask (using only positive thoughts and words) Believe it is yours, Believe you deserve it.

Take positive steps to getting what you want and it will come. Do not worry about how it will reach you, just believe it will.

The Enquirer Clarifies Question

I wrote here about wishes what I wanted and I didn't have doubts or negative thinking about them or about the outcome but regardless of that. I didn't manifest them but got the opposite:(

Thank you for clarity. Here you are saying that you did everything right but you didn't manifest. You had no doubts, you didn't think they were too big and you didn't have any negative thoughts about what you wanted.

You state that you got the opposite...Here's the thing, if you ask for money, all manner of bills will turn up, debts that you had forgotten about lands in your mail box. You find that you are not able to make as much money as you normally make....Anything to do with money starts appearing in your life....This is the 'Breakdown stage.' You have aligned with money, money you owe, money that you could or in this scenario can't make, you may even find that people you know are asking to loan money from you.

Remember, this is when people make another wish, you for example stated, *"I didn't manifest them but got opposite:("* But that was not the case at all, you should have continued to expect your wish, saying that you got the opposite means you had resigned yourself to the fact that you was not going to get your wish and that was the end of the manifesting process for that wish!

You may have experienced the opposite, as a way of telling you that your manifestation was on its way, instead you started the process all over again with a new wish which was, *"I didn't manifest them but got opposite:("* I bet you get the *"opposite"* often!

As I have mentioned to many, 'keep the faith' or keep believing your manifestation is on the way, know that this is just another stage of the manifesting process, know that regardless of what is happening you have asked, believed so it must come.

Sometimes it is hard to think positive as doubts always come through.

I understand that it can be challenging at times to *"think positive."* There are a few things I do when situations are not ideal, I first survey the concern I have. Knowing that I am not being chased by a bear and that my children are safe. I devise ways to correct the situation (after a rant). If the situation is out of my hands, then it is out of my hands, there is no need worrying over situations, issues or concerns you can not do anything about (easier said than done). I then resign myself to the fact that 'everything is working in my favour regardless of appearances'.

Now this will take some practice if you are not use to letting things go, and seeing how it will pan out. You will have to work at this, if you are the type of person who has to get a result, confirmation, or desired outcome to your concern as soon as humanly possible.

This is a Law of Attraction forum, so the advice would be to Ask for an amicable outcome to your situation, regardless of what that is. Believe that God/the Universe is bigger than any issue you may have and it will be sorted one way or another. As mentioned above, do what you can to correct the situation.

Listen for any guided instructions you may get in the form of a hunch, then you wait knowing that 'everything is working in your favour regardless of appearances.'

I have trouble blocking out random intrusive bad things that may manifest although I did not intend too think that thought, and thinking the bad thoughts seem to come with powerful energy that could manifest, fear, anxiousness etc. I quickly try to switch the thought but I worry that the energy put into them is still enough to start the harvest? Is there a technique for reversal of an accidental possible bad manifest.

Thank you for the question. First I need to suggest that if your 'random intrusive' thoughts are interfering with your everyday life, please seek professional help.

Do note that as humans, we have about 60,000 thoughts a day and some may be less than positive. One does not accidentally manifest, as we are manifesting all the time. You are not causing it *"to start to harvest,"* if thoughts begin to harvest as quickly as you believe they do, we would be attempting a "reversal" of these thoughts all day long.

In order to manifest you would need to dwell, believe or act on those thoughts.
As mentioned above, if your thoughts are not causing issues in your everyday life or routine, and perhaps after ruling out professional help, find and use affirmations that resonate with you, whenever you have thoughts that are less than positive.

Response From Enquirer

No it's not like that I promise, it's more over a current situation with a so called friend that was unnecessarily blown out of proportion, and threats were made towards me....I just get negative thoughts in the form of fear. No random intrusive thoughts in that sense. Yes I wouldn't be acting on the negative fear response, I just don't want it in the mix.

Sorry to read that *"threats were made towards"* you. Please ensure you are safe and contact the appropriate authorities if you feel you need to.

When one is living in fear, it can be challenging to think positive or otherwise, as the mind and body goes into fight or flight mode. Please consider your safety first and foremost, then work on healing from this episode in your life.

As I mentioned above, we get many thoughts a day, but brush away the ones that are not conducive to what we are doing or dealing with at the time.

Give your mind something to think of when these intrusive thoughts pop in, an affirmation, a song or use the intrusive thought as cue to stand up and do something, find a cupboard to clean, get the washing done, anything that will have you thinking of something else.

Hi, Let's just say I live with a hardy dose of scepticism these days. I'm constantly waiting for that other shoe to drop.

Thank you for sharing. If you are *"constantly waiting for that other shoe to drop"* You will remain in this state, even when 'good' things happen. Waiting for the other shoe to drop also keeps you in an uneasy state all the time! Which for many, is a vicious cycle.

Do remember what you think about you bring about. What you may find that that is your go to emotion as it has been practised over and over.

In order to get out of that cycle of thinking, I would suggest that you begin each day reminiscing on when something went as plan, nothing went wrong, the other shoe didn't drop and you got your desired out come.

Now this can be something as simple as making a cup of tea....You desired a cup of tea

(I am British so my hot beverage is always going to be tea), you go to the kitchen you put the kettle on and reach for the tea bags and sweetener, you go to the fridge and get the milk. You also get your favourite mug or cup and a spoon to stir the tea and remove the tea bag. You make the tea and sit down to enjoy it. There you have it, nothing dropped!

Now think of a trip to the shops. You got ready, you went to the shops, you bought your items and returned home....No shoe dropping there. Now an event you put together, maybe a childs' birthday party. You sent out the invites, brought all the things needed, the children came, made an almighty mess, little Johnny cried, Susan wet herself, they all had a great time and left. No shoe dropping there either. Unless you are classing the crying and wetting as a shoe dropping moment. I know you're not, as those incidents are just incidents.

You are probably talking about not getting what you have asked for, or perhaps getting some of what you desired but not all of it. When embarking on the use of LOA one has to believe it will come straight off the bat, or get go. There should be no doubt in your mind that you will get what you have asked for.

Here are a few reasons we believe we won't get what has been wished.
The ask is unrealistic for us to conceive getting.
We have never had it before, so why should we get it now!
'believe its too good to be true' or
Something always goes wrong, so I won't get this either, was that last one, your shoe dropping? Why ask for it then?

Perhaps you are just trying the LOA out, to see if it works! It works, because you have managed to manifest *"constantly waiting for that other shoe to drop."* Insist or believe without a doubt that you will manifest the next thing or situation you desire.

Try it with something you class or have labelled easy or small, finding a penny or a pound may come into that category. This will heighten your expectation on using the LOA, by doing so, you bring about people, situations and wished for items, that come to stay and to make your life brighter whether they are wearing or carrying shoes.

Thank you for this forum. I'm going through a really hard time. I've left a toxic family situation with my toddler, currently in a refuge facing Homelessness.
I've been riddled with great fear and I know I've gotten myself here with my fearful thoughts throughout the past 4 months.
I'm trying to be positive and change my mind around so that I start manifesting good things. My question is, how the heck do I do this?
I try every night before I go to sleep to manifest great things for us but it's hard and I find I know what I DON'T want. But when I try to think about what I DO want... I'm always coming back to " I don't know what I want, I just don't want this or this or that" It's just hard and easier to think about what I don't want, it's hard to keep the thoughts on track they always turn into fear, negative and what I don't want. Help!? Where do I start? Why is it so hard? Is this normal or am I just a ball of negativity? Thank you.

First, I must say, well done for being able *to leave a horrid family situation with your toddler*, and thank you for trusting us to answer this question.

"I've been riddled with great fear and I know I've gotten myself here with my fearful thoughts throughout the past 4 months".

Having been through what you had been through, there is no wonder you feel you are " riddled with great fear." Unconsciously you may have been going through this fear for far longer than you have mentioned here.

"I'm trying to be positive and change my mind around so I start manifesting good things. My question is, how the heck do I do this?"

I commend you for trying to manifest "good things," in your current situation, unbeknownst to you, you have began to manifest good things, you have manage to manifest a safe space for you and your child. Please give yourself a pat on the back for that, that in itself is a great feat.

"I try every night before I go to sleep to manifest great things for us but it's hard and I find I know what I DON'T want. But when I try to think about what I DO want... I'm always coming back to, I don't know what I want, I just don't want this or this or that."

I can only imagine the amount of things that run through your mind, after going through the ordeal you have endured. Make a list. This list can be as long as your arm, but make it. By doing this, you put yourself in the 'I want this' zone and away from the 'I don't want' zone. Re-visit your list each night, taking away and adding to it, re-arrange it in priority order, you can even add columns, where I can buy this item, where I could get this item free column. The more you look at or think of what you do want, the less what you don't want will come through, which is 'normal'.

Our minds re-visit what has happened to us, our minds create scenarios of things that could happen to us, our minds create scenarios of things good or bad that we think will happen to us. With our minds having 60,000 thoughts per day it is possible that some of those thoughts are not as positive as we would like. You are doing great, you have taken control of your life and attempting to make it better.

Find affirmations that resonate with you, say it out loud or quietly to yourself, every time a negative or a 'I don't want' comes into your mind. You really are doing well and I assume in a place where further help can be given. You've made it this far, its only onwards and upwards for you.

Response From Enquirer.

Angela Scott Wow this is amazing! YOU are amazing!! Thank you so much for taking the time to comment this!! I actually really really appreciate it!
And you've literally demonstrated in this whole comment how I can change my mind around, better than anyone could have explained to me. You've shown me..Seriously Angela, thank you so much for commenting this.
We moved onto a house July last year and I loved it but I found myself often laying in bed absorbing the love of the house but it was always sad for me because I would always come back to 'how long am I going to be here before I have to leave ' I don't know why I kept thinking it. And all of the threats... I guess you're right.
It was hard to not be in great fear and it has been a very long time. Since early on in my

pregnancy, it began. And my babe is 3.5 years old now ... I've been living in so much fear ...I've been drowning for so long, it's been so hard to come out of. But I will listen to your advice and I will start writing before I sleep and whenever I have a chance! And I will come back here and let you know of our progress. Again, I really thank you for this comment.

Hi, How do you keep the negative thoughts from popping in your mind when you are working to manifest something that seems unlikely?

Thank you for the question. It is always important to believe that we will receive what we have asked for, without belief the process doesn't work. Another very important tasks when attempting to use the LOA is to ensure that what we say (at all times) is positive, especially when attempting to bring about a desired outcome.

The reason for manifesting something is because we don't have it....YET. It would be a waste of time and energy if we attempted to manifest something that is "unlikely."

When a person begins to learn to drive, the first lesson may seem fun and easy as the instructor does most of the work for you, having taken a few more lessons, we find it may become a little more challenging, most of us never think its "*unlikely*" that we will pass the test, as we have put in time, effort and money in order to get the L (Learner in the UK) removed from our car.

Are you attempting to see if the LOA works? It works.

If you feel that what you have asked for "*seems unlikely*" what do you think the outcome will be? Yeah, you got it, *unlikely*. It can be challenging when we ask for something we have never had or something we deem 'big' to stay positive about the outcome, but as we want it, and somewhere deep down we feel that it would be nice to have it, we attempt to manifest it.

So here is what you do to stop "*negative thoughts from popping in your mind,*" find an affirmation that resonates with you and say it out loud, to yourself or silently every-time doubt pops into your head. I often say "everything is working in my favour," and I add "regardless of the current appearance," meaning, regardless of how dire my current situation appears, I will trust this will work in my favour.

The more you say your affirmation, the less room you have for negative thoughts regarding your wished for item, person or situation to enter your life.

I'm struggling at the moment to find myself and what I can do to be happy with what I have.

Sorry to read that you are struggling...Note that whatever you are going through is

something that you are **g o i n g** through, and you will **g e t** through it...Think back, there has been situations in your life, where you thought, this situation is hard and 'im not sure how I am going to get over this one.' Well I'm here to tell you that you did get through it, how do I know? Well you are here now, you got over that situation and you will get over this one.

Seek out any organisation in your area who may be able to help you with whatever situation you are in, they are there to help.

By attempting to change or do something about the situation, you will begin to 'find yourself' because it is 'yourself' that is trying to help 'you'.

Sometimes when we are low, it can be challenging to be happy about anything let alone be happy with what we have! I get it, however if we start small...Just happy I have a roof over my head, hot/cold water, food, clothes, the neighbours, family members, the kids/fur babies.

Take your time and you'll find that there is a lot to be thankful or happy about in your life.

The operative word is take your time, God/the Universe knows your heart and knows that you want to be grateful, thankful or happy for what you have... Come back in a while and tell us you smiled today, and tell us why. You'll get there.

I really need some advice please, how can I stay in a positive mindset and emotional state to welcome positive things when I am currently going through something in my life which is causing me emotional pain?

Sorry to read that you are going through an emotional state at the moment. As I do not know your situation, I would advise you to acknowledge the feeling, if that 'something' is someone, do what you need to do to be safe. Please seek help and advice from any organisation in your area that may be able to help and advise you with your particular situation. Your request is to stay positive.

Sometimes, certain situations like the loss of someone, does not allow us to be in a positive space, unless we can find solace in the knowledge that that person has gone to a better place. Being diagnosed with a condition can also keep us in a less than positive space, again one can find solace in the knowledge that they have sought professional medical advice.

In order to get to a more positive mindset, one can think back to a better happier time and realise that you will be able to experience those feelings again, know that what you are going through, is something you are 'going through' and you will get through it.

Everyday, do something for you, that could be watching your favourite show or youtube channel, taking a walk, having a soak in the bath, surround yourself with people (if you can) that care for you, do something that is solely for you. In doing this you are 'welcoming positive things' back into your life.

As for your emotional pain, I am a psychologist and would need to know a little more about how this pain presents itself. This of course is not the space in which to divulge this type of information. Again I would advise you to seek professional help if you feel the help will be of benefit to you.

Hi I'm new to manifesting.
I've listened to the audio book of the secret and really working hard to positive thinking and gratuity. I suffer with personality disorder and today is not a good day.

I'm trying really hard to be positive and think positive but when I have a "bad day" I just don't know how to remove the anxiety or the stresses inside my head.
Can anyone advise what they do to get themselves back into a positive mindset?

Sorry you have experienced *"bad days."* I would suggest that you contact a medical professional on these days.

It is certainly challenging to be optimistic or *"think positive"* when you are unwell and struggling to *"remove the anxiety or the stresses,"* this is something that may be alleviated medically.

We all have 'off days' and they can be calmed by looking at the situation from 'above.'

If you looked down on what may be bothering you, you would realise that you are not being chased by a bear (although the hormones in our body believe we are). We are safe, we can get help if needed.

This all depends on the situation we are in. If someone has upset us, we can remove ourselves from the situation, although we may be upset, but we are safe and not being chased! What I am getting at is, in the great scheme of things, you are safe and you can get help.

I aim to not allow anyone or anything to get me to the stage where my body believes I am being chased by a bear! It's not worth the physical damage this may do.

Getting back into a positive mindset, will take time..having 'grounded' myself or ranted to whoever will listen, I note that everything is working in my favour,
My dining table leg broke, it must be working in my favour, perhaps I'm going to get a new dining room set.

The car won't start, perhaps I wasn't meant to be on the road at my normal time...This type of attitude takes time, however, the longer you practice the 'its working in my favour' the least time you stay stressed out, and the quicker you turn a negative situation or thought into a positive one.

Response From Enquirer.

Love this. Thankfully I don't need medical help any-more. I have coping mechanisms on how to deal with situations but when I'm on a manic day I struggle to keep focused of my thoughts. I really want to get this right just don't know if I'm doing things right.

You are doing what it takes. You obviously know when you feel up or having an 'off day'.

When attempting to feel better, in fact at all times, we are to use positive or neutral words. The term 'manic' conjures up a situation of being out of our control.

As you aware of how you feel, you can 'ground' yourself, by realising that you are not being chased by a bear, lion or tiger, and as that is the case, you can regain control. Think of it this way, if something terrible happens to someone in the street, or in your home for that matter, you wouldn't be soooo out of control or 'manic' that you couldn't call for help! If you agree, then you may be able to control or calm your 'off day'.

Again if you feel that you are out of control, then you should seek medical advice.

I'm new, I haven't been really active here on on this forum in general much.
I have a...messy....chaotic...toxic and very negative situation at home.
Due to things in life, I live with both parents and they're both constantly negative,
and toxic. I've been learning about law of affirmation/attraction and manifesting. I
really would like to do manifesting but with their constant negativity it's hard to.
Not sure what exactly I'm trying to say, I guess possible advice or just anything?
Lol

Thank you for the question, and as I am unsure of your age I have answered this question in a message and removed the question from the forum. I am sorry that you are experiencing a 'toxic, negative' environment at home.

Again as I do not know your age, you should seek the advice of any organisation in your area who may be able to help. No one should be living in a 'constant, negative, toxic' environment, not even animals! Before embarking on LOA you should consider your safety, that is mental as well as physical.

Attempting to 'manifest' a loving caring home is only possible if all the people involved are willing to part take in the process and want the same thing. Attempting to manifest something for yourself, can be challenging if you are trying to be positive in a negative home, we can manifest anything but your safety comes first.

Response From Enquirer

Hi, I am 27 on Friday. Help from an organisation, the best I can do at the moment is applying for disability and currently it's being reviewed so hoping I get it.

Happy birthday when it comes, the best you can do, is to ensure your safety.

Everything else will fall in place, if you believe staying in a toxic environment, waiting for a disability cheque, then that is what will happen...You being in a toxic environment waiting for money.

Believe in a better outcome and regardless of what situation you are in, it will change.

When I find myself in a situation that appears like there is no way out, I say 'everything is working in my favour, regardless of appearances.' I know you may not speak the way I do, but believing things will work in your favour is a great start.

End Of Questions

We can all agree that we have had negative thoughts from time to time. However, most of us snap out of that thought as soon as we have had a rant, jumped up and down screaming or talked the ear off our best friend. Some people however have negativity surround them in the form of 'friends' and family members, those we can not get away from, even if we tried. What do you do then? Well, after trying to get away from those naysayers, we can be left with that negativity vibe or be in 'low vibration.'

This can be challenging when trying to use the LOA to manifest a better life, situation or item into our lives.

Attempting to get into a better more positive frame of mind is not always easy when one is ill, or in a family situation that festers negativity, ill feelings or pain. In those situations, as you saw above, one is to attend to the root of the issues, i.e seek medical attention or alert a helping organisation and take action, by taking the medication or advice prescribed. Only after one is in control of their situation can they begin to concentrate on themselves enough to create a more positive environment.

Think of it like this:

If you have a bucket that has a whole in it and you want water, you would need to fix the bucket in-order for it to hold the water you want. Unless you are whole, feeling better, feeling in control, can you go on to start using the LOA for wanted items, situations and people into your life. Once you feel in control one has to work on staying positive, not allowing negative thoughts to pop in, as with negative thoughts, comes doubt, feelings of undeserving and perhaps the failure of the manifesting process.

These feelings can have us going round in circles as we begin the manifesting process with a particular outcome in mind, only to falter just as our manifestation is about to enter our lives, we then find ourselves feeling low and doubting whether the LOA actually works. As I said at the beginning of this conclusion, we feel low or have negative thoughts from time to time, However if we stay believing that what we have asked for is on its way, it must come. The best way I have found to help me keep the momentum or stay positive is with an affirmation, mine is, 'everything is working in my favour,' try it the next time you feeling a little low.

Chapter Ten

Everything Is Falling Apart

Everything is falling apart, this can be daunting, even frightening to anyone new to using the Law of Attraction (LOA) in order to manifest a want. Most set out to try LOA and mastering the art of getting what they want. They Ask Believing that they will have their wish granted, they go on to take Action, doing everything in their power to achieve their goal. Then they get to the waiting stage and 'Everything falls apart.'

The car stops.
The washing machine breaks down.
There is a leak under the sink.
...and the cat has run away!

What is happening? Depending on your want, you may find that your 'falling apart' is related. Let me explain. Should you ask for money and vibe on that level, everything related to money attracts its self to you, here's what often happens, you ask for money and follow the steps, you are then immediately informed that there will be no more over time and you are expected to actually stay at work until the end of your shift, (you normally leave thirty minutes earlier). A debt you had forgotten about, turns up and is to be paid within 14 days. You get a parking ticket, you are asked by a family member to lend them some money (...and no, its not the one that always asks).

This is what I coined 'The Breakdown Stage' where everything seem to go belly up, I believe it is also a time of clearing out, a getting ready for what you have asked for to come in. I may have mentioned, in the answer to previous questions, it is at this time many feel that their manifestation will not appear and set about making new wishes, often in anger or frustration, they often voice their dissatisfaction of the LOA and claim that they will not get what they have wished for and or it doesn't work. They then add to their comment or statement that they will never get what they have wished for. These words are often believed and sometimes acted upon i.e they stop looking for that new car, house, shoes or outfit, they stop believing the right man or woman will come into their lives. They may even believe that they are 'stuck' in their current situation. What follows is what they have voiced, believed and acted upon.

I welcome 'The Breakdown Stage' as it signals to me that my wish has been heard and it is on its way. It is at this time I say out loud or silently, that 'everything is working in my favour' and I know my wish is on its way. I begin to look for other signs that my wish is on the way. It's like fighting through the burn at the end of a race, I know that if I push through I will get there, and you should too.

Life happens whether you are in the process of manifesting a want or not, you are to remain believing and open to what God/the Universe sends you, you will have your wish granted or something better than you can imagine. Have a look how this stage affected others.

I've been manifesting and my life's fallen apart since, is this normal?

Thank you for your question. The answer is Yes, this is normal. It may seem like things are falling apart, when really its falling into place.

I call this the 'Breakdown stage'. When everything seem to go belly up! It is at this stage many people halt their manifestations, by proclaiming that 'i'm never gonna get'.... what I asked for, and then they wonder why they did not get what they asked for! The aim here is for you to show the universe that you still want what you have asked for and continue to believe its on the way.

Another reason why things 'break away' is the clearing of the path for new stuff, new people, new situations to come in.

I know it can be challenging but keep the faith the best you can, know that your manifestation is on its way.

Why does it seem like many bad things start happening when you are intentionally manifesting?

In my recent course I call this the 'Breakdown stage'. When everything seem to go belly up! It is at this stage many people halt their manifestations, and wonder why they did not get what they asked for.

The aim here is for you to show that you still want what you have asked for. To answer your question and although I don't like saying it, this stage is a test. Your reaction to this stage is important. I take this stage as an alert that my manifestation is on the way, and even welcome it, so you need to see it as thus. There is a second reason for this stage, its to 'get rid' of some of the things that is hindering your growth.

Here's a few examples: You try to manifest more friends, at the belly up stage, you lose some friends you have had around you for years! Could the reason be, they should have left your life a long time ago (or kept at arms length)? Or will they fit in with the friends you are about to meet? Say you want a new car, at the belly up stage, your current car stops working! Maybe God/the Universe is making space in the garage for a new car.

The 'bad things' are not to be named or labelled, just reacted to, with acknowledgement that your wish has been heard and on its way.

Everything seems to be falling apart! How can someone believe, welcome and manifest so much only for it to all fall apart? Not just one or two or three things, but all of it?

So sorry you are experiencing this right now. Do be aware of your words, *"All of it"* is falling apart? Look at the situation you are in and consider each part of it, pick out the bits that did work and attempt to focus on that. It can be frustrating when we think things are going our way and then it goes in a complete different direction.

Do what you can to change the situation and know that what you are experiencing is happening in your favour.

There are a few reasons why things seem to be working then all of a sudden its turned up side down.

In my recent course, I call this the 'Breakdown stage'. When everything seem to go belly up! It appears like all the hard work of believing, and welcoming an unseen wish has been a waste of time, but how could it be a waste of time, you followed the steps and you should receive. And you will receive, note that life goes on and things happen.

Has the cooker ever broken down just before a family event or a national holiday? It would seem to be the worst time to have happened. Had that cooker broken down at any other time, it would be an inconvenience, but because it was needed for a special occasion it appeared to be more of a catastrophe than the inconvenience it is.

Your wish and the preparations for it, had taken time, effort and maybe money and now one, two, three or more things appear to be going wrong. Through it all, note your wish has not yet materialised, it is still on its way, it is not one of the things falling apart. Remain expectant on what you asked for, remind yourself that you are at the last stage of the LOA process so you must Receive.

I feel like everything is crashing and burning around me. I needed to come here and read other peoples' issues.

Sorry you feel this way. Do reach out to organisations in your area who may be able to help with your situation. I know you have not asked a question, but I feel compelled to respond to your comment.

As this is a LOA forum I would like to remind you that although things may feel like "*everything is crashing and burning around*" you. There has been no reports of any earthquakes measuring 9.5 on the Richter scale! Which may cause everything in its vicinity to crash and burn.

We have to be aware of what we say as the LOA is working all the time and as humans we have a need to voice how we feel, otherwise others would not be aware of what we are going through. As you are aware of the LOA and that voicing catastrophes may bring you unwanted situations.

Try re-wording your speech, or adding what you would like to experience. For example when a person who has the flu is asked 'how are you?' knowing the LOA this person may answer 'i've got the flu, but hope to feel better soon.' This person also takes action by seeking help (medical attention) and following through by taking rest and medication, whilst believing that they will feel better soon.

Another note to remember, when things appear not to be going our way, there is a reason for it. Bare in mind that farmers burn some of their fields at the end of a harvest to get rid of harmful fungi, viruses etc in the hope of getting a stronger crop the following year.

Sometimes things have to fall away in-order for new, stronger/better situations to enter our lives.

I have a question, when things go wrong, does that mean its the start of something good going to happen or is that just me wishful thinking?

Thank you for the question.

When I have asked for something and things appear to begin to 'go wrong' I know at that point that my manifestation is on its way, to answer your question, its the start or the near arrival of my manifestation appearing in my life.

I call this the 'Breakdown stage'. When everything seem to go belly up! It is at this stage many people halt their manifestations, by feeling that their manifestation is a failure, and proclaim or think that their wish will never materialise, this is often accompanied with thoughts of giving up, this causes the whole process to begin again.

This stage is also a time of 'clearing out,' that is people, places and things. Have you ever wondered why your life came together after a certain someone left your life? Or when you moved to a different address, town or country? It works with things too. There is a leak in the roof, circumstances ensue that the government has some incentive that allows you to get a new roof, the car stopped working, here comes the car you've always wanted.

One is to 'keep the faith' and continue to believe that what they have wished for will come regardless of what is happening.

Just because you are attempting to manifest something, does not stop life from happening, things go wrong all the time, it just seems harsher when you are attempting to manifest or just before a national holiday!

Response From Enquirer

Thank you for this explanation, it helped me put things into perspective and give me some faith. Lately for me, things are breaking down at an all time high, it's starting to break me down and lose faith anything good will happen. I just don't understand why it has to get so bad before it gets good again.

Please keep the faith, as mentioned above I look forward to the clear out/ breakdown stage, for me its a sign that the old is clearing out to allow the new to come in.

I sometimes feel the Universe is saying, 'are you sure you want what you've asked for?' As it is at this time we make a different wish...that of 'its never going to work' or 'I'm never going to get out of this situation.'

When things breakdown I feel its your last chance to confirm that what you have asked for, is indeed what you want and expect. Getting through this breakdown, (and you will) will enable you to stand strong the next time you make a wish to God/the Universe, as you'll remember (hopefully) the stages you went through to get what you've asked for.

Hi, I've experienced a sense of disconnection from loved ones, with some family members and friends drifting away. All started after I started my manifestation journey a year ago I'm curious to know: Have others experienced similar challenges and synchronicities during their manifestation journeys? How have you navigated these transformative experiences?

Thank you for the question. Do note that when we start our spiritual journey some people can not come! Some will not understand your need for change, some would like you to stay the person they need in their life.

Some will feel that you are leaving them behind, as they too know they can't go with you. Others will try and bring you back to their level.

Note that God/the Universe tends to separate you from things, places and people that will not enhance or help you on your journey.

If you believe everything is working in your favour or for your good, you will be able to take solace in the fact that you will be alright, you will come out of this season of your transition a better stronger person.

End of Questions

Everything is falling apart, it isn't really! It just seems that way, especially when you are travelling a road less familiar to you. When you embark on the LOA journey or become aware that everything you say or do has moulding powers, you instinctively wonder why your journey isn't straight forward.

Things that were mere inconveniences at any other time in your life, are now catastrophes, as you've become somewhat enlightened. The fact that the car has broken down, may make you feel that things are not going to work out for you. It would appear that many on this journey forget that life still happens, regardless of whether they have changed their lives by becoming more aware of what is happening around them.

These fly in the ointment life situations should be used as signs that something higher then yourself has heard you and your wish is on its way.

As mentioned above, if you have asked for something to enter your home or life, sometimes a clear out is needed before it arrives, to ensure there is space for it. Just like you clearing out the garage for that new car, or the falling out with certain people. This stage allows you to step into your new life experience unencumbered.

Real Questions. Real Talk.

Chapter Eleven

How Do I Heighten My Vibration?

How do you heighten your vibration; how do you know what vibration to be on and how do you know you are there? Are all questions that could be asked regarding high vibration.

Most people know and can tell you when they are in low vibration, they often state that they are feeling low or use the word negative to describe the feeling.

High vibration on the other hand may be a little more challenging to arrive at, as most people are in want when they embark on raising their vibrations for a particular outcome. Albert Einstein said that "Everything is energy" which is based on the idea that all things in the universe vibrate at a specific frequency.

As most believe this is the case, getting on or in the same vibration or frequency of the wished for item or situation should bring it to you. More like a magnet that attracts another magnetic material.

How do you heighten your vibration? You become enthusiastic about your want.
How do you know what vibration to be on? You don't, as you can not see the frequency of a new washing machine or TV.

I would suggest that you begin to welcome your want into your life and home, making space for it and thinking of what life will be like with it in your home, garage or life. The more time and effort you put into its welcome, the closer you are to its frequency, it must be drawn to you.

How do I know I am there? You 'feel' comfortable thinking and talking about your want, you are expectant of your wish and remain in the 'it's on it's way mode.'

The questions below will give you more insight into heightening your vibration.

If you're supposed to match your own vibration with the vibration of what you want to attract, how do you know what that vibration is? Is it the value or feeling you place/have for it?

Thank you for the question.
I believe you should match the vibration of what you want, in-order to do this, think back to when you was a child and wanted a particular toy. Every-time you thought of the toy, you would have a particular feeling! That may have been of excitement, the thought may have made you 'feel' happy. You may have spent time thinking about how you will play with the toy, who you would show or allow to play with it.

Having positive thoughts of what you want is getting in the vibration of what you have wished for. Getting into the vibration of what you want, for me, is welcoming the item or situation. For an item, I would make space for it in my home. Lets say you wanted a car, how would you get into the vibration of the car? As you said, by encouraging the *"value or feeling you place/have for it."*

I would clear out the garage, buy little items that I would like to place in the car when it arrives, I would imagine myself in the car, showing it to friends and family etc. The vibration of the car is where I place it...If I am happy, looking forward to having it, I draw it to me. If I worry about how or when I will get it, that vibration (thought, feeling) will push it away from me.

If I want a particular outcome to a situation, I think of how I will feel when that favourable outcome arrives. I think of who I would tell, how getting the outcome I want will affect me and or my family etc...I also begin to 'Act As If' the favourable outcome is already here.

All you need to do to 'Act As If' a situation has already occurred, is to ensure that you are not worrying about your current situation (i.e without the wished for outcome). Every-time your current circumstance pops into your mind, you act or think of how things would be if you had your want or the desired outcome was here.

So the good feelings and thoughts you send out to welcome your want is the vibration the item or situation is on. The thoughts and or feelings you send out to attract your want is how it will arrive.

Hi, Is it true that you have to be at a higher frequency to use the Law of Attraction??

Thank you for the question.
The answer to your question is two fold. Firstly, you are 'using' the Law of Attraction all the time, as we attract into our lives what we were thinking and acting out, last week, last month, or even this morning. Remember that time you said 'I won't be able to pay that bill'? You said it (Asked) (Believed) and come bill day (Received) the inability to pay the bill.

Secondly, your 'frequency' was at the right level to attract the inability to pay that bill. Everything panned out. The same is for something you want, You Ask, Believe it will come, and Receive, your 'frequency' here is one of expectancy, it isn't at any "higher frequency" it is at your level of belief.

Say you wanted a new outfit, you may start looking for the right pair shoes to go with it, or you may start looking for accessories that would compliment the outfit. You feel happy (you raised your frequency) as you look forward to your new outfit. You do not worry about when or how it will come to you, you just expect it.

So to answer the question about frequency, you can be at any level or frequency you wish, however being at a raised frequency or vibing at the same level of what you want will aid its appearance in your life.

In order to get in the frequency or vibration of what you want is to begin to welcome it into your life any way you can.

Is your aura/vibe, got to be in tune with LOA at all times? Thanks x

I am not sure of your question.
But I will attempt to answer your question in parts, to the 'vibe or frequency' part of the question.

You can be at any level or frequency you wish, bear in mind you are the one that controls how you feel!, however being at a high frequency or vibing at the same level of what you want will aid its appearance in your life.

To attempt to answer the 'tune with LOA at all times' part of your question, heres a question to you, did you know that you are in tune or using the LOA every second of every minute you are alive?

We manifest what we think, say, believe and act out, and then wonder why good/bad things appear in our lives.

Note that the LOA is always always working, listening and watching in order to bring what ever wish we make (or unknowingly) into our lives.

Do I need to raise my vibration to manifest?

Not at all, you are using LOA (or manifesting) every second of every minute you are alive? We manifest what we think, say, believe and act out. Have you ever said, today is going to be a bad day; then found that you had a bad day? You voiced (Asked or proclaimed), you Believed your day would be bad, you may have Acted on your belief, and waited for the dark cloud to follow you for the whole day, the LOA never fails to follow through...you may recall that you had a bad day.

Your vibration was at the level or frequency of a bad day. Should you get up and decide that the day looked liked a bad day, but you didn't believe it would be a bad day, you would be vibing on 'its not such a bad day' and your day may not have been as bad as it could be. You raised your vibration to the level of your belief, and may have had a not so bad a day.

Raising your vibration helps your wish to appear with the same 'happy vibe' you requested it. Raising your vibration also keeps you on task while you wait for your manifestation to arrive, it keeps you in the expectancy zone or mode, and away from doubt or fear that your wish may not be granted.

It's advisable to keep your vibration high when attempting to manifest something in particular, that is, keeping your belief high.

Does anyone have any advice on "getting in the feeling" of having everything you want already? Thank you!

Thank you for the question, here's a question for you: Say you are going out for a night out with friends, whilst getting ready, you may put on some dance music, you may have bought something nice to wear, whilst getting ready you think of what the night may bring, who you may meet, what music you may hear, if you're going out for a meal, you may think of what you may order. All these thoughts get you in the 'feeling' of having a good night out, would you agree?

As children we do not plan out our whole lives (our everything), well most of us do not, we may say we want to be a Nurse, Doctor, Astronaut, and think of what it would be like to be in those professions.

As we aged we may say we want to get a good job, or join a band and be famous, we may say we want to get married, have children etc... and play out those scenarios in our mind.... I can not imagine 'getting in the feeling of having everything you want already' other than a feeling of contentment, perhaps a feeling of accomplishment.

My 'everything' involves sooo many people, I don't know what that would feel like.

What do you call "*everything*?"

A house.
A car.
A partner.
Children.
Money in the bank, is that your "*everything*?"

When using the LOA one has to be specific, but open to what and how God/the Universe brings it into our reality. Lets assume your 'everything' is a house, car, partner, money in the bank and children. One would have to be specific on the area, size of the house and its contents, the car would need the same effort, not to mention the money, partner and the children.

This "*everything*" would need individual 'feelings'. The feeling of getting a new house, would 'feel' different from the 'feeling' of having children! We can manifest most anything however we need to be aware of asking for 'everything' without taking the time to think about the consequences of our not thought out 'everything'.

A gentle reminder: Sometimes people chase "everything" to fill a void, but the real magic comes when you manifest from a place of *wholeness*, not lack. Get specific, feel it deeply, stay open, and be prepared to grow into the version of yourself that your "everything" requires.

How do I heighten my vibration, this is extremely hard to do when life is crumbling. Any tips on how to not give a low vibration when every day it's something else going REALLY bad?

I am sorry you are experiencing this situation at the moment. As I do not know what the issue is (please do not elaborate), I can only advise, that if you feel unsafe, please try and get to a safe place, contact any organisations in your area who may be able to help.

With that said we often use words that may make the situation appear more dire! 'Life is crumbling' evoke images of the apocalypse, I understand that this may be the way you are feeling right now, but you are here with us, writing and reading posts on this forum! I would suggest that you do what you can to change the situation or seek out others who may be able to help. (that can be the authorities, a medical professional, friends or family).

Of course there are certain situations that you can do nothing about, in those situations you often have to acknowledge the sadness or low vibration and work to heal before ones vibration can be lifted or heightened.

Response From Enquirer

Angela Scott Thank you. I won't elaborate but I feel safe I have an amazing family and supportive husband, we just can't seem to exit this negativity but if I was to be honest it's me more than him, he's trying to lift me but everyday is another setback and I guess I'm not as positive as he is.

I do feel things are "crumbling", the second something positive happens, something negative follows.

Thank you for clarity. Your negativity, that you and your husband may be facing or experiencing may not have anything to do with what we on this Law of Attraction forum call 'low vibration,' but sounds more of a domestic personal issue, where you both appear to be 'going through' something.

My advise on negative self talk ie *"the second something positive happens, something negative follows"* may only help in as much as to warn, that what we say, think and in this case write down, we bring about.

Your feelings of *"crumbling"* pricks my psychologists' ear up and would advise as mentioned above that you and your husband seek professional help, as having to be *"lifted"*, not being able to see an *"exit"* and *"everyday is another setback"* calls for more investigation in a safe environment, and not on the pages of this forum.

Again I am sorry you are experiencing this right now, and would advise you both to have a word with a medical professional.

Hello, I was wandering what you find helps, when you are low in energy and want to manifest.

Thank you for the question. When attempting to use the LOA in order to manifest something in our life, we should always rule out practical needs first.

One of the steps or processes in attempting to manifest is high vibration, one gets in a 'happy mood', one is joyful as they wait for their wished for item, situation or person.

Being *"low in energy"* is a symptom. I do not know your situation, or whether you have ruled out any medical issue you may have. If your wish is to be healed from a physical ailment that makes you *"low in energy,"* you should take advice from a medical professional and then Ask, Believing you will become well. You have already taken the action and practical steps towards your goal.

Being *"low in energy"* could mean that you are sad that you don't have something that would help you and perhaps your family, be in a better mood or higher spirits.

For example if your *"low in energy"* stem from a need for money.
Ask, Believe, do what you can to generate more money, listen for guided instruction, in-order to:

Apply for that job you know you can do, but may not have all the qualifications for.
Sell that item you have been thinking of selling.
Start that small business you have always wanted to start.

In other words follow any hunch that you may have during this waiting period. In doing something towards getting your wished for item, situation or person, you will lift your energy and mood.

By heightening your mood, vibration or energy levels, you place yourself on the frequency

of your wish, but I think you knew that, as you know that it can be challenging to have your wish granted without heightening your vibration.

Big 'Hi', I have a question...How do I know at what degree I'm vibrating? Or if my chakras are blocked.

Hi, I do not subscribe to anyone telling another person that 'something' is "*blocked.*" No one can diagnose your situation from the other-side of a computer screen.

To answer your question about to what degree you are vibrating, you ask yourself, what are you attracting at the moment? Or how am I feeling at the moment. That is the degree you are vibrating on.

One tries to 'vibrate' on the level of what they want, for example, if you want a brand new shiny car, what vibration do you think that shiny car is on? I think it is way up there, happy, brand new, shiny, get the picture?

I know life happens and we can't all walk around being HAPPY HAPPY, but one should try and stay as positive as possible when thinking about what they want to manifest in their lives. A way of doing that is to take action toward pulling in your want.

Think about how you will feel when you get your want, who will you tell first, if you need space in your home for your want, clear it out, clean and make it ready for your want.

Do what you can practically do to get your want...That will usher in your want and let it know it is welcome in your life. Your vibration will heighten as you think of your want and that will be the "*degree you will be vibrating.*"

End of Questions

To heighten your vibration is to be happy or welcoming of your wanted item or situation. As mentioned above, one would need to make space for what has been wished. In doing this you can begin to draw the wished for item to you. You are also ensuring that you are in the expectancy zone.

Think of something fun you about to do on the weekend. During the week, when you think of the weekend, a smile may appear on your face, you may even become a little more cordial with others. This is you being on the vibration of your up and coming fun event. Be happy for what you have asked for.

If the item or situation you have asked for is nothing to jump up and down about, show your appreciation for its arrival by thinking of how the wished for item will benefit you and or your house hold.

The mere fact that you are showing gratitude for your want allows your vibration to be heighten and draws it to you.

I have heard a saying regarding money. It goes something like this....Money doesn't stay where its not welcomed. Like anything wished for, making it feel welcomed will cause it to gravitate to you as well as usher you into a more pleasant mood.

Real Questions. Real Talk.

Chapter Twelve

Can I Manifest For Someone Else?

Can I manifest for someone else? Is a great question, and most of us do it everyday, when we say I love you, get home safe, safe travels, enjoy your holiday, keep warm etc. As parents we do it more than most. However, issues arise when the child becomes old enough to want something different! I understand that many cultures believe it is the parents or elders of the family who are to set the young person on a career path they deem fit for that child or young person. I would like to believe that this is done out of love and care for the child and their future!

But after many years of counselling adults who are in careers and jobs that they despise, having being told that they should study a subject they didn't like, and now have no idea what they would like to do instead. I wonder if their family members' wishes had taken into consideration their likes, dislikes or passions. In fact I am of the belief that that young persons' free will had been taken from them. Please do not be mistaken, I have six children of my own and I was and still here to guide them in the direction I feel they should go, but note I said guide! I have a Son who as a child would like to draw, he was not as academic as his older sister, but I felt he would benefit from attending an art school. He is now a Graphic Designer and claims to love his job! Yet another Son who is an architect, but has become a boxer! Go figure! I have another that would 'play schools,' as a child she would line her dolls and soft toys up, and teach them a lesson she had planned the night before, Yep she is a teacher. None of my children have taken the science route to careers, although it would have been nice to have had a fellow scientist in my family.

We all have free will and to attempt to halt or take away another persons free will is not advisable, although this may be done with the greatest of care and love in mind.

When using the Law of Attraction (LOA) to manifest anything, one should always seek out practical steps first. Having seen a friend who has a few too many alcoholic drinks at every gathering and know that they drink an alcoholic beverage every night, in-order to sleep. One may feel that person would benefit from some help to stop drinking as they have voiced the same.

Practically, one should seek out a medical professional who can help, and not take it upon themselves to attempt to 'manifest' that person to stop drinking alcohol. There are so many reasons for this.

Again the same goes for a person you know who is unwell, you may want them well, as they too may want to be well, but this may be on a surface level, as deep down the drinker only wants to be able to control their alcohol intake, not give it up all together. The unwell person may feel, as they have been told by a medical professional that they have a 'life long' condition, they will have to live with it, and they believe they will never get better.

Can you see why it is important that both you and the recipient believe and want the same thing? Let's see you wants what for whom below.

Hello everyone. Are we able to manifest for a family member who is really struggling?

Thank you for your question. I am sorry to read that a family member is struggling. I understand that we want to help those closest to us, and we make a wish on their behalf, every time we say, best wishes, I love you, stay safe etc..however, in-order to manifest something for another, they would need to be on board too. I have mentioned the teenager example many times in answer to this type of question, but I believe it to be true: parents often want the best for their children however, when the child becomes a teenager and want something different, no amount of wishing, affirmation or manifesting is going to turn that teenager into what has been wished for him or her.

You can manifest most anything, however it is important that the person you are attempting to manifest for, believes this manifestation will work.

The reason it can be challenging to manifest for another person, is because we all have free will, which is an important part of manifesting, you are free to believe something will work and you are free to believe it will not work.

If your family member believes that their struggle will end, then that would be a great place to start. They would then need to ask for what they want in-order to stop the struggle.

Therein lays another issue with attempting to use the Law of Attraction on behalf of another. I do not know your situation or the struggle your family member is enduring, (no need to share it here) but you may be assuming this family member would like to end their struggle! Again I do not know your situation, but lets say that family member enjoys an alcoholic drink or two or three or four, they, as I said 'enjoy' their four drinks a day and you may believe that they would like to stop drinking, you know this because that is what they have told you.

In reality that person has only said that they would like to stop drinking because they know, it's what you would like for them. If the family member has a physical illness again they would also need to have the ability to want to get better, as some people reside themselves to the fact that they will never get better.

I hope that answers your question and that your family members' struggle will end.

How do I ensure that my daughter marries someone worthy of her love and respect, so she is treated well in the relationship?

Thank you for the question. Are you aware that no one can "*ensure*" that anybody does anything, especially those closest to us. It may surprise many parents that just because they still feel they know what is best for their adult child, it may not be what the adult child wants (this is something you may never know, as the adult child may want to please you). I understand that as parents we want what we feel is best for our children, I have six children!

You haven't included in your 'want':

Good health.
A good career.
No financial issues.
A nice home.
Children when she wants them.

I can only assume she may want these things too. What she and all of us have is free will, and as I have mentioned countless times, when attempting to manifest anything one has to be aware that attempting to take away, halt or interfere with another persons' free will may create unwanted situations.

We can manifest most anything however EVERYONE involved has to want the same thing....I will not relay the amount of people you intend to touch with your (want) or manifestation. Lets just start with your daughter, I only hope she wants what YOU want for her, then there is the 'husband' YOU want for her, then we have the 'husbands' family who may have to accept your daughter into their family, can you see where I am going with this? ALL these people would need to want the same thing for your daughter.

You may not be able to 'ensure' all your wants from ALL these people involved in your daughter marrying a 'husband' who treats her well. As mentioned above, as parents most of us want the best for our children, but do not attempt to "*ensure*" their adult relationships.

Wish your daughter well, hope that she meets and marries the right person for her, as parents we are there to guide and advise our children. You appear to deeply want to 'ensure' this life for your daughter, only God can do that.

How do I manifest my 20 year old son relationship with a 45 year old woman ends?

Sorry you are experiencing a dislike of your adult sons' relationship. It is important that we do not attempt to evoke another persons' free will as this is not advisable. We can manifest most anything, but should be mindful that we ask with the consideration of the other person, they have free will and no manifestation should attempt to halt that.

Although you may have good intentions for your adult son you should not attempt to inflict or impose your (albeit good) wishes on him. As I have mentioned many times on this forum, as parents we often want the best for our children however, when the child becomes a teenager (or in your case an adult) and want something different, no amount of wishing, affirmation or manifesting is going to turn that 'adult' into what has been wished for him.

Which leads me on to practical considerations. I get it, our babies will always be our babies even when they are grown, as that is the situation here, he is grown (according to the law in England). In order to manifest, one has to be aligned with what they want...There is no aligning with someone who has chosen to be in a relationship with another adult, regardless whether someone or anyone thinks it is valid, good or bad.

Your wish or want is also attempting to 'take away' someone who may give your son pleasure, things or feelings that he does not feel he can get or want from anywhere else.

115

Relationships that sustain the test of time are ones that are conducive to both parties, otherwise they fall away.

Please take solace in the fact that you have done the best for your adult child and still want the best for him.

Attempting or showing contempt for his relationship may not keep you in the one you have with him.

Hi can i manifest that my husband stopped drinking?How.

Thank you for your question. First and foremost, if your are concerned about your safety or the safety of anyone in your household, please seek professional help from AA or any other relevant organisation in your area. I will answer this question assuming you are talking about the intake of alcohol and that the consumption is becoming an issue for your household.

I understand that we want to help those closest to us, however they would need to be on board too. I have mentioned the teenager example many times in answer to this type of question, but I believe it to be true, what we want for those closest to us, may not be what they want or feel they can achieve.

You can manifest most anything, however it is important that the person you are attempting to manifest for, believes this manifestation will work. The reason it can be challenging to manifest for another person, is because we all have free will, which is an important part of manifesting, you are free to believe something will work and you are free to believe it will not work.

If a person 'believe' that drinking will get them through the day, then they are likely to continue to do that, they would need to 'believe' that drinking is causing an issue and 'want' or 'wish' to stop.

Their first port of call is to acknowledge that drinking may be causing some concern, and to seek outside help if needed.

Your husband would then need or want the same outcome as you, he may want to be able to have a few drinks on the weekend, or a glass of wine with his meals. Whereas you have mentioned that you would like him to stop drinking altogether. See the issue in trying to manifest for someone else!

Your husbands drinking appears to be an issue so it is a good time for you both to have a chat about your concerns and his needs.

I want to manifest for someone that I love. Can it still work even though I am not the one who is sick? Does it need to be manifested by the sick person in order for it to work?

Thank you for the question.
Yes, we can manifest for another person, most parents wish for a good and healthy life for

their children, but if the child grows to an age where they decide that they would rather live a different life, no amount of wishing or manifesting for that individual is going to bring about a good and healthy life.

I can understand wanting what we believe is best for another, but if your loved one has decided that they will not get better, they will not get better.

If on the other hand your loved one, is conscious and wants to get better, they will seek medical attention, follow the advice given and above all believe that they will and must get better, then your wishing and believing for or with them becomes more of an incentive for your sick loved one to feel better, but they need to want it too.

If I want something for my family members (kids, hubby), things that they want... and I wish it happens for them! So while I know you manifest your own reality, if this reality is directly entangled with your loved ones, and it makes you feel complete and whole seeing them getting what they want, is this still a manifesting of own new reality? Or is it a block?

Thank you for the question. As parents we are making wishes for our family all the time, whether we are aware of it or not. From parents talking at the school gate, 'No my little Sally hasn't got the measles yet'! That's a wish, mum is expecting the measles! To wanting our children to grow up healthy, wealthy and happy.

There is nothing wrong or 'blocking' to wish something we class as good, for others. Nothing gave me more pleasure than to see my children have a full day of fun, provided by the back garden or a day out, well eaten meals, bath and bed. Most of which I provided. I would have wished them well enough to run and jump about in the garden, I would have wished they finished their meals. I would have ensured that we had gas and electricity, food, toys, the list is endless.

What I am attempting to explain, is I had to ensure that I was healthy enough to provide for my family, being a single mother most of the time, meant I am important in the equation of 'happy family.' So my pleasure or need to see my family happy had my wants (them happy) and my needs (me healthy) intertwined, which for all intensive purposes was my reality.

I understand the feeling of contentment seeing my family happy, you mention this as a feeling of *"complete and whole,"* I am sure you have your reasons for using that term, but I get it, there is a sense of accomplishment to see your family happy. Again there is nothing wrong with wishing your family happy.

The issue arises when parents wish, want and attempt to enforce certain life choices unto their grown children, or other members of their family. We all have free will and if the person you are making the wish for doesn't want or desire your wish, it is unlikely to come to fruition.

Oblige me while I make an assumption of your family, lets say your want or wish is for a better paying job for your husband, as he may have said that he would like a better paying job.

Therein lays the issue, he says he would like a better paying job, when in fact, he would like to go fishing most days, but because of his responsibilities and the need to present as a stable member of the family, he states that he would like a better paying job. See why attempting to wish for someone else, may be challenging?

Lets look at the children, in my scenario here, your children are 9 and 12 years old, you may have wished them certain university degrees, as you know that they would earn a good wage, you may have even allotted a wife or husband.

Would it shock you to know that deep down your 12 year old wants to sail around the world and the 9 year old has secretly vowed never to get married. I know they are only children in my little made up family here, but can you further see why attempting to wish for others, is never wise as they also have the ability to make wishes, secretly or otherwise.

Can you manifest for someone else? For example good luck

Sure, we can manifest most anything, we make this particular wish for others every-time we say 'Good luck.' I am unaware of the reason you intend to wish someone good luck and so I can't help myself, but go through what I believe 'good luck' means.

Let me start by stating, when we say 'Good Luck' to another, we are actually saying 'there is a chance you will not achieve your goal, but I am hoping it leans in your favour.' Another way of saying good luck is, 'what you are embarking on has a 50/50 chance of failing, I hope you get 51% in your favour.' Yep! You are saying all that. I try not to use the words Good luck. The French actually say 'good chance' (Bonne chance). I would say something closer to what is said in Arabic that is inshallah, meaning God willing or if God wills it. which is more fitting for a LOA question and answer.

When using the LOA one is sure, well as sure as their belief will allow them to be. There should not be any thoughts of chance at play here. You ask knowing or expecting your wish will be granted. So perhaps you should reconsider what you intend to 'wish' that someone in your question.

I understand that saying 'good luck' to another is just a way of wishing them well, well that the pendulum lands on their side of the board! See, I can't help myself thinking that way. But I get it, its a figure of speech, just something we have said or heard for years.

There is no figure of speech in using the LOA, that is why one is taught to ask aright. I also understand that we can only be as articulate as our vocabulary allows. Ok I may have gone on too much in regard to how I feel about Good luck, and to answer your question, do be mindful of what you say, and what you are actually wishing for your someone when you say 'good luck'.

Can I use the Law of Attraction to heal someone? It's a family member and she swears to God something is ALWAYS wrong with her!! She is allergic to good news and I swear It does rub off on me. When something good happens she scrambles to find something bad. She also does not take care of herself. So what can I do while using the Law of Attraction to heal her?

Thank you for the question, however I believe you know the answer to your family members' issue! *"Can I use the Law of Attraction to heal someone?"* You can use the Law of Attraction for most anything.

You state that *"she swears to God something is ALWAYS wrong with her."* What is often said here, about what you say and believe? Whether they or you believe that one is manifesting ALL the time, the proof is in what they ALWAYS say. This person even *"swears to God something is ALWAYS wrong with her."* How is it possible to change that?

They are using the LOA to its fullest effect and gets results quickly and constantly (Imagine if they used it for what they actually wanted!) They proclaim that *"something is ALWAYS wrong with [them]"* and without knowing this person, I can tell you that they ALWAYS have something *"wrong with [them]."*

You state, *"She is allergic to good news. It's like when something good happens she scrambles to find something bad."* This person is comfortable in the knowledge that something bad is going to happen. Thinking this way is like an old comfortable pair of slippers, something bad, for some, is a surety. For some, its easier to think something bad is going to happen, than something good.

You go on to *"swear It does rub off on me."* In fact anybody in this persons' vicinity will be affected. As they have shown anyone within the sound of their voice that *"something bad"* is going to happen, then as LOA states, it must happen, when on-lookers see her proof, they begin to believe it too. And there you have it...What you believe, you bring about.

To further answer your question *"What can I do while using the Law of Attraction to heal her?"* With the statements I have given above, do you think you have the answer? If you are still unsure, I will relay what I have said many times on this forum.

It is important that the person you are attempting to manifest for, believes this manifestation will work. The reason it can be challenging to manifest for another person, is because we all have free will, which is an important part of manifesting, you are free to believe something will work and you are free to believe it will not work.

In order to manifest, one has to be aligned with what they want...There is no aligning with someone who has chosen and proven that *"something is ALWAYS wrong with her"* and the fact that you believe *"is allergic to good news."* In these instances, you should work on changing your beliefs.

If you find that your family members' wishes, woes and negative wants are not aligned with what you want in your life, attempt to distance yourself from them, if this is not possible right now, find an affirmation that counteracts what they say.

My mother use to always say, 'Life is hard eh.' I would counteract utterance, really her affirmation by adding 'sometimes,' to the end of her statement.

Stop accepting what this person is saying and manifesting in their life. If you would like things to go right for you, to be happy instead of adverse to good things happening, then change you, stop trying to change (or heal) a person who clearly has other ideas and wishes for their life.

It can be disheartening when a family member, not only doesn't wish well for themselves and as you say *"also does not take care of herself."* You can certainly wish and want the best for them, but they have to want it too.

End of Questions

Can you see why it can be challenging to manifest for someone else? But certainly not impossible, I have spoken about parents at the school gates expecting the measles on their child or children, and inevitably the measles arrive and the parent is not surprised as it was expected, even welcomed. Here the unwitted child did not align with the measles, everybody around the child did. We see one enquirer stating, *"It does rub off on me,"* meaning they were beginning to succumb to the not so positive environment they where around. You could say the environment was contagious!

Often the person who would like to manifest for another wish or hope that that person would catch their enthusiasm to stop drinking or get better. Until both people are aligned with the wish, it can be very challenging to see your best wishes come true for someone who doesn't really want your gift!

Attempting to manifest something, someone or situation for someone is very much like buying a present for that someone, you take your time to pick what you see as the perfect gift, you present it all parcelled up in a pretty box and maybe bows, only to find that the receiver doesn't like or want your gift. You was sure it would benefit them, in these, like all situations of attempting to manifest for someone else, they may never tell you what they really want, and if you knew what they 'really really' wanted, it may alter the relationship you have with that person, you may view them differently.

Take the wife and mother enquirer above who wanted gifts for her family, in my scenario, her husband and children may have secretly wanted things that they never utter to anyone, let alone the person who felt she 'knew' what would make them, in her mind, happy.

Get help for the person you want to manifest for, encourage them to speak to a professional, if you could help without 'making or manifesting it right' you would. Allow children to grow and find their passion, then guide them in the direction that may enhance that latent God given gift/talent.

Chapter Thirteen

Using Other Methods To Manifest

This book is all about using the Law of Attraction, but as it is Esoteric in nature, I get questions relating to other methods of manifesting items, people and situations into ones life. I see these 'other methods' as add on's, and a way of keeping you in the expectant mode. I believe while you use these other methods, you are actually using the time between the waiting stage and receiving your want with exercises that will keep you in the vibration of your want.

I preach LOA, so it often surprises me when I get questions related to the use of other methods. I will not be telling anyone to use a different method as, for me, LOA is tested and proved in my life, plus I have faith, belief and trust in the source from whence my manifestations come, that of God.

I do however, find some other methods used to manifest very interesting, I say if it works for you, go for it. It is important to me that I keep God in mind, and in whatever I do, so some methods wouldn't fit with my beliefs.

I haven't manifested anything, I wanna learn different types of methods
I watched some people who are manifesting with meditation, using crystals, writing in special (not cheap) notebooks and I was wondering if I need all of these?

Hi, Thank you for the question. You state that you *"haven't manifested anything,"* the truth is you have manifested something, you have manifested 'not manifesting anything', which is something! You go directly to asking for other *"types of methods,"* as it would appear as if the LOA hasn't worked for you, and you would like to move on to a different method. Let me address the issues one by one.

When using the LOA one has to be very mindful of what they say as it is one of the steps of the LOA, which is always always working. When one voices or proclaim a thing, believe a thing and act upon a belief it must manifest. As I mentioned above, you actually manifested 'not manifesting anything'.

Here's how you did it, you said it, you even wrote it down, this is something you believe, as now you would like to *"learn [other] types of methods."* The action you have taken is contacting me and seeking out other methods. You Asked, Believed, you took Action then your manifestation arrived in the form of *"not manifesting anything."* In order to attract or manifest something you want, you just follow the steps, Ask Believe, take Action and you will Receive.

You mention meditation to manifest, great idea, as it keeps you believing that your manifestation is on its way. The use of crystals, as I am not fully versed with its use for manifesting particular things, people or situations, I can not speak on that option. You go on to state that there is a method of writing in a notebook..... Why has the notebook or pen got to be expensive; isn't it still just writing on paper? Buying other items to help is fine, but this shouldn't cause you financial hardship, I think that defeats the object, especially if you are asking for money!

You should find and use any method that 'feels' right to you. There are many many methods out there. However the simplest ways are the best.

As mention above Ask, Believe, take action (do whatever you can to achieve your want) then wait, leave it to God/the Universe to bring it to you. While in this space of waiting you may get a hunch to do something or go somewhere, often this is guiding you towards what you have asked for.

The Law of Attraction is like gravity, it must come if you do not halt its progression to you, by not believing or by deciding how, by whom or when it should come. Using other methods, while you wait is conducive to keeping you in the expectant mode and on track to receiving what you have asked for.

Hi, I am seeing repeated numbers every day all day long when i look at the clock its 11:11 then 1:11, 2:22, 3:33, 4:44, 5:55 then back to 11:11 Sometimes the percentage on my phone will match up with it too it's just constant repeated numbers no specific ones... I'm constantly googling the meanings but is there a meaning of just seeing multiple of the same numbers no matter what numbers they are?

Hi, Thank you for the question. It is said that seeing multiple numbers all the time, should assure you that you are in tune with your guardian angels and that they can converse with you. They have at last got through to you. Perhaps they are just trying to reinforce the message they have for you. Nothing to worry about, it's great that you look up the numbers and act or acknowledge the messages.

I very rarely see Angel numbers am I doing something wrong?

Thanks for the question, you are not doing anything wrong, however, you may not be 'still' or 'quite' enough to see them...They turn up on a bill, a receipt, on the clock, on a notice board, a car licence plate etc. They will come when you are ready to see them.

What is the 369 method?

The 369 method is repeating your chosen affirmation (or writing the item you want) three times in the morning, six times in the afternoon and nine times before you go to bed.

Does anyone have any good ideas on how to identify what state you're in? like different methods like writing on paper and also stuff that can be done on the fly in the field?

Thank you for your question. You ask *"how to identify what state you're in?"* How do you feel? That is the 'state' you are in! If your question is actually, how do I change my state/vibration, as I asked above, how do you feel?

You certainly can write down the state or vibration you would like to be in, or you can just decide to be in the state/vibration you want to be in!

People often have a goal or vibration they want to be in when using the Law of Attraction, they tend to want to be on the vibration of the item, person or situation they are attempting to manifest or bring into their life.

Many believe that if they 'align' with the item, person or situation they are wanting, it will help manifest it quicker.

For me, aligning with the wish you have made, keeps you in a believing or hopeful mode, once you keep on believing you will remain expectant that your wish will manifest in your life.

You ask about "different methods," I am unsure if you are asking, 'can writing on paper bring about a particular vibration?'

As mentioned above, you certainly can write down the vibration you would like to be in, but finding an affirmation that resonates with you, would be quicker and repeating it in your mind can be done anywhere at any time.

Hello! tonight is the full moon, and if i know correctly, it's not really advised to start manifesting when there's a full moon, but rather around a new moon. How many days after the full moon has passed am i "allowed" to start manifesting?

Thank you for the question. Do note that you are 'manifesting' ALL the time, you manifest or make wishes with your thoughts, deeds and voice. As this is the case, there is no good or bad time to manifest.

Some believe that there are 'better' times to manifest, this may be the case if that is what you believe.

As using the LOA is about Asking, Believing and Receiving, nothing in the basic three steps state that you should or shouldn't Ask, Believe or you'll Receive at a particular time!

We have been given the right to use our free will, so whenever you decide to manifest a particular thing, person or situation it is up to you.

I am curious, if it is the case that one is not 'allowed' to manifest something until a particular time. What happens when or if the washing machine breaks down and I want a new one, do I wait until there is a new moon to ask for it? I know that the LOA is working every minute of every day and so does not put restrictions on when you ask for something, and there is the fact that we are asking for things most of our day.

Such as:

I hope I wake up on time.
I hope I get a chance to cook breakfast this morning.
I hope there isn't too much traffic today.
I hope the train isn't too full.
I Hope I get into work on time.

All these hopes are wishes, and that is before we get into work! Imagine if you had to wait!

Did my 11:11 at 11:11 manifest of all wonderful and positive things
I was overcome with vibrations and could really feel connected
And now all afternoon I feel defeated. Any advice would be appreciated

So sorry you feel defeated. You say that you *"Did my 11:11 at 11:11 manifest of all wonderful and positive things I was overcome with vibrations and could really feel connected."* At the time of writing this I note that you are on page 111 of this forum. 111 seems to be following you.

1111 it is said, stands for new beginnings, its a message of encouragement and support. You are on the right track keep doing what you are doing. Keep your chin up.

We tend to feel down or things go belly up just before a break through. It's a time of cleansing, we often loose things and relationships around this time.

Keep believing that things will work out and they will.

Hi, just a question I have seen a few of these repeated numbers, what's the significance of the numbers like 11:11 and I've seen other numbers. Is it Law of Attraction/numerology type thing. Genuine question I like to know more.

The Law of Attraction is esoteric in nature and so is seeing repeated numbers, which is not unusual.

They are sometimes called Angel numbers, it is where one would see a particular sequence of numbers often three or four i.e 111 or 7777, these numbers can pop up anywhere, you look up and you see the same number on an advert, it would be as if this number follows you around. You may wake up at 3.33am then see that number on the clock at 3.33pm as you happen to glance at the clock...or you may be out and see 3333 on a car number plate, you go round the supermarket and find that you have spent £33.33.

These numbers are believed to be your guardian angels trying to converse with you. The numbers you see carry a message whether it is multiples of three or fours. Look up their meanings, it's great that you are acknowledging these numbers.

Hello, is there anyone here who actively practices manifestation? Could you advise me on what herbs to use for manifestation, what they are intended for, and how to handle them? Or perhaps something else besides herbs, like something that could help me with manifestation? Thank you in advance for all the advice.

Thank you for your question.
You ask is anyone here in this Law of Attraction forum, *"who actively practices manifestation?"* We and you do, all the time, every time, we think a thought, say something that we believe or take action with a belief in mind.

But I think I get it, you would like to know about a different type of manifesting, that of the use of herbs. I am unable to advise you on the use of herbs for manifestation. As for *"something else besides herbs, like something that could help [you] with manifestation?"* I can only offer LOA, if you have a question, I'd be happy to offer my advice.

I saw a post that said 'Create an aura so powerful that all shady energy directed at you, naturally bounces back to its original manifestor' How do you do that?

An aura this strong is grown by being your authentic self, wishing everyone you meet with love and the best they can be. Wishing everyone you know love, and the best in life. Ensuring that every interaction with ANYONE, is conducted with love in mind.

I find it very difficult to manifest something into reality I know a method called 3 6 9 where you write down your affirmations daily but I wasn't consistent.

Thank you for the question. As you are always manifesting, you have manifested finding *"it very difficult to manifest something into reality."* It is very important to be aware of what you say, (at all times) as LOA is always always working.

The process of manifesting is Ask, (say) Believe and Act, follow those steps and you will always Receive. I understand that you believe you haven't manifested anything.

Let me walk you through how you managed to *"find it very difficult to manifest something into reality."*
You have said (Ask, voiced), you have even written down "I find it very difficult to manifest something into reality."
You Believe that you *"find it very difficult to manifest something into reality."* Your belief has brought you here (Action), to seek out advice on changing your ability to manifest something into reality.
Two steps down, do you know what must follow? You got it, you must Receive.

In order to manifest 'something' you do want, you follow the steps! Change what you say, this first step is very important, you could use words like:
'I want to manifest...'
'I will manifest...'
'I am going to manifest...'

Start with something you believe is small and wait for it to arrive.
Here, try my £1 test: Ask for a pound or dollar, whatever your currency is and wait for it to appear, this can show up in an old purse, a coat pocket, in an ad for a pound off, in your inbox as a voucher, someone may buy you a coffee worth a £. Try it this week.

You mention the 369 method. Affirmations are a tool to use when waiting for your wish to manifest into reality. By saying or writing down your want, you are aligning with what you want, you stay in that expectant mode or zone until your want arrives.

Do remember, what you say or think about, you bring about.

What are some really good affirmations especially when waiting for decisions or asking for help in a situation?

Thank you for the question.
I believe that affirmations are personal, they have to resonate with you. Find ones that do just that, they will be easier to remember and recite, as they will feel and sound more real to you.

I tend to use 'Everything is working in my favour.' As well as your affirmations, busy yourself with other things, clear out that cupboard or the garage.

The busier you are the less time you will have to doubt or worry about the outcomes you require or need.

How many times should you affirm for something during one day?

Thank you for your question.
Every time you think of what you want, you could affirm.
Every-time you think of your current situation you could affirm.

The affirmation should be something that resonate with you so it comes naturally.

End of Questions

Enquiring about the LOA may lead you to other methods of manifesting, I believe that any method that enables you to stay on task or stay expectant on your want will help to welcome your want into your life.

Whether you're using the 369 method, aligning with angel numbers, or setting intentions under the New moon, the common thread is focus, faith, and energetic alignment. As I mentioned above, I feel the use of any other methods serve to keep you expectant, during the waiting stage.

Also mentioned above, as I believe my manifestations come from God/the Universe, I know that what I receive will be sent to benefit me, as everything is always working in my favour.

Chapter Fourteen

Ask Me Anything LOA

This chapter is born from the many different topics raised by the forum members. The questions range from is LOA real to I want another child but my husband does not, what should I do? All questions are answered with LOA in mind.

Is LOA natural or Artificial?

Law of Attraction is a 'Law' of the universe, like the Law of gravity, 'what goes up must come down.'
You are using the Law of Attraction every day, in what you say, do and think about!

Try it tomorrow...Ask for a yellow ball...It will show up in an advert, or on a bill board, or someone will talk about a yellow ball...Let me know when you find the yellow ball.

How does it work? Does it work the same for everyone?

Hi, Thank you for the question,
Here's how it works: You ask believing you'll receive it and it shows up. Yes it works the same for everyone. However not everyone believes the same way.

Some may believe in the beginning, then when the item, or situation doesn't appear within a given time, they believe it didn't work, when in fact LOA is always working, so the person who 'believed' it didn't work, had their wish of it not working come true.

There are others who believe without a shadow of a doubt that what they ask for will appear and set about making room for it in their life.....
Want a new car...clean out the garage.
Want a partner...clear out the old one and make space for this new person to come in.
Want a new home, sort out your finances, start viewing homes, virtually or in person, buy something small that you will only use when you move into your new home....Get the picture?

There are others still that can only manifest what they believe they deserve!

Hey all,
I have a question, every day I have been reading posts randomly some pop up. They mention the things I'm manifesting to get fixed or resolved. Some ppl have the same issues others are just mentioning the exact issue but without my hassle, What does this mean? Also I see my manifestations in others, what I envisioned for myself is happening for others. I can't move to or go ahead with my plans till I get this approval from council and it's been 10 months of torture and lost money.
I'm hanging on super tight. Thinking about it daily and affirming my vision, praying and meditating. I asked for signs that it's coming and each day I see those signs! Please help me unpack this.

Thank you for the question. Many people ask me how to align with what they have asked for, you have done just that, with everything showing up in your eye sight, take it as proof that what you have asked for is on its way.

Other people ask me how to manifest, but you also have that down, as the proof that yours is on its way shows up in the posts that you have been seeing.

Many people will find out that the person down the street, won the exact amount of money they had been wishing for, or their colleague got the job, car or house they wanted, at the moment you are having it show up in your eye sight! You have asked, you see signs of your want...It follows that the only thing left to happen, is for it to be tangible.

Be happy, act as if you've received proof that yours is on the way and it will come, as what you are doing is actually working.

Do note that it is at this stage many decide that they will not get what they have wished for as it seems to be popping up everywhere else instead of in their life, home or bank account. They then begin to believe that they will not receive what they have asked for and thus, they do not receive their want or wish.

Don't consider other peoples journey, they may have Asked, Believed and Detached quickly, causing their wish to be granted quickly, they could have had to wait twice as long as you, but did not agonise over the issue (in public).

Keep the faith, knowing yours is on the way.

I want to hear how or if the LOA applies to Hurricane Helene & the LA Wildfires most recently? I'm not posting this to debate or argue with you. So, I'm not including in this what I think because I genuinely, want to know what you think about these two disasters in relation to the LOA.

Thank you for your question. You mention my personal opinion, that is 'Hurricane Helene & the LA Wildfires' are disasters, for me they are natural disasters.

Everything that happens applies to LOA in that it is your personal thoughts and beliefs about these disasters that matters.

My personal thoughts are that of hope and safety to those escaping these disasters. For those who are no longer with us due to these natural disasters, I hope their families can continue to heal and rebuild their lives and home.

Can you manifest something you really want even if it weren't meant for you?

Thank you for your question. Sure, we all manifest things, people and situations that do not benefit us in the long run. Some of us set out to manifest things, people and situations knowing it may not be the best for us or those around us, but do it anyway.

You can manifest most anything good or not so good.
The process is always the same...Ask, Believe, Act and Receive. The answer we would like to know from you is, what have you been up to?

A response to my reply from another forum member.

If it wasn't for you..you wouldn't manifest it.

Thank you for sharing.
We are always always manifesting. This means that sometimes, we manifest things that may not truly serve us or those around us. Just because something appears in our lives doesn't automatically mean it's aligned with our highest good.

Some people deliberately manifest things, people and situations that do not benefit them or the people they have close to them.

Think of the times we've received unexpected money, perhaps from work, a gift, or what we believe to be the fruits of our manifestation. Instead of using it wisely or saving it for what really matters, we sometimes rush to spend it on something we don't really need. Later, we may find ourselves short. That item, no matter how appealing in the moment, wasn't meant for us at that time. Yet, we convinced ourselves that the money appeared to justify the purchase. This shows how easy it is to mistake a momentary opportunity for our manifestation!

The same applies to relationships. People sometimes attract or manifest partners who, deep down, they know aren't right for them. But they indulge in the connection, hoping it will evolve into something meaningful. Later, when the relationship becomes strained or harmful, they realise that what they thought was a blessing was actually a lesson or perhaps a sign of someone more aligned with them or their purpose, on the horizon.

We must understand that not everything we draw into our lives is meant to be kept. Some appearances are simply signals that something greater is coming. If only we have the patience to wait for it.

We are always manifesting. The key is to discern whether it is what we asked for, by asking ourselves, "Did I attract this, is this truly what I asked for, or is it a sign of something better to come?"

When it comes to manifesting what's your single biggest struggle or frustration?

Thank you for your question. You ask, *"When it comes to manifesting what's your single biggest struggle or frustration?"*
Let me ask you a question? Are you aware that what you think, talk or in this case write about often, you bring into your life; and how would you have members of this forum answer this question?

They would have to THINK about their *"single biggest struggle or frustration,"* then they would need to WRITE down their *"single biggest struggle or frustration"* and perhaps, re-read/SAY what their *"single biggest struggle or frustration"* is. That is three times too many in my book!

Asking this question and getting others to join in with you is counter productive to using the Law of Attraction!

As the Law of Attraction is always always working and works with our thoughts, what we say, write down (often) and what we do.

Looking, seeking an answer to the *"single biggest struggle or frustration"* will ensure you have (or find) struggles and or frustrations when using the Law of Attraction.

Here's some advice given to another member who asked the same question:

How a manifestation appears in your life may be different from how it appears in another persons life. Just before a manifestation arrives, there can be what I call the 'Breakdown stage'. When everything seem to go belly up! It is at this stage many people halt their manifestations, by proclaiming 'i'm never gonna get'..what they have asked for, or begin to voice their 'frustrations' and or 'struggles' causing the whole process to begin again.

The voiced frustration is a wish (Ask) the frustration is Believed, then they detach from the situation (part of the process most do not use). They then receive these unwanted situations as they have followed the process of Ask, Believe and Act. These unwanted situations may seem to appear, so much quicker than other wishes because the process is completed quickly.

So you see, your frustration or struggle is and may remain your frustration and or struggle because you've added it to your process of using the Law of Attraction.

Follow the process of Ask, Believe, Act and you will Receive, now this is to be done regardless to what is happening in your life.

If the roof starts to leak, still expect what you asked for.
If the washing machine stops working, still expect what you asked for.
If the person down the road gets the exact thing you've asked for....you get the gist....expect what you have asked for.

Keep believing and don't give in to any frustrations that may arise and what you have asked for will arrive.

I'm just wondering what's everyone's biggest frustration so far with the Law of Attraction?I'm not trying to bash it - far from it - I'm trying to see what the common problems or frustrations are to see if there's a way around them.
Thanks for sharing!

Thank you for your question. I understand that you do not want to *"bash"* the Law of Attraction, but to have members or even yourself list their *"biggest frustration so far with the Law of Attraction"* is counter productive to using the Law of Attraction.

The LOA is always always working and works with our thoughts, what we say, write down (often) and what we do. Looking, seeking or *"trying to see what the common problems or frustrations are"* will ensure you have common problems or frustrations to see!

How a manifestation appears in your life may be different from how it appears in another persons life, and so what you call a "frustration" may not be a "frustration" to me. Thus no "common problem."

There is a particular stage, however, just before a manifestation arrives, I call it the 'Breakdown stage'. This is when everything seem to go belly up! It is at this stage many people halt their manifestations, by voicing their 'frustrations' at the LOA and stating that 'it isn't working,' causing the whole process to begin again.

The voiced frustration is a wish (Ask) the frustration is believed, then they detach from the situation (part of the process most do not use). As the process or steps of the LOA are complete, the unwanted situations will appear, so much quicker than other wishes.

There is no *"way around"* the use of LOA, you Ask, Believe, take Action and you will Receive....Nothing in between, regardless of what is happening, you continue to believe what you have asked for and it will arrive.

Can anyone please please tell me how to manifest properly as I have had absolutely no luck with it so far. Cheers.

Thank you for your question. Sorry to read that you *"have had absolutely no luck with it so far."* The 'it' you refer to, I believe is the Law of Attraction (LOA). Do note that you are manifesting ALL the time. In fact you are manifesting *"absolutely no luck with it so far."*

When using the LOA one has to be conscious of what we think, say and write down, as words, thoughts and deeds have moulding powers.

To use LOA to the desired outcome, all you do is Ask, Believe, Act and you will Receive. You proclaim (Ask or say) you *"have had absolutely no luck with it so far,"* which is something you (Believe), and so you (Act) as if you do not know how to manifest, which will have you seeking out forums, youtube channels that will help you *"manifest properly."*

You will receive advice, because you are unable to *"manifest properly."* If the advice you have been given does not resonate with you or your beliefs, you stay in the mode of *"I don't know how to manifest, I've had no luck."* What do you think the result of all that type of thinking, speaking, seeking out or writing brings you? Yes you got it *"No luck."*

Change your words, thoughts, and deeds, know that you are always manifesting and you will see the change in your manifesting journey within a day.

Try the £1 test, Ask for a pound or dollar, whatever your currency is and wait for it to appear, this can be in an old purse, a coat pocket, in an ad for a pound off, in your inbox as a voucher, someone may buy you a coffee worth a £. Try it this week.

I Manifest Nothing. All the things I manifested never came or maybe I just don't know how to manifest.

Sorry to read that you *"manifested nothing."* This is not actually true, you manifested not manifesting and you may find that *"all the things,"* you attempt to *"manifest, never come."*

As we manifest ALL the time, it is important that we are very careful what we say and write down!

When using the Law of Attraction to manifest, we must Ask for what we want, Believe it will come, and then take Action, what have you done to show God/the Universe that you are ready or expectant on the want you have asked for?

If you want a new car, clean out the garage, buy some new smellies for that new car...Go visit a show room, test drive the car you want.
If you want a new home.....Do the leg work, enlist an Estate agent, view properties, imagine what your life will be like living in that new home, get rid of anything in your present home that you do not use and will not be taking to that new home....You get the gist.

Depending on what you want, make a conscious effort to do something, anything towards getting it and then expect it to arrive. Life goes on while we wait, so don't be discourage when the opposite turns up, its just a sign that what you have asked for is on the way.

When attempting to manifest a certain thing, that thing in all its form may turn up.....The one that many see is, debt, when money is requested. I know someone who wanted more money and a debt turned up that had occurred six years ago, they had no idea that it had not been paid. It is at this stage many people start the process all over, when they voice their frustrations or proclaim that *"I manifest nothing, all the things I manifested never came."* What do you think happens then?

You ASKED or stated *" I manifest nothing"* you BELIEVED *"all the things I manifested never came"* and so you manifested (received)....Nothing. Change the way you speak about the use of LOA, I understand you feel this is your truth, but the way you speak and what you believe may be causing nothing to turn up for you.

Try re-wording your 'truth' with something like:
'I will manifest ....'(add the thing or situation you are attempting to manifest).
'I believe my......' (what you want) 'will turn up soon'

Stay believing that what you have asked for will come, and don't limit how, who or when it will come to you. Try the £1 test, Ask for a pound or dollar, whatever your currency is and wait for it to appear, this can turn up in numerous ways and or places, someone may even buy you a coffee worth a £. Try it this week.

I am struggling to manifest anything.

Hi, Sorry you feel this way, you are manifesting all the time, in fact you are manifesting *"struggling to manifest."* Try and change the way you speak about what you want in your life.
Here's how to use the Law of Attraction: All you do is Ask, Believe and you will Receive. *"struggling to manifest,"* is a wish, (it is voiced), *"struggling to manifest,"* is believed, what comes next?
Also the use of "I" or "I am" is a wish, anything said after I or I am has happened, is happening or will happen.

There are other processes, but the basics are above. Ask for something you deem 'small'. Believe and wait for it to appear. The Law of Attraction is always working, you are manifesting all the time, what you manifest is down to you.

Try the £1 test, Ask for a pound or dollar, whatever your currency is and wait for it to appear, this can be in an old purse, a coat pocket, in an ad for a pound off, in your inbox as a voucher, someone may buy you a coffee worth a £. Try it this week and let us know how you got on.

So I have been manifesting for 6 months for one particular thing.
I have asked God to show me signs in particular a white bird. Today I picked up a toilet paper brand I never use and noticed at home it had a white parrot on it. I also got some biscuits for my kids to decorate and when I got home my daughter goes oh a white dove. There were two white doves on the packaging. Does this count as my manifestations and vibrations being heard? I was so shocked!!

Thank you for the question. You asked for a sign and got two.

Yes they were signs that you are being heard, just a note here, you are being heard all the time.

Did you ask for a sign that your want is on its way? If so the answer is 'it's surely on its way.'

You state that you have *"been manifesting for 6 months for a particular thing."* You are manifesting all the time, we do this with our thoughts, speech and deeds.

It would appear that you have been believing, waiting or wanting for a particular thing for 6 months. You have been shown signs that it is on its way, now prepare for it to enter your life, your home, garage or bank...

As I do not know what you have asked for you will have to do the leg work, is their room for what you have asked for to come in? de-clutter if you need to, throw or give away things that are taking up space, clear schedules to accommodate this wished for item, person or situation. By doing what you can to welcome your wish into your life, it will usher it in sooner.

Keep expecting it...Do come back and let us know when it arrives.

I am in no way trying to paint myself as a saint. However, I struggle with manifesting as I always wonder why the universe or God would grant me a want or a need when others have greater needs. How does one overcome such a block?

Thank you for your question. I understand that you would *"struggle"* to manifest as you do not believe you will be granted your wish or want. You state that you feel that God/the Universe have others more needy than you, again I can see why you have found it challenging to manifest.

There can be many reasons we do not get what we ask for, after attempting to follow the steps of LOA.

Here's a couple: Not being realistic at the start of the process, some may ask for more than they believe they will receive, for example, asking for a £10,000 per month salary when they know the company and their experience or qualifications only warrants a £5,000 per month salary.

(This does not mean, if this person genuinely believed they should have a £10,000 per month salary they will not be able to receive it).
Another reason we do not get what we ask for, is knowing or believing we do not deserve what we have asked for.

I will use a scenario based on an author like myself, Imagine an author has written the best book they have ever produced, they know that it would help thousands of people and could possibly out rank any large selling books on the market, but feels they shouldn't put themselves on the same pedestal as, lets say, J.K. Rowling. As a psychologist I would want to know why you felt this way, because the last time I looked, J.K. Rowling is a human being and an author, same characteristics as the author in my scenario. A little like what you are going through with not painting yourself as a saint issue!

Take some time to look up the personal story of anybody who has succeeded in their field and you will see that most started from humble beginnings. One of the things they will all have in common is belief and trust in the product they produced, themselves or a higher power.

Do you believe that God/the Universe has enough for everyone who asks;

For help.
For food.
For money.
A new home.
A job.
A wife, a husband etc? If your answer is yes, then there is enough for you too.

Whenever you ask for something, think of a large bag or warehouse that has your name on it, everything in that bag or in that warehouse is yours, (note everyone has a bag or warehouse too) and all you have to do is ask for some of its contents. I think Abraham Hicks calls this the vortex.

Remember LOA only works by what you believe.

Do you have any suggestions for shutting out the internal doubt that sometimes makes itself known when working on manifesting?

Thank you for the question. Internal doubt comes when you either don't believe you will get what you have asked for, or feel that you don't deserve what you have asked for; which is it?

Instead of asking for one million ask for one hundred thousand, instead of asking for a six bedroomed house ask for a three bedroomed house or an apartment, instead of asking for a job that pays 15k per month ask for one that pays 10k per month. Get the picture?

Be realistic in your ask. There is nothing wrong with asking for that million, six bedroom house or 15k a month job, if you believe you WILL get and deserve it.

Ask for what you want and set about doing all you can to welcome it into your life.

If its a car, clear out the garage, if its a house move, start packing, get rid of things you will not be taking to your new home, do all you can to receive what you have asked for and start acting as if you already have it.

Act as if you have that six bedroomed house, ensuring every room in your house is as tidy as it would be if you had that new home, dress as if you have that 10k per month job (even if your just going to the supermarket), window shop as if you have the money you have asked for, put items in your online 'basket'. Start making lists of what you will buy with your wages or for that new home.

With all that said the most important process is to believe you will get it, do not worry when, where or how it will come, just know that it will.

Does insecurities play a factor in manifesting?

Thank you for the question. Insecurity about the want or wish you aim to manifest will play a big factor in what, when and how you get your manifestation.

As we are manifesting ALL the time, we get what we believe and what we align with.

Wishes asked for drearily will turn up drearily, slow and may not really fit the situation. Wishes asked for desperately with a need for speed, are violently received.

Insecurity or non belief in what you have asked for will not bring about your manifestation, but more insecurity.

Ensure your want is realistic, you've got to believe it is achievable.
Ensure you feel you deserve what you have asked for.
Then go about doing what you can to achieve this want, by doing this you keep your mind on your goal or prize, leaving no room for insecurity to seep in.

How do you recommend dealing with unpleasant intrusive thoughts that appear during manifesting. I sometimes experience intrusive thoughts as I am imagining my manifestation fulfilled. For example, if I imagine living in my dream home, I'll have obtrusive thoughts about it broken into by violent robbers.
Ive worked through some of my underlying beliefs and have realised that part of me didn't feel deserving of the manifestation. However, will still experience the intrusive thoughts now and again. Be great to hear your thoughts

Thanks for the question. What I have learnt is that we are so use to things not working out

for us that it is 'comfortable' for things to not work out. A comfort zone type of place, here we know what to do and how to feel, because we are use to it. We have experienced this numerous times over many years, so we have it down! Then we try to change the comfort zone feeling with manifesting or thinking about what we would really like in our lives and we encounter intrusive thoughts. It is as if our mind wants to get back to its comfy slippers, that of 'things don't work out for us.'

135

So here is what you do....Find a time or situation when things did work out for you, the stars did align, you had a great outcome to something you wanted, then tell yourself that things do work out, remind yourself (your mind) of the instance when things worked out, by doing this you give yourself (your mind) proof that things can actually work out, so manifesting a home in which no one tries to break in is possible.

Often we can only believe when we have proof, and as believing is a great part of manifesting, it is needed.

Find an affirmation or two that can be said, out loud or silently when you have an intrusive thought about your wish fulfilled, the more you train your mind to 'look for' or expect a counter affirmation to your intrusive thoughts the less you will have them.

Just another quick tip, make sure you want or wish is believable to you!

Wishing for a Ten Million pound house, when you believe you could comfortably live in a Five Hundred Thousand Pound house, will have intruders of the mind trying to get in, keep your wants realistic and you will be able to manage the manifestation process and the wish when it arrives.

What is the difference in technique when removing obstacles during manifesting when something appears nearly instantly and when something being manifested seems to never arrive?

Thank you for your question. I believe you are asking, what technique do you use to remove obstacles, for manifesting things instantly, and what technique do you use to remove obstacles when the thing you are attempting to manifest seems to never arrive. Come close, let me whisper the answer...YOU'RE THE TECHNIQUE.

The technique is whatever YOU believe will be the outcome of your wish. If you believed what you asked for is an 'easy ask', and it would come quickly because it wasn't anything 'difficult' or 'big', then you have removed any obstacle (although there was none in the beginning, an obstacle is something you have conjured up) surrounding that wish.

You also detached, meaning you didn't have any thoughts or concerns around when, how or who this want would come, and you got on with the business of waiting, or being expectant of your wish. That is the technique you used.

Want to know what technique you used for the things that *"never seems to arrive?"* Or perhaps you already know, having read the first part of this response....Just a note here, doesn't it defeat the object of asking for something if you feel that you have to jump over hurdles or obstacles before getting what you want.

Remind me of the process of using the LOA....It's Ask, Believe and Receive, there is no jumping over obstacles in that equation.

So back to the technique you may have used to ensure, yep to ensure that your manifestation *"seem to never arrive."* Think back to how you started the process in-order to manifest this thing that "seems to never arrive."
Did you have thoughts of 'this is big' or 'this is going to take a long time to come,' perhaps

you thought 'I will never get this'. What were your thoughts around this wish?

If your thoughts were as they were when you manifested instantly, then wait, take all the practical steps you can. If you asked for a house, go visit some, if it was for a partner, go to where they are likely to hang out, if it is for a new job, go seek it. You could also start 'acting' as if you already have the thing you have asked for.

When using the LOA we Ask, Believe Act (take action or and Act as if) then we Receive. The manifestations that "seems to never arrive" are on the way, your belief is the obstacle!

How do you stay optimistic and believe that your manifestation will come to fruition. Especially when you can't see how it can possibly come true.

Hi, Stating that *"you can't see how it can possibly come true."* will not bring your manifestation to you.

Staying optimistic is not always easy, but you make it more challenging by not believing you will get your manifestation.

Know that you will get what you asked for or something better, this is called detachment and will help you stay on task i.e *"stay optimistic,"* as it will help you stay in the right mindset.

Another part of detachment is not worrying or spending any time on how your manifestation will come, just know it will. This stops you halting or claiming that your manifestation will not arrive and keep in the right mindset or vibe for it to get to you.

Response From Enquirer

Thank you, this is exactly it with me, I worry so much and its incredibly difficult to just stop worrying! I do try so hard to stay focused and imagine it happening and be optimistic about it, but I can't detach myself from worrying or being anxious, I have no idea how, it just doesn't seem to work, I can't shut it off no matter how hard I try.

I understand that there are some situations that causes us to worry instead of wait. Do you know that we sometimes worry as an act of 'doing something'!

Try this...Get ready for what you have asked for. Get ready for that person, organisation or situation to give you a favourable response. Believe the answer will work in your favour, whatever the response or answer is.

Please note the amount of times you utter a less than positive thing about yourself:

"I worry so much"
"its incredibly difficult to just stop worrying."
"I cant detach myself from worrying or being anxious."
"I have no idea how, it just doesn't seem to work."
"I can't shut it off no matter how hard I try."

Also note that everything you say after 'I' is what has happened, is happening or will happen! Try today, to change everything you say after 'I' to something positive, worrying causes more harm than good, for you and or the situation.

When you think of the situation, add a positive outcome to it, this will take practice but will stop you worrying so much.

Hi, I've just joined and wanted to ask a question …. I've tried manifesting many, many times and have failed (many, many times). Let's just say, my circumstances are not good and I am most definitely not where I want to be in life.
Here's my question: can your manifestations go to someone else? Someone close to you?
It's something I've been thinking about a lot, it seems that everything I've asked for has gone to my daughter - the holidays, the car, the money, absolutely everything. She and I are very, very close, we speak every day and see each other regularly. Recently, I've gone into manifesting 100%, I'm doing breath-work, mantras, affirmations etc and last week I put out to the universe that I wanted £15,000 - a very specific amount to pay off my debts and pay for a holiday. Guess what, last week my daughter received £15,000 she wasn't expecting. Surely this is no longer a coincidence? Help and insight would be appreciated. I love her but I don't want her to have everything.

Thank you for the question and welcome to this forum.

Firstly you are a mega manifestor (I'll explain later) As a mega manifestor you should not be thinking, saying or writing *"I've tried manifesting many, many times and have failed (many, many times)"* or *"my circumstances are not good and I am most definitely not where I want to be in life."* What you think, say, write and believe you bring about.

Secondly to your question *"can your manifestations go to someone else?"* The answer is NO, what is for you is for you. The *"holidays, the car, the money, absolutely everything,"* even the recent £15,000 was PROOF that yours was on the way! You should have jumped up and down and said 'Mine is on the way,' 'Mine is on the way.' The minute you gave her gifts the side eye! (I know you love her) you halted your manifestations.

Why? because you are a mega manifestor, most people ask me how to manifest, but you have it down and the proof that yours is on its way, shows up right next to you.

Many people will find out that the person down the street, won the exact amount they had been wishing for, or their colleague got the job, car or house they wanted, but you have it show up in your eye sight!

Be happy for her, act as if you've received proof that yours is on the way and it will come. This proof is you aligning with what you have asked for, everything you have asked for has appeared but you end the process, that of Ask, Believe and Receive, you stopped it at the Believe stage as you didn't believe it was coming to you, because it arrived at your daughters door step.

That was her manifestation, you state that you and your daughter are close, is it not possible that she could have had the same wish or want you had?

What you have been doing up until the wants arriving for your daughter, is what you should do, but don't stop there, wait, expect and believe that yours will arrive.

What to do if we attract the opposite of our wishes or if another one get your wishes?

Thank you for the question and welcome to this forum. When I have asked for something and things appear to 'go wrong' or the 'opposite' turns up, I know at that point that my manifestation is on its way, to answer your question, its the start or the near arrival of your manifestation appearing in your life.

I call this the 'Breakdown stage'. When everything seem to go belly up! It is at this stage many people halt their manifestations, by feeling that the wishing process is a failure, and proclaiming 'i'm never going to get'..what they have asked for, along with thoughts of giving up, this causes the whole process to begin again. This stage is also a time of 'clearing out,' that is people, places and things.

Have you ever wondered why your life came together after a certain someone left your life? Or when you moved to a different address? It works with things too. Have you ever had a machine, car or cooker break down only to find someone was giving away the said item or you find the item at a knock down price? This is the clearing out for better to come in.

Regarding others getting your wishes.......You should start jumping up and down and saying 'Mine is on the way,' 'Mine is on the way.' Its proof that yours is on the way. Many people will find out that another person, either won or was given the exact amount they had been wishing for, or their colleague got the job, car or house they wanted. You have it showing up right in-front of your eyes! You have aligned with your wants, that is why it is showing up. Act as if you've received proof that yours is on the way and it will come.

The minute you begin to feel that others have got your wish, you are accepting that you won't get yours. No one can get your wishes they are your wishes, just like you can not wish for someone else, they have to wish or want for themselves. What's yours is yours. Stop telling God/the Universe that they gave your wish away, this keeps you in the state of 'i'm not gonna get mine', instead of 'they got theirs so mine must be on the way'.

Response From Enquirer

Angela Scott - Oh this is a good way to look at things ... thank you for this explanation .. It has helped me keep positive .... When I was feeling the universe wasn't working for me ... it's just taking a little longer than I hoped ... but it's still coming ... thank you xx

Yes it's still coming. The Law of Attraction is always always working, you are manifesting all the time, what you manifest is down to you.

If you ask for something, God/the Universe sets in motion the process for you to get it, if half way through (normally when the manifestation is about to arrive) people get despondent and make another wish 'it's never going to come', 'I never get what I ask for.'

This starts the process of manifesting a new wish, 'never coming' and 'never getting what you ask for'........get it? We may have these thoughts, but the sooner we dispel them, the quicker we get back to the waiting for our want to manifest.

How can you tell when a manifestation is close.

Thank you for your question.

Some manifestation are near, when things seem to go wrong or in the opposite direction to your wished for want. In my recent course, I call this the 'Breakdown stage'. When everything seem to go belly up! It is at this stage many people halt their manifestations, by proclaiming that 'i'm never gonna get'.... what I asked for, and then they wonder why they did not get what they asked for!

The aim here is for you to show the Universe that you still want what you have asked for and continue to believe its on the way.

There is another sign that your manifestation is near, this is when you see or notice that someone else has just been given or won what you asked for, experiencing this, shows that you have aligned with your want, i.e its in your vicinity, its close by.

Keep believing regardless of the circumstances, yours will come.

Hi! I started to learn about manifesting a couple weeks ago. Mostly because of videos on TikTok. I started to manifest and I believe 100% in it. But are there signs for when your manifestation is about to happen? For the last couple of days I've been seeing angels numbers everywhere and I also saw a video once that said everything goes bad before your manifestation comes in. The past two nights I've had two very vivid dreams about what I'm manifesting. I know I will get what i'm manifesting and I trust the universe to bring it to me but are those signs saying my manifestation is about to happen?

Thank you for the question. Yes, the video you saw that stated *"everything goes bad before your manifestation comes in,"* may be right, it is at this stage that people believe that their wish is not going to be granted. As they make another wish by saying 'this LOA doesn't work' or 'I never get what I ask for'. I call this the 'Breakdown stage'. When everything seem to go belly up!

This stage is also a time of 'clearing out,' that is people, places and things. Have you ever wondered why your life came together after a big shake up, someone left, you left, something in your life changed in a big way. This shake up includes things too.

Another consideration, just like any other time in your life, things happen. Going through the process of using the LOA to manifest is no different, life happens. However, the things that 'happen' or the life changing situations that occur and are connected to your want being on its way, often are like for like.

For example if you ask for money and unexpected debts turn up, or a friend or relative (who don't normally) ask you to loan some money. You ask for a new car and your old car stops working, in these instances, you can be sure your manifestation is on its way, because you have aligned with your want, your want is showing up in all its forms, you just have to remember that this is also a stage or a process of you getting what you want.

You should keep the faith' or as you are currently doing, knowing you "will get what you're manifesting and trust the universe to bring it to you," stay steadfast in this belief regardless of what is happening as you have asked and believed so it must come.

Can I manifest more than one thing (multiple) but none are material things?

Thanks for the question. Whether you are asking for *"material things"* or not you can ask for multiple, (more than one) things. However, you need to ask for what you feel comfortable with, remember it has to be what you believe will manifest, so if that is one thing at a time, then do that.

If I want to manifest a house, I want it fully loaded;
The furniture (in side and out).
The window covering.
The bed sheets.
The flooring, you get my gist.

Being realistic is an important part of manifesting. You know you are being realistic when you can think and talk about your want with ease. If you believe you can have, then you can have it, just Ask.

I am not sure if I will say this right, but when asking the universe the manifest one thing but ten other things come to mind, can I just redo my question and start over or do I just go on with the new question?

Thank you for your question. If I want a house, I think of ALL the other things that I want in that house, that's the wall covering, the floor treatment, the furniture inside and outside..you get the gist.

There is nothing wrong with wanting things, however thinking of a house its contents and then thinking or wanting a new job, new clothes and a full fridge of food etc may be a little challenging.

Pick something that you can concentrate on, and when other things come to mind (and they will) use an affirmation to put them on the back burner, i.e. I want the house and I'll get the shoes later or I want the new car and I'll get that bag later.

We have thousands of thoughts a day and it is for us to dispel or accommodate those thoughts. You can *"redo the question"* or as mentioned above concentrate on what you really want.

Please note, if a child wants a particular toy, have you noticed that they stick with wanting that particular toy, that is how you should attempt to be when trying to manifest.

Does it take a long time to manifest things?

Thank you for the question.

Time is relative, some people believe that manifesting large sums of money takes longer than small sums of money...But what do you call large sums of money and what do you consider small sums of money? What do you feel is a long or short time?

What you should consider is the process Ask, believe and leave it to God/Universe to present your wished for item, person or situation at the right time.

Hi guys. How do you deal with people around you who will remind you of your past self (decisions, mistakes, events). I ask because Ive been having difficulty totally ignoring that as if I owe an explanation to them. Can anyone relate to this?

Thank you for the question.
I am not quite clear what you are asking however, If you are 'around people' that make you feel uncomfortable.......Do what you can to stop being around them.

I understand that this can be difficult if you live with this person. However, if you cared for someone, would you make them feel the way this person is making you feel?

Again I am unclear of your situation, (please do not elaborate) but I am reading traits of a not so healthy person and abuse, this may not be the case, but if it is...Please get help from any organisation in your area.

Attempting to 'manifest them better or for yourself to *"totally ignore"* abusive behaviour is not the way to go.

When manifesting I have a qualification, do I study as usual or do I study whilst affirming I'm just recapping information? So that my asking don't come from a place of lack.

Thank you for the question, when manifesting we tend to think of the finished product...for example the holiday - We think of laying on the beach, we don't think of having to save the money to get there, or having to ask for time off, or who will house, plant or pet sit. Take wanting a car we do not think of the metal, the factory it will go to or the workers.......you get the gist.

Think of the finished product....Nevill Goddard said we should 'live in the end' meaning we should not think of the 'getting it' but the 'got it'. That is why we 'Act as if' Acting as if allows us to imagine what life would be like if we had the thing or situation we want to bring into our lives. You are taking action which is a part of having your wish come true.

So yes you should study as normal as you are expecting that qualification 'in the end', you are showing God/the Universe that you want this qualification and so you are doing what it takes to get it. It is certainly not coming from a place of lack, because you are aligning yourself with what you wished for.

Sitting doing nothing and wishing you have a qualification won't bring it to you. We do our part God/the universe does the rest.

How can i manifest passing my most important exam that's in 3 months? And also how can i manifest getting better at mathematics?

Thank you for the question, we can manifest most anything.
On a practical note, in order to pass a test one would need to study, understand and revise for the test or exam. Once you have done that you are on the way to passing.

Ask, do the work (study) and believe you will pass. Imagine your self passing the exam, what will it feel like; who will you tell first; how will you celebrate? Get a picture of someone passing their exam and pin it where you can see it everyday, it will be as if someone took a picture of you, when you passed your exam.

In-order to get better at mathematics, you will need to take the practical steps and ask God/the Universe to make you "*better at mathematics.*"

One can manifest most anything, however, I could ask God/the universe to make me better at drawing, but at the moment I really am not skilled at that art.

I'm not sure how long it would take for me to be good, let alone "*better*" at it. You have to have an aptitude for the subject and believe that you will become "*better*" at it.

I understand one of the important steps to manifesting is to take "action" but what exactly is meant by this? Please could you kindly explain/provide an example so I can better understand what action I need to take? Thank you.

Thank you for the question.
There are two types of actions one should take when using the LOA to manifest.

The first is practical *"action."* If you want something, do what you can to get it i.e If you want to buy something that you can not afford, your action should be to start saving, or taking extra hours at your job. If it is money you need, the action you should be seeking out how can I make more money. If you want a new car, what would you normally do in this instance? Well its the same when using the LOA, you take the action to sort out your finances, you test drive the car you want.

In taking these practical steps or actions, you are showing God /the Universe that you are doing something to get your want, you are also 'acting as if' (which is another type of acting, but we will deal with two here), the acting as if, comes in the form of you doing something towards getting what you want...which in turn shows that you believe you will receive your want (A big component of using the LOA.)

Then there is 'guided action.' I answered a question earlier for a person who wanted a 'large sum of money,' as well as other things they needed to consider, they were advised to listen or beware of any guided action. (Guided action is a hunch you may get) For this person, I suggested this can be something like...applying for that job, they had seen advertised, start a business, sell that item that had been in the attic for years.

This is God/the Universe helping (or giving you guided actions to take) in-order to get the wished for money. Getting that job, you've had a hunch to take, may pay the exact amount of money you want, just for joining the company, your business may take off the minute you start advertising, that artefact that had been forgotten about in the attic, is now worth the money being sought.

Say you want to move house, you get a feeling to check a particular Estate agents (Realtor) page, and find a suitable property, you want a particular outfit, which has been out of your reach for sometime, you get a hunch to check out a different part of town, in search of this outfit, when you do, you find it half price and the right colour and fit. 'guided' action is a hunch, a feeling, a light bulb moment that is sent by God/the Universe to guide you to what you have asked for.

When you have done all you believe you can to bring what you have asked into your life, you wait...While waiting you believe it will come.

Hey! I told the universe that it can't change what I said, and now I regret it and I would like him to change it or is it too late?

Hey, Did you know that you are using LOA (or manifesting) every second of every minute you are alive? We manifest what we think, say and act out. So change the narrative, thinking or saying *"I want to change what I said"*, will have you wanting to change what you said. Instead state that 'I have removed what was said, as if it was never said' or words to that effect, make it make sense to you. When any doubt around what you had commanded appears, repeat an affirmation until you believe it has been removed.

Hi, I read somewhere - 'Your path is more difficult because your calling is higher.' Please explain.

You may find that people who have a big calling on their lives, have been through a 'hard life' Here's a few:
Fredrick Douglass.
Harriet Tubman.
Albert Einstein.
Eckhart Tolle.
Oprah.
Richard Branson.. I could go on, but you get the gist.

I believe it is to make us stronger, to be able to follow our path and share what we know with the world.

Response From Enquirer

It's just sometimes I feel that each time I get up someone knocks me down and its hard.

First, I must advise you to ensure you are safe, and if you feel you are at risk in any way, to get help from any organisation in your area who may be able to help. I also understand that you may not mean that that 'someone, knocks you down' physically, however I have learnt that anybody that makes another feel 'less than' are to be kept at arms length. I don't know your situation and the "*someone*" doing the 'knocking down' can be a someone you live with!

Take a look at your life and see where you can put a little distance between you and that 'someone'.

If that someone or that *somebodies* is at work, start TODAY by speaking to a supervisor of your HR department, perhaps you need to find another job (easier said than done) but by taking a step, God/the Universe will see that you are making the effort to change your environment.

Yes I agree it can be challenging but as what you read above states, *'Your path is more difficult because your calling is higher,'* you may have something to share with others who have been in your situation.

After you have overcome the situation you are in and this "being knocked down," you may be able to see a red flag a mile off, and be able to advise others.

I have had a really bad day. I've cried all day and feel like all the hard work I had done is ruined.

Hi, Sorry you are experiencing this.
Firstly if you often have *"really bad days,"* in which you are crying all day, you should consult your local medical professional as they may be able to help.

Secondly, nothing you have done with good intentions is wasted.

That also means doing better next time, or starting over..Your hard work is always counted. As I do not know your situation, I can only advise on the tears and how you state you feel right now.

Wipe your tears and carry on as you always do...take baby steps, you'll get there, as it would seem that you have a goal to reach.

As mentioned above, there is nothing wrong with starting over, as you are here, you have a chance at a do over.

Trying to work out how to let go of the detail and control of the outcomes and just trust the universe, but it's hard!

Sorry you are feeling this way.
You state that you are finding it hard to let go and let God/Universe do its work!

Consider this, when you turn a light on, do you wonder how the electricity connects to your house from the grid; then from the electrical piping to the switch? If you work for a large company, do you think of how they will pay you this month, where they will get the money from, or what they had to do to get it?

Here's an easy one, when you was a child and asked for a present for that special day, a birthday or religious day did you wonder where the gift will come from, or how the money is going to be generated in-order to buy that present? Your likely answer to those questions is NO, NO I do not wonder, worry or contemplate the who what and where. See where I am going with this?

All the above items, and situations you expect to appear. The light, the wages and as a child the present. Do you know why you expected it? Because you commanded, worked or asked for it. All the above had you doing something for what you required.

Why ask for something then set about working it out the who what and where for God/the Universe?

It really defeats the object of asking, wouldn't you agree? Your *'it's hard'* in your question is the 'hard' work you are putting in to working out the who, what and where this item or situation is going to come from.

Here's how the Law of Attraction works you Ask+Believe= Receive. Trying to sort it out yourself is not in the equation.

Thank you. Just a quick question, I have been successful with manifesting success for my business. However I have a very difficult legal case at moment. Would manifesting help with this?

Sure manifesting can help with a legal issue, what makes you think it wouldn't? Are you thinking 'man' (the justice system), is bigger than God/the Universe or perhaps you are thinking that you can only use manifesting to 'get something tangible'.

Whatever your thoughts, you may have to change them,

as what or who you believe in to grant you your wish, is what will grant you your wish! What I mean is if you believe and leave it to the justice system to grant you a favourable outcome, then you will remain in the same doubt (situation) you are in now.

If you believe God/the Universe will give you the best or a favourable outcome, then you can begin the work needed for the outcome you would like.

Who or what ever you believe in, bare in mind that everything is working in your favour regardless of the outcome.

Response From Enquirer

So I don't know where to start. There is corrupt police and my ex involved in this. Manifesting has worked for the success of my business and health though.

You start where you have always started when trying to manifest something for your business and health, what could be bigger than manifesting something regarding your health?

It would seem that you hold the corrupt police, your ex and the justice system in such high esteem, you feel they can not be beaten! However, I could be wrong. What makes them bigger or stronger than your will to manifest better health? Nothing in my book.

You have manifested a great outcome before and you will do it again. Nothing is stronger, bigger or greater than who or what you conjured up to grant you your wishes in the past.

Visualise the outcome you would like, ensure you are not disliking any one or any system involved.

Ask for the outcome you would like, think of how you will feel when you get the outcome you would like.

Find affirmations that will keep you believing you will get the outcome you want.

On a practical note, seriously consider why you want justice, it must be for the right reasons, remember there is also the law of Karma, nothing done unto you has gone unnoticed.

Response From Enquirer

Thank you. I think my anger at the police is holding back my manifestations so maybe release anger and then try manifesting again.

How do you know if your manifestation has worked or if it's just coincidence? Do you just know? Because I think I might have manifested some stuff

Thank you for the question. Do be aware that we are manifesting ALL the time, so if you have asked, believed it would come into your life and it arrives, it was a manifestation. Coincidences don't grant wishes.

Hey everyone, When someone treats you disrespectfully, you can change it by sticking to the version of this person that is respectful, right? The circumstances don't matter, so you put them aside until your manifestation comes true?

Thank you for the question - *"When someone treats you disrespectfully, you can change it by sticking to the version of this person that is respectful, right?"* Right.

However, it does matter what you do after you have changed the "version of [that] person" in your mind.

No manner of affirmations, wishing, wanting or waiting "until your manifestation comes true" is going to stop the abuse or 'dis,' that's 'dis-respect' or the feelings of 'dis-trust' you experience, if you keep this person close.

Anyone who abuse or in this instance dis-respects you should be kept at arms length. I understand that this is not always easy if you live with this person, you should let them know how they make you feel when they dis-respect you, and ask them to refrain from doing it. If they do not stop, you need to re-think their intentions towards you....

Someone who 'loves' you would not take pleasure in hurting your feelings.

Consider this....You want to manifest or keep a drinking glass from breaking, but you constantly put it at the edge of a table! You are not doing all you can to keep the glass safe, you're hoping you'll be able to manifest it safe.

You're the glass! Keep yourself safe and wish that dis-respectful person well, ideally at arms length.

I've got a question: What role does secrecy play in manifestation? Are we to keep secrets or be vocal about our desires and dreams? I've read and experienced success and opposition with both. Any thoughts?

Thank you for your question. Shouting your want from the mountain tops will have it fall on deaf ears, on ears that will add positivity to it and ears that may add doubt and jealousy to it. You should choose wisely who to tell and who not to tell.

Do note that even your closest friends, who wants the very best for you, may add doubt to your wish, in the form of 'I don't want her to be disappointed, when it doesn't show up'! If I want another house, there will be no secret amongst those closest to me that I want another house.

However, I may not mention, in detail what I am doing to get it. I do not mention the affirmations I am saying and writing down, the other rituals that I follow everyday to bring this house to me. The checking on my finances, the house viewing etc. Those things I keep to myself.

Before sharing your desires and dreams, consider what you hope to gain by sharing. If it is purely to proclaim your happy thoughts, great.

If it is for any other reason, perhaps you need to think carefully about your intentions.

Hi, I am trying the mantras that I have seen…I have a question sort of. I said a mantra to Archangel Chamuel and the answer I got was a dream of my ex (so I guess he was my soulmate) and not any-more. Does that sound right?

Thank you for your question, You dreamt of an ex, I don't think that means they are or was

your 'soul mate'. You also mention an Archangel, I do not know the significance or correlation between your dream and the Archangel.

Hi! I'm new to this Forum. I recently joined because I would to know different between manifesting, praying and meditating.

Thank you for the question. I have a question for you, why do you attempt to manifest; why do you pray; why do you meditate?

People pray for many reasons, to give thanks to their God/higher self or entity, they may pray to ask/or beg for something. Many people meditate to get inner peace of mind or to focus on something they want. All people manifest and manifest everyday, every minute of every day, even if they don't know they are doing it.

You are where you are today because you manifested it.
You live in the house you do, because you manifested it.
You have the money you have (or don't have) because you manifested it.

We make wishes when we speak, we believe what we say, we act as if what we believe is true and we detach (a process of manifesting) and there you have it! You have manifested something, which can often be something unwanted. Do note, the same process is used for wanted items, people and situations.

I am unsure if there is a difference between manifesting, praying and meditating.

What I do know is that people manifest, pray and meditate for different reasons.

Do your thoughts for attraction need to be said out loud or can they be said in your head? Do you need to repeat the thought or is once enough?

Thank you for the question.

Thoughts for attraction can be repeated 'in your head'. But I find if I start off by repeating something out loud, it is easier to repeat in my mind.

Repeating a thought out loud or silently re-wires the mind to begin to believe the thought.

Doing it once and getting results, takes practice and a great belief in what you want.

Hello, Can someone help me to manifest 5 seater and a tv stand am giving birth 28this month I would love to have them items before I gave birth.

Hi, Congratulations and thank you for the question.
Picture yourself sitting on the 5 seater watching your TV on your new stand. Every-time you see the TV think of it on the stand you want.

When thinking of the 5 seater, feel how comfy it is, what colour is it, what material is it made of...Tell friends and family that you are looking for a 5 seater and TV stand.

Look on those free sites, you may see your ideal stand and sofa, plus they may even deliver it for you....Just believe it will arrive before 28th and it will arrive....or something better!

Does anyone here feel overwhelmed by the demands of work and personal life? What are the LOA solutions you have found?

That sounds like a lot of overwhelming!

Anything that is making such demands on you to the extent that you feel overwhelmed, needs to be addressed.

Look at your work life, is there anything you can do to remove stress?
Look at your personal life...Who is stressing you?

There is no affirmation, spell or incantation that is going to stop demands on you but you.

Feeling overwhelmed is a you thing, and really need to be addressed personally not spiritually.

If I want another child but my husband doesn't how can I go about manifesting this?

Thank you for the question.
I believe your question is: 'How can I get my husband to be alright with me having another child, although he doesn't want one.' If I am right in my assumption, this is a you sitting down with your husband and discussing this want issue, not a manifesting issue. We all have free will and you will be attempting to take his free will from him.

We can manifest most anything, but we have to beware of the consequences of trying to 'make' someone do something they would rather not do! We often think that what 'we' want will benefit the other person or persons involved, but that is the issue, the other person would not be involved, they are often unaware that they are spiritually being summoned to do something.

Consider this, how would you feel if someone came to me or anybody else and asked them to help them 'make' you accept another family member into your life and home for the next 18 years, and this is to be done without your consent?

I got an apology that I've been waiting for for a year and a half!

So pleased that you got the apology you felt you needed. but note that you kept that 'feeling' of 'I need an apology' for a whole year and a half.

I am sure you had forgiven this person a year and a half ago!

But note we should learn to accept an apology from all those who didn't give it. This frees us to get on with our lives, without the thought of what that person did or said to us, in the back of our minds.

I read this post: 'I pray you heal from things nobody ever apologized for.'
This is something I really need to focus on. The person and situation I need to forgive directly links to what I'm trying to manifest. Thank you for your comments.

I am sorry this is your experience. I do hope you heal soon.
Sometimes in life, people intentionally hurt us and carry on with their lives,

sometimes people unintentionally hurt us and get on with their lives, never turning back to see the effects of what they said or did to us.

In these instances self care is important, waiting for the person who hurt you to 'make' you feel better, is giving that person even more power over you!

Thinking or waiting for that apology that may never come, is imprisoning yourself. Set yourself and the other person free from owing you anything....write it off as a bad debt.

By forgiving that person you allow yourself to self soothe.

Do note, only you can do this for you.

I heard in other books that Universe does not have a memory. Telling the entire world not to listen is comical. The universe will listen to every thought because this is how the law works. So the universe keeps attracting what we think and it won't stop because we want it to in some cases. is it true?

Thank you for the question.
The LOA is always always working, so it would follow that the Universe is always listening, to what we voice, think, act out and write down, however in order to manifest a thing, one would need to believe it.

We have over 60,000 thoughts a day, so imagine if we had to 'stop' the Universe from granting every unwanted thought.

The important thing to remember is that the belief is what gets you the wish granted, although the Universe heard all the other semi, half hearted wishes.

What's the difference between Affirmations & Mantras?

I don't think there is a difference between an Affirmation and a Mantra.

They both can be described as an affirmation as they both can be used for the same thing.

An Affirmation is the action or process of affirming something or being affirmed, like something you would repeat to keep your mind on task.

A Mantra is a word or sound repeated to aid concentration in meditation.

For me affirmations and Mantras is Sankalpa, which is an intention formed by the heart and mind.

What to do for making people to start prioritizing me and being scared to lose me? Going out of their way to do things for me and stuff.... I always expect this to happen... but the opposite usually does.
People make promises then forget or text nicely one day and are super busy the next etc... I have to continuously ask for the same bare minimum stuff.
How to make the people around me become people who I can truly rely on.
How to make them fearful I'm mad over something instead of not caring if I'm mad or upset and me having to just accept what is
Hope that makes sense.
If someone sees I'm upset they should reach out as many times as necessary to make me happy.
The 3D is the opposite where even when I speak my mind and try to communicate nicely things always go back to extreme bare minimum where I just have to accept what is or I'll literally have no one....

I do affirmations and feelings and stuff... I listen to recordings... Meditate...

It sounds like you would like someone to value you. You use words like 'prioritise and scared to lose you.' This treatment is taught or commanded. You have already taught the person you are seeking this type of treatment from, how to treat you. Why would they change? They already understand that you will accept *"the bare minimum"* so that is what they will give.

You also use words like *'How to Make'* somebody do this or feel like that. You state that you want people to be scared, fearful that you might be mad at them (that whole sentence sounds like abuse to me!) why would you want someone to feel abused? How would you feel after you've made someone feel like that. How would you feel if you was *'made'* to feel that way? (Do note if this is your reality, please contact any organisation in your local area who may be able to help).

We all have free will, can you imagine someone coming to me or anyone else, and asking them to show them how to make you start doing all the things you feel you should have from the people around you?

Free will allows us to choose to accept *"the bare minimum"* or not to accept *"the bare minimum."*

That means you need to change YOU, when you change, the people around you have no choice but to change too.

You would need firstly to start treating yourself how you expect to be treated, you should be willing to be alone until the right person, who treats you like a priority appears in your life.

I do not know your situation, but you need to rely on you and not expect the many things you want from others *(To be given more than the bare minimum, to be prioritised, to be feared, to be scared that they will lose you. To reach out until they are sure you are 'happy')* I won't go on.

When you give yourself all the above....You teach people that that is the way you insist on being treated and that the 'bare minimum' will not be accepted.

End of Questions

There has been a large mix of questions in this chapter. The overarching topic was one of belief, what was believed and what was not believed.

A persons' belief often ensured their actions, if you believe that you can not manifest, have internal doubts or feel that there are obstacles in the way, you often voice that opinion. Here you have completed two of the LOA steps, the only step left is to Receive.

Believing that someone else received the wish asked for ensured the end of the manifesting process for some of the enquirers, as the action that followed and the voiced opinion or frustrations regarding the process, encouraged another wish to make its way to them.

To the questions posed, 'what is your biggest frustrations in using the LOA'. It would appear that I don't want anybody to seek out what works or what does not work whilst using the LOA. This is further from the truth, what I am trying to portray is the fact that the LOA is always working and seeking out what doesn't work will inevitably bring what 'doesn't work.'

In-order to investigate the use of LOA one should consider what they did last time, when attempting to use the LOA! Consider how quick or slowly it 'worked.' What they intend to do this time, how they feel about the wish, is the wish 'big' or 'small' and to consider whether adding a size to the wish actually mattered. Do they feel this wish will be granted and whether they believe they deserve the wanted outcome. Seeking out what worked as opposed to what didn't work has a better outcome for the seeker.

There were questions asked about signs that the manifestation is on its way, often these signs appear in the form of the exact opposite of what was asked for. Money brought debt, a new car can sometimes bring the breakdown of the current car, with all that said, life also continues to happen, the washing machine, although not a wish, breaks down, there is a leak under the sink and the cat ran away, many enquirers faulter at this stage and instead of seeing this as the clearing out or breakdown stage they see it as a stumbling block and often, the end of the manifesting process.
Which brings us back to believing in the wish asked for, and waiting for it to arrive, regardless of what has appeared or is happening in our everyday lives as a wish is not granted until you Receive it.

Real Questions. Real Talk.

Chapter Fifteen

How Do I Get New Friends?

We are humans and social beings, we need other humans to thrive, for love, the need to be wanted, to feel that we belong and our identity.

Have you ever watched 4 or 5 year old children as they meet for the first time? They stop what they are doing and stare at each other, during that time they seem to be having a telepathic conversation, as within 2 minutes they are best friends, running around, playing together as if they had known each other for some time.

I don't think we loose that, but as adults there are physical attractions, societal norms or restrictions, there may be cultural and religious considerations that take place when we, like the 4 or 5 year olds stop and stare or glance at someone.

We make assumptions or impressions of people we meet, putting them in their little box in our minds...That person is a grandma, that person is a middle aged man, that person is in her early thirties, that person seems nice, that person appears dangerous. Those group of people are etc... The list of tiny boxes we have in our heads are endless, and are there to keep us safe, they enable us to experience the person on first meeting them, as we pull from our mental filing cabinet our assumptions and stereotypes of the people we meet.

With those assumptions comes the need to belong to one or two or a few of these groups of people, it enables us to form our identity, by letting us and the world know who we are, who we appear to be, or who we want to be. Most people want or need the company of others and there are a myriad of reasons why, some are mentioned above.

Throughout this book, we have seen the attempt to use the Law of Attraction (LOA) for needs and wants. Finding friends is no different.

I always maintain that one should consider practical means before embarking on attempting to use LOA for help.

When trying to make friends, most think of what they want from a friendship without considering what they bring to the table! Many make lists of their wants in a friend, but find it hard to match their wants in themselves.

It is important to ask ourselves 'would you like and want to make friends with you?' If like attracts like what do you need to do or change in-order to meet the type of person you would like to meet?

Lets see who wants to meet whom below.

Hi all, How do i manifest friends?

Thank you for your question. When using the Law of Attraction one has to take practical action.

What type of people would you like to meet; Are you the type of person you would like to meet; Are there things about you that may need changing or developing?

Where do you go to meet new friends?

In order to meet like minded people you need to frequent places, groups and events where like minded people meet.

Are you into a particular sport? If you are into football, attending tennis matches may not get you close to people who are into football.

Attend hobby classes in your local area, volunteer at a animal shelter etc...If you don't get out much, find online groups of like minded people and participate in the group activities. After you have considered the practical steps, just Ask, Believe, Act and you will Receive. Ask for what you want, Believe you will Receive your want and take practical Action.

Start imagining what life will be like with the friends you want in your life;
Where will you go?
What will you do together?
How often will you be in contact?
Will you go on holiday together?
Where will you go?

Once you have asked for this want, be open as your new friend or friends will turn up anywhere, at the bus stop, on the train, in your local supermarket.

Your new friend or friends could be your neighbours and had been there all the time, maybe you just needed to open your eyes and perhaps put your phone away.

So how can I visualize new friends I don't even know who will match my high vibration or frequency if I haven't even met them because I want new ones because me and my old friends are pulling away they just avoid me nowadays please

Thank you for the question. Lets look at your question:

"So how can I visualize new friends I don't even know who will match my high vibration or frequency if I haven't even met them"

You have in-effect said: 'I can not visualise anyone who will match my high vibration or frequency, because I need to meet them first and 'judge' whether they meet my high vibration or frequency.'

When asking for something or someone to enter your life, you leave it up to God/the Universe to work out the ins and the outs i.e, you leave the how, who what and when to God/the Universe.

If you could have done it yourself, you wouldn't need help or direction.

Here's the process, you Ask, Believe, Act and you will Receive. God/the Universe will place people in your life that will be of benefit to you in making lasting or productive friendships.

Do you believe that people will be placed in your life to be judged on whether they are worthy or not of your friendship? If your answer is no, then you are half way there.

Believe that only the right type of people will appear in your life, note that they may enter your life to learn something from you or that you may learn something from them....Believe that everyone presented to you is a valid part of your journey.

In the other part of your question you state;

"I want new ones because me and my old friends are pulling away they just avoid me nowadays"

It would appear that you have already asked for new friends and your wish is on its way to you. This stage of the manifesting process is what I call the 'breakdown stage'. Part of this stage is when things seem to 'Break down' or 'Break away,' its function is to 'get rid' of some of the things that is hindering your growth.

Here's a few examples: You try to manifest more friends, at this stage, you lose some friends you have had around you for years! Could the reason be, they should have left your life a long time ago (or kept at arms length)? Or will they fit in with the friends you are about to meet?

Say you want a new car, at this stage, your current car stops working! Maybe God/the Universe is making space in the garage for the new car. The 'bad things' are not to be named or labelled, just reacted to, with acknowledgement that your wish has been heard and on its way.

So Ask, Believe, Act as if your well placed, well vetted friends are on the way.

Spend your visualizing time, thinking about where you and your new friends will go, what will you do together and how happy you will be to have these new people in your life.

Leave the 'are they, will they' to God/the Universe.

Hi there, I want to manifest more people into my life. I have a strong healthy relationship with my partner but I lack platonic connections. It seems hard to meet new friends in your 20s. It seems like most of my connections are very surface level and I long to meet people that I can connect with spiritually.

Thank you for the question.
Did you know that you are using LOA (or manifesting) every second of every minute you are alive? We manifest what we think, say and act upon.

In your short sentence, you have said *"I lack platonic connections", "It seems hard to meet new friends in your 20s"* and *"most of my connections are very surface level."*

Can you see what you are commanding to stay in your life? Let me remind you, a lack of platonic connections difficulty in meeting new friends in your 20's and very surface level connections, which has already entered your life because you believe and state it.

It is important that you become aware of what you say, as we tend to make wishes without realising we are doing just that. I understand that the above statements are what you believe is your reality, but attempting to use the LOA one learns the importance of the spoken word.

Did you know that everything said after 'I' is a wish? Anything said after 'I' has happened, is happening or will happen in your life.

Start believing that you will have platonic friends in your 20's, and that they will not be *"surface level"*. Stop *"longing"* to connect and start believing that you 'will' connect with people spiritually.

On a practical level, think about where you go to meet people! If you go to places where you believe *"surface level"* people go, what type of people do you think you will meet there? The golf club, might not be the place to meet people who enjoy tennis, consider your intentions on meeting new people, ensure it is pure.

Consider what you can offer those new friends you would like to meet. Be open to meeting genuine people who will connect with you spiritually. I understand that, just wishing or visualizing new friends may not bring them into your life.

Take a look at you, what do you have to offer these friends you would like to come into your life; would you like to meet you?

Spend some time, changing or developing the person in you that you would like to meet.

After taking the practical steps of 'getting out there,' believe that any one who crosses your path has the potential of being a friend. Get on with the life you do lead and God/the Universe will bring people into your life, that will benefit or enrich your life as well as theirs.

How can I manifest a girlfriend?

Thank you for your question.

Where do you go to meet new friends?
What type of girlfriend would you like to meet?
Are you the type of person she would like to meet?

In order to meet like minded people you need to frequent places, clubs, bars, groups and events where like minded people meet. If you don't get out much, find online groups of like minded people and participate in the group activities, some people use online dating sites.

After you have considered the practical steps, just Ask, Believe, Act and you will Receive.

Ask for the type of person you would like to meet. Believe you will Receive your want and take practical action.

Start imagining what life will be like with the type of girlfriend you want in your life, where will you go, what will you do together, how often will you be in contact...Will you go on holidays together, where will you go?

Think about what you can offer that special someone who will enter your life, and be open to the different types of people that will begin to arrive.

I would like to use the LOA to attract women. But I get irritated with the anti-men rhetoric and another part of me does not care about relationships because I love my freedom. What can I do to fix my focus?

Your focus is your focus, you should be you and not change your "*focus*" because society says you should be a different way. If you want to change your focus for you, then you should embark on reaching that goal. I will address your main wants in this answer.

You state that you would like to attract women, but immediately add a trait or flaw that she should not have. You then go on to state that you do not want a relationship as you would like to keep your freedom.

It is important to know what you want, its also good to be somewhat specific, but when using the LOA one should believe that God/the Universe will send what or whom is best for us. As you are looking for a girlfriend, comments heard from the same sex may "*irritate*" you, but what is said should not share the same sentence as what you are wishing for yourself. There are many women out there that are not what you class "*anti-men,*" (however, I am unsure what you mean by that.)

You state that you would like to attract women, but you don't care about relationships. We have relationships with most people we allow in our lives. I take it you mean a long term, long lasting relationship! If this is the case, you should ask for the type of person you want in your life and she will appear.

Ask believing you will receive. As mentioned before: On a practical note, get out there, go to places where you can meet new people, when you do meet someone, be clear of what you want from the relationship. However, ones focus can change before, after or during the relationship, and that goes for you as well as the person you meet.

Hi , I am new here. My greatest challenge and what has been affecting all areas of my life is the fact that I have no friends. I have tried and had many friendships none of which ever lasts. Can you imagine wanted to talk over something that bothers you but have absolutely no one to call? I have workmates and very few family members but no one i consider a friend or no one who considers me a friend. How do I manifest good friendships or even one friend?

Welcome and thank you for the question. I am sorry you are experiencing this issue. As LOA is always always working to bring into our lives what we think, say, and do, one has to be aware of what we say.

You state that *"My greatest challenge and what has been affecting all areas of my life is the fact that I have no friends."* This is a very big statement to say over your life! You essentially start off by commanding a great big hurdle, *"My greatest challenge,"* see where I am going with this? You then state that it *"has been affecting all areas of my life,"* then you go on to state that it is a fact, *"I have no friends."*

It is really important that we are careful what we say....I can think of many great challenges in life, and having no friends, is not one of them. The fact that you state *"it has been affecting all areas of your life,"* shows a glimmer of hope as you put the statement in the past tense. *"it has been,"* although I am unsure you intended to do that. All areas of your life may not have been affected by not having friends! It may be a fact that you feel you have no friends and that if you do make a friend, that friendship will never last. *"I have tried and had many friendships none of which ever lasts."* Again it is important what we say and think regarding our lives.

You state there is *"no one I consider a friend or no one who considers me a friend."* If we go into friendships knowing it will never last, do you think that friendship will last? If we meet people who we would not consider a friend or a likely friend, do you think they will become a friend? If we meet people with the thought that that person or people will not consider us a friend, do you think they will consider any type of friendship with you?

Just as you have manifested the issues above, you can manifest friendships that will last. First you need to stop saying or writing any issue you may have in a negative way, and imagine a life filled with caring friends. The image you are asking us to conjure up *"Can you imagine wanted to talk over something that bothers you but have absolutely no one to call?"* is not one, anyone on this forum would like to manifest just by thinking about it.

On a practical level, think about where you go to meet people! Do not only think of what you can gain from a friendship, but also what you can offer to another persons life. That is consider your intentions..no one wants a friend who only talks about what is bothering them...Many of us in this group have or had friends like that!

Ask God/the Universe for caring friendships, be willing and open to consider friendships outside your norm, do not exclude anyone. Get on with the life you do lead and God/the Universe will bring people into your life, that will benefit or enrich your life as well as theirs.

Hello. please any tips on attracting love, when single full time parent, live in a small village and work from home, so not meeting lots of people as no car and approaching 50 but would like to be in a nice relationship, so just looking for a few tips thank you kindly.

Thank you for the question. When using LOA we do not put hurdles in the way, you write *"Single, full time parent live in a small village and work from home, so not meeting lots of people has no car and approaching 50"* as if this is a deficit! Do you believe the above mentioned are going to cause you a problem reaching your goal; or perhaps it will be challenging? What you believe is what you bring into your life.

Attempting to manifest half heartily will get you your manifestation half heartily.

Here's what you have:

You are free and single.
You are a nurturer.
You live in a small village...Everybody knows somebody who is looking for what you are looking for, plus somebody knows everybody, so you'll be able to get a rundown of your prospective mate.

You work from home, you can schedule a meet up easier than working 9-5 from a office building in which you have to commute...You work from home, that means online...! Which is where many many people meet each other! No car, walking is good for exercise, there's public transport, s/he may have a car.
Approaching 50!? have you seen what 50 looks like these days? Go look!
You could be approaching 80 and want a partner, if that is what you want, it is what you want...Age has nothing to do with wanting what you want.

Be optimistic, you have loads going for you, plus the fact that you are willing to ask for tips on how to meet that special someone shows that you are willing to work on yourself, to be the best you can be for yourself and the lucky person who meets you.

Response From Enquirer

Thank you so much. So I think it will take a bit of time to change my thinking but this is a really helpful answer so very glad that I asked. x Thank you so much.

Can someone explain if everyone is me pushed out then I have caused all the issues in my life including the relationship problems ?

Thank you for your question.
To use Neville Goddard's 'Pushed out' statement, we meet who we are, what plays out in our life is a mirror of our thoughts. STOP. Decide TODAY that you are going to change the things that do not serve you in your life. Decide that you will have a harmonious relationship. Believe that everything is working in your favour (this can sometimes be challenging) but stick with it.

The LOA is working ALL the time, in what we think, say and do, so you have the power to make a change. Start by believing that your life will change, believe that you will meet people who will bring benefits to your life and you to theirs, smile more, appreciate the small wins in your life. Do not spend too much time thinking of what you may or may not have 'caused' in your life. Today is a new day and a new you.

Response From Enquirer

I'm afraid that when I say this, the universe will answer me "I'm not listening because you told me so..." Does the universe remember what I said yesterday?

We create what we believe, if you believe the universe is saying *"I'm not listening because you told me so..."* then that is what will be so.

However, think about a child that has been told off in-front of their friends, the embarrassment could have them wishing all sorts of 'bad' things on the person who told them off! (Thank God, these things don't materialize straight away!)

It is the intention and the feeling that God/the Universe reacts to, your intention at the time may not be your intention now! Although you said a thing yesterday, it may not be how you feel about it today. It's todays' intention, belief and feelings that is taken into account.

The universe often speaks in THREE/FOUR WORDS, (Go there, don't do that, he is lying, go check the cooker) not often in full sentences. Find an affirmation that you can use every time the "*im not listening*" comes up and note that the LOA is always in motion and is always listening.

End of Questions

I wish all that are currently seeking new friends, well. Asking for friendships is slightly different from asking for a car or a pair of shoes. The process is the same, Ask, Believe Act and Receive, but friendships are personal, not something to use, wear and disregard when you are done. Friendships remain our history, whether it leaves lasting good memories or a scar.

My assumption is that people who want to meet new friends, tend to be around potential friends. Perhaps they are not open or approachable, perhaps they have a wall up, there could be a plethora of reasons.

To ensure you are not the reason people do not engage, it is important that you take a look at yourself and ask a few questions, 'would I like to meet me?' 'What do I want from a friendship.' and 'What do I have to offer a new friend.' People come into our lives, for many reasons, but one thing is for sure, they come to teach us something, often about ourselves.
Whatever you want from a new friendship ensure you approach it with the intention of providing good memories.

Chapter Sixteen

How Do I Get My Ex Back?

After the initial shock of breaking up is over, like grieving, one may go through the stages, some quicker than others. Many of us get to the stage of acceptance of the situation or come to the realisation that this person was in their life for a season but it is now over. Others as you will see would like to return their lives back to it's norm, surprisingly things will never be the same, as the break up, like any heated argument, things may have come to light that need to be addressed, things may have been said that shone a light on short comings and thus taught the couple about each other as well as themselves.

Having made the decision to try to get their ex back, many tactics are put into place. I always suggest that one thinks practically when embarking on any decision of the heart, well any decision that involves another person. My first thoughts are, if they wanted to come back, they would. Nothing, in most cases, is stopping this person from reaching out.

As mentioned in the last chapter, we are social beings and creatures of habit, if that is the case, when we bond with another person we tend to want to keep it that way. So I can understand why many of us want our Ex (Ex Partner) or SP (Special Person) back or to have things return to our norm, even if that norm may not be in our best interest or of the interest of personal growth.

To re-cap, we need social interaction as we are creatures of habit and when an intimate bond has been made, we tend to want to return to that norm. It's our free will to want or decline all of the above.

Free will, will leave another grieving, free will, will leave a partner and kids, to begin a new life with another. Free will, will decide not to text or respond to calls. As we all possess free will, one would assume we all know that it can be asserted at anytime. However, as we will see, the free will of the pursuer remains intact, as they use it in an attempt to get their ex back, ignoring the fact that the ex has free will too. How is this fair?

Often in a break up situation one is emotional and perhaps rational thinking takes a back seat. This is understandable as they want their lives which they may feel has been shattered, back together, their norm if you will, and so set about trying to or taking action to make it so. And we are back where we started at the beginning of this introduction. I will try to tell the enquirers below all of the above. But we will start with a 'prayer' from Evangeline (Not real name).

Evangeline's Prayer

I feel like I'm losing the man I love. His name is Roland. It feels like he's drifting further and further away from me.
I pray for him each and every single day. Heavenly Father, I pray again asking that you fill Roland's heart with nothing but love for me.
I pray that you touch him in a way that I can't, letting him to realize nothing but the good in me, all the good I've done for him, and that I'm the woman for him.
Heavenly Father, I pray and ask that you blind Roland's eyes to any other woman that isn't me. Lord, I pray and ask that you touch Roland's heart to never want to hurt me again and to always want to do right by me.
Heavenly Father, I pray and ask that you soften Roland's heart for me and fill his heart with nothing but love for me.
Lord, I pray that you bring us together in a lifelong, loving, faithful, happy and committed relationship with you as our guide every step of the way.
There's not a day that goes by that I don't thank you for placing Roland in my life Lord. I send this prayer up to the heavens in the mighty name of Jesus, Amen

Dear Evangeline (Not real name),

First I would like to suggest, that if you feel you are being abused in any way, please contact any organisation in your local area that could offer you help. With that said and as you have posted your prayer publicly, I am compelled to respond.
There are a few points I would like to propose that you consider.

We all have free will and that love should be reciprocal (not one sided), would you agree? It would appear from your 'every single day prayer' or wish that you would like to evoke Roland's free-will to *"fill [his] heart with nothing but love for [you]"* and for you to become *"the woman for him,"* you would also like him to be blinded! *"to any other woman that isn't [you]."*

On a practical level and with free will in mind, If you have to beg, pray and attempt to manifest these things, is this really the person for you? Should Roland not feel these things for you 'naturally'? Staying on the practical level, it would appear that you have been *"hurt"* by Roland, when you say *"I pray and ask that you touch Roland's heart to never want to hurt me again."* The first time is enough times, why are you waiting around for *"again?"* Shouldn't that special person in your life want to naturally *"do right by [you]?"*

With all the changes you have '*prayed*' for above, ask yourself, are you trying to create a completely different person? Perhaps a person who is already *"loving, faithful, happy and committed [to the] relationship."*

You thank God for *"placing Roland in [your] life."* Do be aware, that people come into our life to teach us about ourselves, what lessons do you feel you have learnt so far, about yourself and Roland? I believe that God would want you to be happy and in a loving relationship, not one that has you feeling the need to publicly 'put it out there' in the Universe, the wants, needs and wishes of the major changes required, in-order for you to be happy and in a loving relationship. I believe your time is worth so much more, than to spend it every-day pleading about anyone who warrants such a prayer.

I was doing a manifestation and my ex text me instead of the person I was trying to manifest. This has happened a couple of times. Can anyone tell me why?

Thank you for your question. When attempting to manifest a certain thing, that thing in all its form may turn up. It is proof that your manifestation is on its way and that you are aligning or vibrating on the same energy as what you have asked for. You may have asked for a person you find physically attractive, you may have asked for an intimate partner, you may have asked for a companion. There may be traits of your ex, so all 'like things' will start to enter your space, that is, in your eye sight. You may notice similarities to the person you are trying to manifest in people you meet, the delivery person, a cashier, you may see someone who looks like that person, at the bus stop, in the supermarket, in the car that pulled up beside you at the lights.

The one that many people experience is debt, when they have requested money. I know someone who wanted more money and a debt turned up that had occurred six years ago, they had no idea that it had not been paid and was summoned to pay it within 14 days. People often see the exact thing they want being given to someone else, like that promotion you wanted, being given to someone who joined the company after you, that new car you took a fancy to, being delivered to a neighbour. Take it as a sign that what you have asked for is on the way.

You are almost there, don't loose hope, it is at this stage many people start the process all over, (they put into motion a new wish) when they proclaim, say, and or believe that they 'are never going to get' what they have wished for, they may also begin to believe that they had actually manifested what they see in front of them, instead of waiting for what they asked for, like your ex texting you. Take the text from your ex as a sign that your manifestation is on its way, and keep expecting what you wished for to show up.

Hello! I have a problem, I broke up with my SP for over 3 months, we are in no contact. For over a month he has blocked me everywhere. I started the manifestation, but I can't keep myself in the state of fulfilled desire. I always check if he unblocked me, I'm disappointed that he doesn't write to me, that he refuses to communicate with me. I'm starting to lose hope. Can you help me with some advice? Have you been through such situations, did you manage to reconcile with your SP? I feel like I can't any-more and I'm afraid of falling into despair.

Hi, Sorry to read that you feel that you are *"falling into despair."* I do not know your situation or your responsibilities, however if you feel that you need mental health help, please contact your local medical professional or any organisation in your area that may be able to assist you. With that said, it would appear that your sanity depended on this one person contacting you! I can not imagine putting the state of my mind in the hands of another. I get it, it hurts when one breaks up, and for some I guess, enough to feel that they are *"falling into despair."*

Lets look at what we do know about your situation. You broke up with your SP 3 months ago, they haven't contacted you and they *"refuse to communicate with [you],"* they have even gone as far as to *"block"* you! You go on to say that you are *"starting to lose hope."* The no contact and the blocking is a great indication of your SP's feelings towards you.

I am not sure what advice you would like, perhaps you would like me to tell you how to reconcile with your SP, if this is your question I take it you would like to change this persons' mind, and for them to love or like you. If this is the case it would appear that you are attempting to take away this persons' free will. This is not advisable. No manifestation should attempt to halt another persons free will. It would also appear that this person has used their free will to block you!

Spend your time and energy on YOU. You need to heal from this break up, you need time to soothe you, care for you and love you. In order to enter or re-enter into a healthy relationship, one has to be healthy! When you have healed, ask for the right person to enter your life, if that is your ex, they will return, but be open to receiving the right person for you at the right time.

Hello All,
I am trying to manifest my SP. He said we were not compatible and ended things over text. I know I am the best that he could do - and I mean it.
The reason for the breakup is because a 3P (3ʳᵈ Person) was involved. They are now dating and so called to be "in love." I can't stop resenting this 3P and whenever I try to visualise - what naturally comes to me is that "he is my boyfriend so stay away from us"
I really cannot get over this resentful feeling but this is what feels natural to me when manifesting. I know that when I have these thoughts its hard for my SP to feel the love that is in me. The resentment trumps my better part. Has anyone gone through a similar situation and actually won the battle? Thank you!!

Thank you for the question. We can manifest most anything, but when using the Law of Attraction one has to be practical, lets look at your situation.
" I am trying to manifest my SP. He said we were not compatible and ended things over text." A few considerations here: You are trying to *"manifest"* someone who has ended the relationship. I won't comment on how you received this information! What are you trying to manifest? I take it you would like to change this persons' mind, and for them to love or like you. If this is the case it would appear that you are attempting to take away this persons' free will. This is not advisable. No manifestation should attempt to halt another persons free will. It would also appear that this person has used their free will to date and "be in love" with someone else! See what free will allows us to do!

As well as attempting to change this persons mind, you proclaim that you *"know [you are] the best that he could do - and [you] mean it."* I am not sure how you arrived at that conclusion, as no one can be sure that they and only they are the best person for another.

This leads me to another process of using the Law of Attraction, one can only Ask Believe and trust that God/the Universe knows what's best for us, and will send the right person at the right time to share our lives, in the case of love or intimate relationships, we can only hope this will be for a life time.

When using the Law of Attraction, resentment is also not advisable, should your wish be granted, resentment would feature in the manifestation, perhaps over time the other person resents you, their job, where you both live, you may resent your in-laws or who this person has become.

I'm just throwing anything out there! Here's a real possibility, the 3P may resent you, should you manage to 'manifest' your SP back. This may not be a concern for you, but I would want my relationship to be blessed by all the people I know, I would not like to think that there was any resentment attached to my chosen relationship.

Speaking of the 3P what would you have God/the Universe do to or for them? Be-careful now, words and thoughts have moulding powers, and what you wish for another you wish for yourself. Again when using the Law of Attraction one should leave the who, how and when to God/the Universe, in doing this you ensure that you get what is really best for you and not what you believe is good for you.

Ask for the right person to enter your life, if that is your ex, they will return, but be open to receiving the right person for you and note that there will be no resentment on any-ones' part concerning your relationship.

You also ask *"Has anyone gone through a similar situation and actually won the battle?"* Maybe some members have been in a similar situation as we are all adults here, you may get mixed responses, but consider your words at all times, especially when using the Law of Attraction....should you really need to go to war in order to win a battle; should there be a battle at all?

How do I manifest a text from sp when it involves a serious topic and convo that needs to be discussed? He falsely accused me of lying all the time but i have stopped. He has said he's giving me another chance, so how do i manifest him agreeing with what i had wrote and communicating properly? Then how do I manifest attention from sp?

Thank you for the question. We can manifest most anything, but when attempting to use the Law of Attraction we have to be practical. I am unsure of your age or the age of your 'SP' but I take it, they have free will to pick up a phone and call you in order to have a conversation, should they WISH to do so!

Lets look at my statement. If someone WANTS to get in touch they WILL. We all have free will and attempting to halt or control another persons free will is not advisable. You ask: *"so how do i manifest him agreeing with what i had wrote and communicating properly?"* The Law of Attraction should not be used as a puppeteer, making people do this and that. Can you imagine someone having that type of ability/power over you? We can not 'make' another do anything.

Have you considered why you felt you needed to *"lie"* in the first place; as you state that you *"have stopped!"* What was you trying to make your SP believe? Another consideration here, after your SP agrees with what you have written, you go on to ask *"then how to manifest attention from sp?"* Please be aware that not all attention is good attention, one has to be aware of what they ask for. I understand that you may mean good, caring, thoughtful attention. What if you get a different type of attention; and does it matter what type of attention you receive from your SP?

I would ask for an amicable outcome to anything that had been said. In this way God/the Universe will give you the best outcome for you and the person involved.

Ok, so my sp is 'bettering himself' by 'cutting me and her off' cause he doesn't know who he loves. (he still is in contact with her but is also with me in a sense, since i'm not blocked anywhere and our Spotify playlists are all up) i already know they are gonna end fast, and he's gonna realize he misses and is in love with me, how would i manifest it to happen quickly?

Thank you for the question. For me the answer to your question starts and 'finishes' the minute your SP feels that not being with you is *"bettering himself."*

The answer is then cemented (for me at least) when you mention that you are in a bidding situation with another person. Your SP has used his free will to distance himself from you! You go on to 'check' that he hasn't blocked you when you say *"i'm not blocked anywhere and our Spotify playlists are all up."* I believe, you then take this to mean he is still in contact with you! I do not want to give you a description of what being in contact with another person is, what I can say is, not being blocked *"anywhere and [your] Spotify playlists are all up"* does not mean you are in contact. You state that *"he still is in contact with her."* Is that contact any different to the contact he has with you? I ask just to understand what you mean by contact.

From what you go on to say: *"i already know they are gonna end fast, and he's gonna realize he misses and is in love with me."* I need to ask, does that mean he is in a relationship with the other person? Didn't you say he had cut her off? I am a little confused. The last statement above is really your question, you would like him to end what he has with the other person and to realise that he misses and is in love with you, this you would like to happen quickly!

Before I answer, lets do a quick recap: Your SP was in some sort of relationship with you and another person, he feels that he would be a 'better' person if he distances himself from you and the other person. You still believe that you are in contact with him as he hasn't blocked you. You know that he will end what he has with the other person and come to the realisation that he misses and loves you. You also want this to happen quickly.

When someone shows you that they are not interested or go to the extreme to 'cut you off', hear and see what they are showing and telling you. This person has distance himself from you, but you hang on to the fact that although you have been 'cut off' you are not 'blocked'. Not to mention the fact that he feels that he would be a better person without you. Regardless of all of that, you would like him to come to the realisation that he actually misses you and that he loves you. Not to make this answer any longer.

The LOA is not to be used after practical steps have been taken to show you that another does not want you in their life, right now. Here's another practical step, work on you, ask yourself what would it feel like, to have a person in your life that wants and loves you. What would their actions be, would they feel that you made them a better person; would they show you how much they missed you when you have been apart?

Above all I have said, where does your boundaries lay with being wanted, loved and cherished. The LOA is not to be used to change or make another person do or say anything, that is why God/the Universe gave us free will.

Hey all, so i have been on my manifestation journey, it began as a way of feeling super confident and attractive in every way, as well as to get attention and love from my sp.

I've been feeling super fulfilled and happy and living in the end which makes me feel warm and fuzzy inside. HOWEVER, my sp triggered me today, by posting another girl on his story. (This ended up being his mate's sister so nothing going on there as I clarified with his mum) but I don't want to spiral and lose all the work I've made. Any tips?

I do also believe his mate is involved somehow, nothing but bad vibes from him.

Hi, Thank you for your question. I am so pleased you are *"feeling super fulfilled and happy and living in the end which makes [you] feel warm and fuzzy inside,"* and that you are on your *"manifestation journey [which] began as a way of feeling super confident and attractive in every way."* This is great for you. But then your statement seem to take a sudden turn, you state that you also used the LOA *"to get attention and love from [your] SP."* Shouldn't this be given and received freely? I will return to this part of your LOA wish, hope or need in a moment.

Note that when you set out to manifest things like the need to feel *"super confident and attractive in every way,"* you felt *"fulfilled and happy, which [made you] feel warm and fuzzy inside."* Life may have seemed great. Attempting to use the LOA as a string to attach to another inorder to 'make' them do anything, in your case it was to 'make' another pay *"attention and love,"* can course unforeseen consequences, as you attempted to take away a persons' free will.

Perhaps this is what you are experiencing at the moment, a lesson in the use of free will, as you state that you was triggered today because your SP used his free will and posted *"another girl on his story."* I don't want to nick pick, but do you mean he has posted yet another (plural) girl on his page; Is this girl posted instead or as well as you on his page? Either way, you will not be able to answer this question inorder for me to respond to you in a timely fashion, so let me make an assumption.

Regardless of whether your SP posted a picture of a girl instead of you or he has posted yet another girl on his story, it seem to upset or should I say *"trigger"* you. It even caused you to investigate who the girl was, as you state, *"This ended up being his mate's sister so nothing going on there as I clarified with his mum."* Should you have had to do this, whilst in a loving, caring relationship? It is not for me to point out that you should have felt the need to ask your SP about what he posted on his story, and not have it *"clarified with his mum."* It would seem that there could be some trust issues as well as other people in your relationship, (the girl/s on his story, and his mate). Maybe you should be *"feeling super fulfilled and happy"* as well as *"warm and fuzzy inside,"* in your relationship! Should there be a reason, within a loving, caring relationship to make you feel that you may *"spiral and lose all the work [you've] made?"* Perhaps not.

Do note that you can not "lose" the work you have done, as you are always doing work, that work can be to bring about wished for situations, or items into your life, you can also be working to bring about unfavourable situations or items into your life!

It is important that you are aware of your thoughts and deeds right now, especially when 'triggered.'

While you was doing what you felt was *"the work,"* you felt good, as it was working for you. Continue to ask, believing that what you are going through will come to an amicable end. Ask believing that everything will work in your favour. If it is a healthy loving relationship, then ask for it believing that you will receive just that. Do note that you can not 'make' another give you their attention or their love, as it belongs to them and they have free will to do with it what they will.

I'm been trying to manifest that my sp be nicer to me, but he is growing colder. I guess my question would be how to manifest or affirm correctly. I have been trying for 3 months but get hot and cold.

Thank you for the question. I am unsure what the 'not nice' behaviour from your SP is, however if this is any type of abuse, you should seek help from organisations in your area. It would appear that you would like to know whether you are manifesting or affirming correctly in-order to stop your SP from being hot or cold. As humans we have our off days and that is understandable, but I am sorry to see that you have been waiting three whole months for someone (anyone) to be 'nicer' to you. Any body who is not 'nice' should be kept at arms length, you should not be waiting around for three months of your precious life to find out whether this person is going to be nicer, hot or cold towards you.

We teach people how to treat us......Right now this person has taught you that they will give you bits of nice (hot) and bits of not nice (cold) and they will dictate when this happens, it doesn't matter when this occurs, because they know you will be waiting. The saddest part of this enquiry is the fact that you have been waiting to find out how nice or not nice this person is going to treat you! This is not nice.

You can not 'make' people do anything with or without the LOA, the reason is, we all have free will. Your SP has free will to be nice to you or not, you can only change yourself, you also have free will to accept your SP's treatment of you or not. For you the times when your SP acts like he loves you may out-weight the times he is not nice (cold).

I am here to tell you that a loving, caring relationship should not have hot and cold times. It should be a constant 'warm' loll. God/the Universe will not send a 'SP' into your life to treat you like an option! You will know whether a person is for you or not for you by their actions!

Response From Enquirer

He has just been ignoring me for no reason, we haven't had any arguments or anything I could justify his attitude some times, as he acts like he loves me and wants to marry him and other times he just stop texting or calling for no reason for a few days.

It still remains, you are waiting around to be validated! His *"just ignoring"* appears to be acceptable to you! Think of a loving relationship.....Do you see any ignoring or no contact *"for no reason for a few days;"* in those thoughts? Or do you see any, he loves me, he loves me not, in your imagined loving relationship?

We all have free will and your SP has the free will to *"act like he loves [you] and wants to marry and other times he just stop texting or calling for no reason for few days."*

The actions of someone who wants to be with another in a loving caring relationship is very different.

How would I manifest my x back if they're trying to move on, and me realising it might have been me who caused this because I never felt valued by him.

Thank you for the question. You ask *"How would I manifest my x back if they're trying to move on."* The answer is in the question! However there are a few practical considerations here: 1) He is your ex, so he has left your life and 2) he is trying to move on. Firstly he used his free will to leave your life and he has free will to attempt to come back, he has made a choice and one shouldn't attempt to interfere with anothers' free will.

I understand that you would like things to return to what was 'normal' for you, and that we, as humans attempt to rationalise, what went wrong. It would seem that you have considered why this person is not in your life and come to the conclusion that you are to blame for your ex using his free will to leave. Do remember your ex had the free will to stay!

The second consideration is your ex *"trying to move on."* Before we go any further picture this..Your ex is an arrow and he is put in a bow and has been propelled. Your question is *"How would I manifest my x back if they're trying to move on."* or 'How do I stop someone who has left (propelled) and set to get on with the next stage of their life (In flight, aiming for his target)?' With the bow and arrow in mind, and the fact that we all have free will, can you see that it would be challenging to answer your question.

The LOA is not to be use as a magic wand in-order to reverse actions made by free will. It is important for you and your ex to heal from the experience of the break up. Consider what you have learnt from the relationship you was in, and when you feel ready Ask for a partner you feel you can value as well as one that will value you.

Can I manifest my ex?

Thank you for your question, note that you can manifest most anything. Your question is very vague.

There are a few considerations you could bare in mind.
What led to the break up?
Have you and your ex learnt from the break up?
Does your ex partner want to return?
If your ex wants to return to you, what is stopping them from contacting you?

After a break up one should use the time apart to heal, getting back together is not a remedy for the pain caused. Use this time to work on you, when you feel ready Ask for the right partner to enter your life, believe that the right person will arrive at the right time.

How do I manifest a specific person and get them to conform.

Your question concerns me slightly, I will start with the advice I give everyone with a LOA question. It is important that one starts with practical steps first.

Does your specific person know that you are interested in having a relationship with them; what is stopping your specific person contacting you or you contacting them? These are some practical considerations before attempting to use the LOA.

To revisit your question, I believe you are asking me to give you instructions in-order to make another human being *"conform,"* strong word! What would they be conforming to? Don't answer that. There is a largely known concept called free will. Just like you are free to contact this specific person they are free to accept or decline your advances. To wish or want another person to "conform" is to take away their human rights, freedom to act as they will, their liberty and free will.

We sometimes believe we know what is good or could be great for another, especially if we have romantic feelings towards them, but it still remains, they have thoughts, feelings and a mind of their own.

It is important when using the LOA that we consider the other person or people our wish or want will affect, regardless of what we believe are good intentions, we should not attempt to take their free will away from them, for our own gratification.

In considering the ability to make another conform, have you considered someone asking me for the ingredient or steps to make you *"conform?"* If I had a formula to give that worked, you would perform as if you didn't have a mind of your own.

Consider a relationship in which a person did what you wanted all the time! A loving relationship should be reciprocal not one sided. In-order to usher someone special into your life, ask, believing the right person for you will enter your life, without the need to *"conform"* but uses their free will to love and care for you.

How to manifest my lifelong soulmate? I've written him down several times and visualized what it feels like to be with him. I dream about him all the time but it seems he's only in my dreams.

Hi, Thank you for the question, I see that you have done what one would expect, when using the LOA, you have Asked, from what you have said, you have taken Action with visualising. All you need to do, is keep believing that your lifelong Soulmate will arrive.

While you wait there are a few things you could do. Take practical steps, are you going out to meet your soulmate; or are you on line; signed up to dating sites? You certainly could do both.

Go to places of interest to you, as you may want to meet a person with some of your interests, attend sporting events that are of interest to you, check out your local community billboard or community centre to see what's on, attend a show or a class that is of interest.

That was going out, now look within. Ask yourself, are you the best version of yourself for your Soulmate; is there any personal growth you need to attend to? Consider your current life with him, does he really fit in; have you made your life and home ready for him to come in? Have you cleared your schedule for 'date-nights' each week? Have you cleared your house for him to come in, does he have a drawer to put his clothes in, if you want him to live with you.

The waiting will not seem too long, once you occupy yourself with getting you, your life and your home ready for him to come in.

Does anyone have any suggestions on how to get my ex back?

Thank you for the question, when using the LOA one has to first think on a 'practical' level. Consider why you broke up in the first place, have you or your partner learnt from the cause of the break up? A loving relationship should be reciprocal not one sided, does your partner want to get back together, if they do, I take it that there is nothing stopping them from reaching out!

Another consideration, can you imagine me giving one of your ex's or any random person advice on how to get you back? We can manifest anything, but should be mindful that we ask with the consideration of the other person, they have free will and no manifestation should attempt to halt that. Ask for the right person to enter your life, if that is your ex, they will return, but be open to receiving the right person for you at the right time.

Has anyone manifested moving in with their SP? I have a key to his place and I am there several days a week but I want to live together permanently.

Thank you for the question. Many many people live with their SP, not sure this has anything to do with 'manifesting it' and more to do with both people talking and reaching an agreement in regard to commitment or taking the next step!

I can think of many instances, where someone has a key to a house they don't live in and go there several times a week! What commitment plans have you made in this relationship? Is it to visit "several days a week?" What commitment plans has your SP made in this relationship? Is it to allow you a key in-order for you to be there "several days a week!" What is your next step?

Can you manifest a specific person. How does it work?

Thank you for the question. You can manifest most anything, however, your question is not clear. What would you have this specific person do or be in your life? Do you know this person? Does this person want to be in your life? I am unable to answer your question until I am sure of what you want. Please note that everyone has free will and as an adult we have the means to contact people we are 'interested in.'

Attempting to use LOA to "manifest a specific person" you know, would be attempting to take away that persons' free will.

Response From Enquirer

It's an ex girlfriend. The breakup was over taking the time for us both to grow as individuals and fear of a blended family. There are still some feelings on both sides.

Thank you for clarifying your question, however, one has to be as specific as they can be, whilst remaining open minded. In your case you would need to specify whether your wish is to get back together; that you both simultaneously *"grow as individuals"* or that you both stop fearing "a blended family."

Being open minded would be to ask for an amicable reconciliation whilst you both work through your issues. You state that there is *"still some feelings on both sides,"* if this is the case why can't you both work out what is best moving forward?

Attempting to make an unclear wish, may lead to an outcome you don't want. Manifesting something you want and what you believe another person wants, is not the way to go. As mentioned in most answers to LOA questions regarding SP's, it is important that you consider practical action before attempting to manifest anything to do with your relationships.

I need help!!! This guy and I have been talking for 2 months and we really connected. We decided today that we aren't in the same place in our lives and I'm pretty upset. I have some work on myself to do. What can I do to boost my confidence and feel secure? And how can I get him to not stop thinking about me?

Thank you for the question. Sorry to read that you are upset, which is understandable. Boosting your confidence, is a daily task, feeling secure is subjective. Believe that you will be able to boost your confidence and take action. You could start with daily affirmations, find ones that resonate with you, say them out loud or silently when you are not feeling confident.

To answer your question of *"how can I get him to not stop thinking about me."* I believe that you would like to know how to remain in another persons thoughts? Consider this, how would you feel if an ex came to me, and asked if I could help them to ensure that you kept thinking about them?

It would seem that you have accepted that you and *"this guy"* both are not in the same place in your lives, and you have partially released him, you intend to hold on to 'a little bit' of him, so he isn't actually free of you as you have sought out advice on how to have him think about you. We have to be careful with our wants, as what we feel is good for us may not be good for the person the wish or want is directed at.

If the other person has already voiced their position or desire, they too have made a wish, you trying to over ride that wish is not advisable. What could possibly happen, 'I just want him to think about me,' you may say. Therein lies the issue, you may not be aware of the importance of asking aright, that is ensuring we are somewhat specific in our wishing and

pure in our intentions! None of this is true with wanting someone to *not stop thinking about you.* How would he function, what if his thoughts as they do belong to him, turn into thoughts of you that you are not agreeable with?

You have released him, so you should let him go. Continue with your self care, as you need it now more than before. When you feel ready you should ask for the type of person you would like to enter your life, someone who has his own thoughts and is heading in the same direction you are in life.

Hey, I wanna manifest my sp, we know each other for almost 5 years, in the beginning he told me that he likes me, but few months ago, his ex comes back and now they're together. And now it's like I'm a stranger to him. I tried many techniques, videos, affirmations, but it feels like it doesn't work. What would you recommend or any tips? I would be so glad.

Thank you for your question. I have a few questions, but understand that you may not be able to answer in time for me to respond without too much delay. So I will make some assumptions.

You state that you have known your SP for almost 5 years, how did you know your SP; was he your partner? Did you know your SP in person or was this an online friendship? I feel that if he was your partner you would not state that he 'likes' you. With the information you have given, it sounds like your SP was a 'friend' and nothing more. He has now fulfilled the role of friend and partner in the one person, so has chosen not to communicate with you as he did before this person returned to his life. This is just my assumption, I have no way of knowing this is true.

I will further assume that you had a friendship with this person, that has come to an end. However you do not see it this way. You have set out to change, what has been a friendship into a Special Person, perhaps a partner, as you have *"tried many techniques, videos [and] affirmations."* You go on to say that *"it feels like it doesn't work."* There may be a few reasons why your many techniques and attempts to manifest this person into your SP did not work. Perhaps they were only meant to be a friend.

The other reason many people are unable to turn a friend into a SP is because we all possess free will, that is free will to contact you, free will to decline your advances, free will to contact his ex and rekindle a relationship with them.

It is important that we think of the other person involved, when attempting to change their life! As mentioned above, this person has free will and has made a choice you are attempting to change. You are also attempting to halt this persons' free will, which is not advisable.

Consider your life, spend time to focus on yourself. Do ask yourself, what would a relationship feel like, with a person who wants to be in your life, what will it feel like to be contacted everyday by someone who wants to be in your life. If you are not feeling or seeing this from someone who said they 'like' you, then realise that perhaps they are not the type of person you should spend your time trying to 'get', manifest or ask others for recommendations to bring closer.

Hello, I'm on my journey now to manifest my sp, as well as improve my self concept. I'm already very loving towards myself but I wanted to know what everyone does PHYSICALLY that improves self concept?

Hi, Thank you for the question. It is good that you are trying to improve yourself while attempting to manifest an SP. Many are just interested in manifesting an SP without working on themselves.

I am unsure one needs to do anything physically in-order to improve self concept however, it really depends on what you call "*self concept.*" If it is to heighten your self esteem, then you should do what makes you feel good. Structure your day so you do something for you solely for at least an hour...bath, face mask, window shopping (these days, called scrolling shop websites) or add stuff to a wish list, video (inspirational) a film.

When we spend time pursuing what makes us feel good, we feel good about ourselves and heighten self esteem.

We show ourselves that we matter. When self esteem is heighten we expect others to hold us to the same esteem and are less tolerant of those who do not.

Getting that hair do or cut, having that face mask, relaxing and enjoying what makes you happy will make you smile more, your physical outward appearance will change.

However if you want to do something 'physical' for others to see, we would need to have a different conversation.

So, from what i've read here, manifesting your ex back is not a good idea?

Thank you for your question,
It is never a good idea to manifest, wish, magic or try to manipulate someone, anywhere, that is to you or away from you. As people come into our lives for a reason and always to teach us something about ourselves, for example:
What did your ex teach you?
What did you learn about them?

The need to have someone return to your life is understandable as we all yearn for equilibrium in our lives, or what we claim is our norm. It is often that norm that we reach for when we want someone to return.

I further understand that this can be a painful time. Take the time to grieve for what you had. Use this time to care for you, as a break up is life changing and you need self care.

We all have free will and it is important that we consider the other persons free will, your ex exercised their own free will when they left your life, they have the free will to return, as well as you have the free will to decline or except them back.

As I have said to many, you can manifest most anything. If your wish is to have your ex back, start the work on yourself, heal from the pain you have endured, consider the lessons you learnt and then ask believing you will receive a loving relationship, be open to who appears in your life, if you are to re-kindle a relationship with your ex, they will return.

Is it possible to have 2 soul mates as in married to 1 and have a connection with another person and no matter what you try the connection is still there.

Thank you for asking this question. Are you calling the one you "*feel connected to*" a soul mate, in-order to feel better about a potential extra marital relationship? I am not aware of the contract or agreement you have with the "*1 [you are] married to,*" but if you are permitted to have *"2 soul mates"* then feel free.

As to answer your question of the possibility of having two soul mates, I would need a definition of what you call a *"Soul Mate,"* as there are many definitions of *"soul mates"* out there!

What I can tell you, if what you are about to embark on, is lightly to hurt the *"1 [you are] married to,"* you would be wise not to encourage the "connection" you believe you have *"with another."* We all have free will and should the *"1 [you are] married to,"* decide to become "*connected*" to what they called a soul mate, how would you feel?

It is always important when delving into anything esoteric (LOA or soul mates) you consider all the people who could possibly be affected or effected by your action or wishes.

Lovely people, can you please help me manifest that my partner and I are back together stronger and better than ever. I'm doing the inner work but I would deeply appreciate all the positive loving support.

Thank you for the question, I am unsure if you are asking for support and or advice to ensure your current relationship with your partner is stronger, or you are asking for support in getting your ex partner back and the relationship stronger. Are you and your partner back together? You didn't call that person your ex, so maybe you are together. I will attempt to answer the question in two sections.

If you are together, you both need to be as clear as possible as to what you want out of the relationship, if you want one thing and your partner want something different, using the LOA may not work in your favour. You both need to come to some agreement as using the LOA to 'make' another person 'do' or not 'do' something is attempting to take that persons free will away and is not advisable.

You state that you are doing inner work, which is always encouraged, while you are there you may learn something about yourself or your partner that may strengthen your relationship.

If you are apart from 'your partner' before using the LOA one has to first think on a 'practical' level. Consider why you broke up in the first place, have you or your partner learnt from the cause of the break up?

A loving relationship should be reciprocal not one sided. I take it that there is nothing stopping them from reaching out to you should they wish to return!
Another consideration, can you imagine me giving one of your ex's or any random person advice on how to get you back; how would you feel knowing that?

We can manifest most anything, but should be mindful that we ask with the consideration of the other person, they have free will and no manifestation should attempt to halt that. Ask for the right person to enter your life, if that is your ex, they will return, but be open to receiving the right person for you at the right time.

Hi everyone I am new to this forum. I have been manifesting for this special guy for a long time I have been writing down my affirmations. Believe me I was so nervous going up there to see him but I had to shake it off. I've never been that much in love with someone like him before. Its something inside of me that just feels like I need to protect him if that makes any sense. You can call me crazy if you want to. Lol my question is what more can I do to bring this guy closer to me?

Welcome to this forum, I am a little confused by your question.
You state that you *"have been manifesting for this special guy for a long time"* Do you mean you have been trying to manifest *"this special guy"* into your life? Am I to assume that you are now together; but you would like to be closer?

You also state that you *"went up there to see him,"* where is up there? Have you spent time with this person; or do you *"love"* him from afar? As your question is about LOA I will answer it as thus. But first on a practical level, does this person know how you feel about them, if not, why not?

In reviewing the way you appear to feel about this person and the fact that you would like him to be closer to you, I take it, he doesn't feel the way you do towards him? A loving relationship should be reciprocal not one sided, you both need to want to be closer to each other, for LOA to work in your favour. The *"more"* you can do, would be to talk to this *"special guy"* and find out what he wants from a relationship with you. His actions so far should have spoken volumes to you, but being able to ask him how he feels about you and hear what he says may give you an indication of his intentions towards you and whether they match the *"love and the need to protect"* that you have for him.

On a spiritual level your affirmations will not revoke another persons' free will. If this person knows how you feel about him and is exercising his free will not to be in your life, the way you would like him to be, then no amount of manifesting will bring him closer to you.

Hi,I know some people will throw up in their mouth over this, but I would like to manifest my ex back. I'm pretty good at manifesting things I just don't know how I do it if that makes sense. How can I manifest a happy and healthy relationship with this person? Like if I'm manifesting them I can manifest the good parts and none of the bad parts. This is my world and they are just living in it right?

Thank you for the question. I am pleased you are *"pretty good at manifesting things,"* It may become challenging when we try to manifest 'people.' The reason for this is, we all have free will, which is an important part of manifesting, you are free to believe something will work and you are free to believe it will not work. Although you may have good intentions for another person, you should be mindful to take into consideration that they have free will too, and no manifestation should attempt to halt that.

On a 'practical' note, consider why you broke up in the first place, have you or your partner learnt from the cause of the break up? Does your ex want to get back together with you; if they do, I take it that there is nothing stopping them from reaching out to you!

You mention wanting only the good parts of this person back in your life. We all come with both, If their bad parts are something you do not want returning, it may mean that there is personal work needed to be completed by your ex, do you think you have given them enough time to complete this work; and do they even know that you feel they have 'bad' parts that need addressing? With all this 'fine tuning' are you sure you are not trying to manifest a whole different person? We do not have the power to take 'parts' of a person and discard the rest, we also do not have the power to decide what is good and bad about a person, we only have the power to accept or decline that 'whole' person with or without these 'parts'.

A loving relationship should be reciprocal not one sided, you both need to want 'a happy, healthy, warts and all relationship,' for LOA to work in your favour.

As we have free will, we have the ability to Ask for what we want, and yes we can be specific, however, because we are human and not an all seeing knowing God, we are unlikely to get every single detail of another human being ticked off our wish list of traits, habits, likes, dislikes, good and bad parts.

This is why we Ask with an open mind and not restrict God/the Universe with tick boxes!

You ask, *"is this my world and they are just living in it?"* Consider a random ex saying the same thing, and seeking out ways to make you exist in their world, with only your 'good parts'!

When using the Law of Attraction, one has to be mindful that what we deem good for us, may not be good for the other person or people our manifestations may intend to include, that's intentionally or coincidentally.

Ask for the right person to enter your life, if that is your ex, they will return, but be open to receiving the right person for you at the right time, with the right 'parts'!

My dear, I am asking about "the way I am doing things"... like for example I am thinking thoughts about my sp, I think "he loves only me." After two to three days I had difficulties to flip it to "my sp loves only me," and I think this all day. Then I tried to think about him and his appearance comes up before his name comes up in my mind. I have to flip it x3 so his name comes up first then his appearance, is this the correct way??? Will my manifestation come to fruition??
Is thinking about his name his appearance and saying my sp loves only me, should get my manifestations?
I try to think that he sent me a friend request on Instagram. But my mind doesn't create his image or his profile pic of Instagram my mind CREATES image of something else or beyond that topic. So I force my mind to create images of his Instagram pics while thinking of him. Me doing this thing now, will it bring my desire? will I MANIFEST him in my reality or not?? Mam.... please respond madam I hope you will reply.

Thank you for your question. I believe you are asking whether what you are doing in-order to manifest an SP is correct or not, and will you get your manifestation. In your ideal world what would you like me to say; and can I really give you an answer to this question? Before I attempt to answer your question I am assuming you both are adults!
As you have asked me this question, you are or should be aware of how I feel about attempting to halt another persons' free will. It would appear that you want nothing else but for *"my sp loves only me, and I think this all day."* As this is the affirmation you are using, it

should resonate with you, i.e it has to sit comfortably with you, it should flow off your tongue or you can easily recite it in your mind. It should take no effort when saying and believing it.

There are a few considerations here:
Firstly the issue of a persons free will to call you, get in touch some other way, Instagram for instance, should give you an indication of their 'will' to be in your life! But that does not seem to be your concern as all you want is *"my sp loves only me."*

Secondly, one should be very mindful of what they ask for! Imagine, you and this person got together, got married and or had children....You have asked that *"my sp loves only me."* I understand that to mean no other prospective love partner, but your wish is for this person to love only you. Not his parents, his extended family members, his friends, your friends, your parents and family members. Lets not get into your SP loving the children you may have. Do be careful of what you wish for. It is important that you Ask aright!

You then go on to have your mind conjure up his name before his appearance, you state that you had to flip it x3 in order for this to happen in your minds eye. There are a few considerations here too, you ask, is this the correct way? Ask yourself, what difference does it make whether his name or his image appears first in your mind. It is concerning that you have to *'force'* the idea of your SP's image to appear in the sequence you want it to. Visualising your SP is not coming naturally! As you have also had to force the need to conjure up your SP sending you a *'friend request'* on Instagram, which leads me to believe that you may have never met this person but would like to drag this person into your life, and it would appear that you spend your whole day at this task.

When attempting to manifest a love interest in fact any wish, one is to be open to what God/the Universe presents you. I understand you have your sights set on a particular person, but what if that person isn't the best you can have in your life, and does that matter to you, maybe not! However we should ask for what we want adding 'by divine right' meaning you are asking that this person comes to you with the blessing of God/the Universe. In making that affirmation you assure your self the best outcome for you, in this instance, the best partner for you.

I'm manifesting my ex back. (A very complex situation, please don't judge, it feels right for me). it's been going really well. obviously, I understand that what's showing up in the 3D isn't always true, it's what's in our mind, because we create the reality.
i'm just really struggling. we went from no contact, to talking again (and we had a good friendship thing happening), to him reaching out to me, he even asked me to go out with him again! He asked me to go out two weeks ago, and then radio silence.

We've been talking still, here and there, but it's not the same. he's not reaching out any-more, and he said "maybe we'll go out" and then "no, we're not going out." Today he told me that he has another partner, and that they've been out multiple times. (apparently been out multiple times since he asked me out two weeks ago) Turns out, that's a lie, he hasn't been out with anyone (his family enlightened me). But, he still has another person pinned on his snapchat which is suppose to be his "new partner."

I don't know what to do, it feels like it was all going super well, and I had a great mindset happening, and things were showing up for me in the 3D, it was fantastic. But now nothing has happened for two weeks, and i'm starting to feel sad again. I feel like I don't know how to come back from this. I don't know what to do.

Thank you for your question. I will first answer the *"i'm starting to feel sad again,"* part of your question. I am sorry you are feeling sad, consider why you feel sad! You haven't heard from a person who *"asked [you] to go out two weeks ago, and then radio silence."* They are *"not reaching out any-more,"* plus "he told [you] that he has another partner." What more does he have to do or say to let you know that he is getting on with his own life as he sees fit?

Maybe he had to go to the depths of lying to get that information through to you! As you caught him in that lie through your investigations, (*"his family enlightened me."*) I understand that you state that we are not to judge as this feels right for you, but as you have asked and without judgement I will tell you what I believe to be true.

On a practical note, I have two points: No person who wants to be in the life of another, would mess them around like the events you have mentioned above. And you should not put your happiness in the hands of another person. It would seem that this person allowed you to feel happy for a while, as you state *"I had a great mindset happening, and things were showing up for me in the 3D, it was fantastic. but now nothing has happened for two weeks, and i'm starting to feel sad again."* As I have mentioned many times in this forum, no amount of wishing, affirmation or manifesting is going to make another person do what you want them to do! Everyone has free will and we shouldn't try to halt that in another person. In order to manifest, one needs to be aligned with what or who they are trying to manifest. There is no alignment here, this person appears to have the power to make you happy or sad, they also appear to be getting on with their own life, regardless of what their family member said or what you gleaned from 'snapchat.'

I understand that you feel that this person would make your world 'fantastic,' but I assure you, you are the only person who can do that. We tend to teach people how to treat us, if this person calls and says 'lets go out' you may say 'okay,' then this person does not get in touch with you for two weeks. While you sit, wait, attempt to manifest a response and become sad, they call and ask you out again, happy to hear from this person, you say 'okay' then 'radio silence' ensues, what do you think you are telling or teaching that person? Better yet, what are you telling yourself? Perhaps its, he holds your happiness and his acknowledgement of you will make you happy! The only person who should hold that power is you.

Make you happy and a happy friend/partner will attach themselves to you. Make you happy and your future partner will endeavour to keep you happy.

Make you happy and most of your days will be 'fantastic'. In fact you will learn how to make you happy.

Attempting to create *"what's showing up in the 3D"* is a way of staying in a suspended reality, and not what is actually happening. Stop for a moment and think of you and your happiness, you mention that what you are being subjected to *"feels right for you."'* You could 'feel' better, much better, if you put you first and attempt to give yourself the care and attention you may be seeking elsewhere.

I need some guidance. My husband of 20 years started an affair in July last year, he has now move in with the person he had the affair with. Our house just sold. We have four small children. I want him to come home and mend things here. I've tried manifesting. I've been doing it all month and nothing is working. I feel delusional.

Thank you for sharing. I am sorry you are experiencing this situation. I hope you and your children are safe. Perhaps in your ideal world, your husband, you and your children would be living happily in your house. In reality this is not the case. Although there may be many reasons for this, one of which is free will. Your husband utilised his free will to 'move out with his affair partner.' Attempting to evoke another persons' free will is not advisable. We can manifest most anything, but should be mindful that we ask with the consideration of the other person, they have free will and no manifestation should attempt to halt that.

Although you may have good intentions for you and your children, you should not attempt to inflict or impose your (albeit good) wishes on your husband.

You state that "I want him to come home and mend things here, I've tried manifesting. I've been doing it all month and nothing is working." What you are aiming to do is not unlike what many parents do for their children, they often want the best for their children however, when the child becomes a teenager and want something different, no amount of wishing, affirmation or manifesting is going to turn that teenager into what has been wished for him or her.

This leads me on to practical considerations. Your husband left a 20 year marriage, children and house. Mending things, may not be on his mind, if it was, you wouldn't be attempting to evoke his free will! And as mentioned above the teenager would need to want the same things as their parent, for any manifestation to work. One has to be aligned with what they want...There is no aligning with someone who has chosen to be elsewhere.

I understand that this situation can be devastating as your life may have revolved around your marriage, children and home. It is time to think about yourself and your children, it is time to heal from this upheaval, your children will be watching you closely, needing more from you, as their world as they knew it is turned upside down. In years to come they will note how you handled this disruptive situation, and may copy your way of dealing with discord in their lives. I don't want to go all Psychologist on you or cause you to feel you have more of a burden than you already have, but your thoughts should be on you and your children, not someone who clearly has other things on their mind.

Is there any recommendation on how to manifest contact with a sp

I may not be able to give you any 'recommendations' but perhaps some practical questions you could ask yourself.
Do you know this person; if so give them a call, or 'slide in their DM's'.
If you know this person why are they not returning your calls or messages?

Perhaps your question is how can I 'make someone do something'. If that is the question, attempting to evoke another persons' free will is not advisable. We can manifest most anything, but should be mindful that we ask with the consideration of the other person, they have free will and no manifestation should attempt to halt that. Ask for the right person to enter your life and they will appear of their own accord.

Hey, great Forum. I recently went into no contact with my husband for about a week ago. I was in a really good head-space, very confident in myself, working on bettering myself, and I manifested him to come back to me and he literally reached out not even 30 minutes later. But now I feel like that has caused me to overthink because I don't know if it's luck or I actually manifested him. Then it kind of caused me to second guess.

Thank you for sharing. You state that you was in a *"good head space, very confident working on bettering [your]self, and [then you] manifested."* You followed the steps to manifesting. You Asked, Believed, Acted 'As If' and Detached very quickly.
Let me walk you through your steps:
You (Asked) wanted your partner back or at least wanted him to reach out to you.
You Believed he would.
Your 'Acting as if' or Action, was you remaining in a good head space.
You Detached.

The term detachment may be seen as no longer interested in a want, but that is further from the truth, when one detaches from their want, they still care about the want, still know what they will do when the want appears in their life, if they didn't care about the want or wish, it wouldn't be a desire. Detaching aids the person to stop being held ransom by the want. In essence one does not worry or even care about how it will come, they just know its coming. Its the how, when and who that one detaches from.
Having followed the LOA Steps and aligning with what you wanted, it took 30mins.

Your wish was granted *"but now"* you say, you *"feel like that has caused [you] to overthink"* and you are unsure whether it was luck or you *"actually manifested."*
If I find a rare coin on the beach, just as I asked for money, is it luck or did I manifest it? Why look a gift horse in the mouth; Do you feel you deserved what you wished for? Or perhaps there is a case of 'be careful of what you wish for' going on here!

You decide, in fact you can decide whether it was luck or you manifested your partner back. What you know and or believe will play itself out in your relationship with your partner! There is a difference between a game of chance (luck) and following a tried and tested law in-order to bring something into your life.

When we work for what we want, some of us cherish our gain more. Ask yourself a few questions regarding your relationship, what you want from it, what has your partner taught you about yourself and about him. You have free will to change your mind, you decide what you want and what or who you don't want in your life, you can also decide how they play a part in your life! So you made a wish and it came true. You can make a different wish anytime you wish!

I'm trying to manifest an ex who came back into my life after 5 years for companionship, someone to have conversations and a laugh with and to support me with my dad who has Alzheimer's as I've no other family and have health problems.

Thank you for sharing. I am sorry you have had to experience health problems and that your father has Alzheimer's.

You state that you want a relationship with your ex back, as he has returned to your life after 5 years:
1) For companionship.
2) For someone to have conversations with.
3) For someone to have a laugh with.
4) To support you with your father.
5) To be another family member.

What you have described there, is a home help! When using the Law of Attraction one has to be careful not to attempt to take anyone's free will away from them.

Can you imagine someone using the Law of Attraction to attract you to come into their life as a 'home help?'

A loving relationship should be reciprocal not one sided. You have cemented what you want from this person, but only willing to give conversation and a laugh! People need more than that from a relationship.

Sharing a life together, I believe means giving and receiving. One sided 'love' means only one person gets what they want. When we embark on a relationship, we should have an idea what we bring to the table, as we already know what we want from the other person.

You should first find the support you need for your father and yourself, then seek a partner to share a life together. It is important that you don't just see your ex, as someone to be used!

Ideally, when embarking on an intimate relationship, one should become the best they can become, given their circumstances and have an idea of how they will enhance the other persons life. The LOA is not a magic stick to command another person to do as one wishes, but a way of enhancing ones life, a way to enable us to live the life we are meant to live and to share that with others around us. When you feel ready, Ask, believing you will get the best person and or relationship for you and your family.

So I know we can manifest love.. but can we manifest a certain person we want back in our lives? I had a few good weeks where I really believed, and now I'm doubting myself.. any advice please?

Thank you for the question. You are right, we can manifest love, I am assuming the person you would like to return back into your life is a romantic partner and hopefully someone you intend to love.

Although you have started your manifesting journey there are some practical considerations, does this certain person want to get back together with you; if they do, I take it that there is nothing stopping them from reaching out!

As you are aware we can manifest most anything, but should be mindful that we ask with the consideration of the other person, they have free will, that is free will to reach out, you also have free will to contact them too, via everyday channels, the phone, online, social media etc. If these practical steps have been exhausted, it may lead you to wonder if it is this persons free will that is keeping them from you, and as I state no manifestation should attempt to halt that.

Ask for the right person to enter your life, don't doubt yourself, keep believing if you feel you want a special person in your life, if that is your "certain person" they will return, but be open to receiving the right person for you at the right time.

I'm currently manifesting my ex. We broke up and tried to work things out, but then he left me hanging 2 months ago for another girl unexpectedly. Since then we have only argued and he has shut me down multiple times saying he's not in love any-more and we stopped talking. A month ago I started manifesting, just working on my self concept, etc. He texted me tonight. My current area is flooded and he asked if I was doing okay. I didn't see the message but an hour later he texted again saying I know I'm the last person you wanna hear from but I do hope you're doing okay. What's my next step? (Third party is still involved as I know of!)

Thank you for the question. Ask yourself why and when you decided you needed to know what your next step is regarding your ex partner.

Let me do that for you. A month ago you started to work on yourself, which I commend you on that, as it is the right thing to do after a break up. You took pride in working on yourself and was going through the grieving process, as you had resigned yourself to the fact that your relationship had ended. What changed?

I can help you with that too. You got a text asking if you "was doing okay," as you mentioned the fact that your area had flooded, I believe your ex wanted to know if you was safe and whether the waters had washed away your home, its contents or even you. The *"are you okay"* didn't mean I have left my current partner, I am in love with you and want to get back with you! Or perhaps you felt it meant all of that.

It would appear that your ex is able to articulate himself quiet clearly, as he had made it clear that the relationship is over with his actions when he *"shut [you] down multiple times"* with his speech by *"saying he's not in love any-more"* and with he's none communication

"and we stopped talking." As you have become aware, when a couple breaks up, they do not immediately stop caring for the other person, you had made a bond with this person, which can be difficult to unravel, hence the grieving process.

It really isn't for me to tell you what your next step is, as you already know what to do. All I can advise is, as I have mentioned above, your ex articulates his feelings towards you very well, and I believe if his *"are you okay"* was to mean more than "are you okay" he would have expressed that to you.

End of Questions

In answering the questions above my attention is drawn to what is missing from most of the enquiries and or is rarely mentioned, noticed or acknowledged, that is, why their partner left in the first place, and whether they have learnt anything from the breakup

about themselves or the other person. Unfortunately many do not get to know the real reason the partner left. It could be the involvement of a third party, it could be they had no intention of staying pass a certain time or event! Perhaps after years of dissatisfaction they had decided to leave. In fact they have decided to assert their free will for a different life. How easy do you think it will be to return a person to a life they were not happy living?

I have also noticed that when we ask for items, cars, houses, sometimes situations or even new shoes, we are happy to detach, meaning we leave the where, how, why, the area or colour to God/the Universe. We don't necessarily worry or think of it deeply enough to become extra specific. Here's an example: I want a house, I say where I want this house, I may request three bedrooms. Being presented with a two bedroomed house, I accept the house as there is a walk-in cupboard on the landing upstairs, which is adjacent to a large bathroom. I make the bathroom smaller, using some of its floor space and the cupboard into a box room, giving me my third bedroom. I did not manipulate anyone, I didn't expect the walls to move into place and align themselves to give me my third bedroom. I accepted what I was presented with and worked with the house to the satisfaction of the house and myself.

However, when our wish is for an SP we become territorial, using the house scenario, it is as if we expect the exact floor plan we have in our mind, (the SP to live up to our specifications)

we also expect that the traits and or abilities that God has given the SP to be removed (their free will). The house like an SP, will not move in the direction we have commanded.

We tend to believe that we have the right to demand that the other person complies, this we do with good intentions, or so we think. Perhaps we think that our love is strong enough to give the other person all they will need, by being with us! One enquirer felt she "was the best he could get." I do not doubt that she really believed this. Is it that we become blind to the needs of the other person; and want to satisfy our own needs? Evangeline actually wanted Roland to become blind to any other possible need he may have! It is for this reason I remind readers that love should be reciprocal and not one sided.

At the stage of wanting an ex back, are we wanting to get back to our norm and to stop the hurt of the breakup, do we do this by attempting to take control of the only thing (or person) that has caused the hurt? I have more questions: Perhaps we are trying to fill the hole the ex left behind in our hearts, or is it that we don't want another to experience the love and perhaps the care we had from them. I understand this is a book about LOA and not one of psychology, but it makes me wonder.

With all my thoughts on the subject of getting an ex back using the LOA, I still believe one should work on their self after a break up, take care of their health and any children involved. After the grieving process they should consider what they have learnt about themselves, i.e the practical steps I am always talking about.

Then when they feel ready, Ask for a loving caring partner, be open to who presents themselves, by this time, they are likely to see red flags clearly, and know whether they are willing to accept or decline any advances from a potential partner. In doing this they go into a relationship knowing what they want and what they can offer. But always knowing they asked, believed and trusted that God/the Universe has sent the best person to share their life.

Conclusion

I hope you enjoyed reading the questions and answers in this book, I hope it opened your eyes to the way you view certain wants in your life and how you go about requesting it using the LOA. I hope you will be able to steer a friend in the right direction when you see them going down the, I won't say wrong road, but the longer road of reaching their intended goal of manifesting.

I have some added notes below to consider when embarking on the use of LOA.

The book starts off with the need for more money.
I noticed that when we Ask for a particular amount of money, again we don't think of the who or why, we insist on that amount and believe that it will solve our immediate problem. We are not open to the problem being solved as we have decided we know definitively what is needed, just like getting an ex back (only that person will do, and with out the use of their free will). It is for this reason that I often state that we should be open to what comes.

Being open allows for the bill or whatever the stipulated amount was to pay or to do in our bank account to be cancelled. Let me explain. If you felt you needed £1,000 to pay a bill, repay a friend and buy some essentials.

Being open allows for that bill to no longer be requested at all, or a plan to be put in place so the outstanding amount can be paid over a longer period of time.
These two eventualities were discounted as you had decided that you must pay x amount towards the bill.
Lets look at what you had decided regarding your friend and the essentials! Being open could allow for the fact that that friend had told you that they didn't need the money back for another few months, but you insisted that it would be paid by a certain date and you want to honour that.
Being open will allow you to notice things around you, you may notice that that supermarket in town, is about to close and they want to get rid of their stock, or that a friend needs to empty their freezer as they have had to extend their plans abroad for several months. Being open allows for all the above to happen.

Being closed and rigid gets you the £1,000 as you would have followed the LOA steps (out of desperation). You would have pleaded (Asked) Believed it was coming (because you couldn't see any other way of getting this money) and you did whatever affirmation you could find to keep you in the waiting to Receive that £1,000 mode.
For you at this stage, there could be no substitutes and nothing else would do.

Receiving the £1,000 this way, we find that there is no give, there is no stretch with this money. You find that it is not enough, for-example the bill incurred added interest you wasn't aware of. The amount you had planned for essentials has you putting some of them back on the shelf as the price for some items have shot way up. Or that cheap supermarket you had intended to visit when you got your £1,000 had closed down while you was being closed minded to where your essentials was going to come from and where you was going to spend it.

The insistence on a particular amount of money to solve a problem attempts to take away the will of God/the Universe whose will is to give us what is best for us.

Looking for a job, or want a promotion? Ask for it, believing you will be presented with the best job for you at the right time with the right benefits. You noted that in the pursuit of securing a job or a promotion some was in tears, others were *"so low"* another was *"disheartened"* yet another was *"confused"* waiting for an answer that was about to dictate their lives.

With this type of cognitive dissonance occurring, should they get the job, they stay in the job longer than they should, giving more hours to the company than their family, staying one more year, as this will be the year that they pick me, *"I work so incredibly hard"* one Enquirer said, it was as if she felt that 'they should see me.'

Sometimes our thoughts are just as far as we perceive our current situation. We sometimes put our working life in the hands of others...what if we look a little further, perhaps within ourselves and ask the question, 'what do I really want from my working life,' instead of what is expected of me. I write in my book 'SELF=YOU' (SELF=YOU, (2017) Angela Scott, SELF=YOU, Chapter 4, Amazon) how I would work a night shift then drive to my day shift, get home at 2pm do all the things single mums do, sleep for five hours and get up to go to my night shift again, all under the guise of keeping a roof over my childrens' head.

Why wouldn't I ask for a better work life balance?
Why wouldn't I ask for enough to live the life of my dreams; instead of hoping, wishing and some times praying that another human being would pick me!
Pick me for that job.
Pick me for that raise or promotion.

We should pick ourselves. Its a pity that we don't know that we could have the life of our dreams if we only believe. I wouldn't want you to think that I don't believe in climbing the ladder of your chosen careers, however it is how you climb it that comes into question here. When all that is needed is for us to ask, do what you can to enter the field of your choice, get the qualifications, if needed, attend the interview, give the post 100% and expect to raise, but not by the hand of a boss. If you feel you deserve a raise ask for one, if you feel you deserve a promotion, ask for one.

Remember you entered that company as a prize, not just another face, body or number. If you feel like that, then that is not the company for you...I understand this type of attitude only comes after deep contemplation with ones self in-order to believe they are worth more than to be dangled on a piece of string, waiting for it to be let go or pulled in and knotted into the fibre of a company. Getting to know your worth is for another book, for now, know that you will be an asset to any company, you wish to grace with your services.

We have the money and the job, the book now turns to moving homes.

Wanting or needing to move home is often a bitter sweet experience. Take wanting a new bigger home for your family, you get through the ups and downs of packing up and moving in the knowledge that the new home will be just that, a new bigger home.

Having to leave and find a new home because of safety or financial issues isn't as welcoming as the stress endured by the family above wanting to move in-order to have a bigger space to live and grow.
We have established that moving is stressful and for most, the biggest expense they will encounter.

With all that said I can see how it could be challenging for many to let go and let God/the Universe sort it! It's not God/the Universe that may have to live next door to party people or people who have 4 or 5 dogs 3 cats and a parrot. It's not God/the Universe that has to pay the mortgage or rent. We know moving is stressful, but it doesn't have to be that way. What if I told you that I found, rented and moved into a house within a week, it is possible. I also bought a property and got the keys within 30 days, it can be done. But you have to leave it to God/the Universe, your wants and needs are known to God/the Universe.

I have moved too many times in my life, from buying, renting to getting evicted several times. I know better than to worry over who the neighbours are or how they may behave, in fact I have never considered the neighbours. Maybe because I had other considerations. Using the LOA to get you that new home, if used correctly will get you a home that you didn't think you could afford, in an area or country you could only have dreamt of.

Leaving it to God/the Universe will have you move with minimum stress, sounds like I am trying to sell the LOA, maybe I am because I know it works, as it has worked for me numerous times. Use the LOA the minute you decide to move home, know that you and your family will be catered for. The new home will be closer to work, schools, parks and shopping centres, if that is what you want. My last note here, consider the LOA as your Top Class Estate agent (Realtor) and God/the Universe will get you the right home, at the right cost, in the right neighbourhood at the right time.

Health concerns come to most of us, at one time or another, seeking Better Health is often thought about, many take action and enjoy the fruits of their labour, with a stronger healthy body, for others there is a need for medical assistance and for a few, the use of the LOA. Most wants in this book is regarding people, places, situations and things. The only two chapters that deal or enquire about wanting a bodily change is 'How Do I Get Better Health' and 'Can I Manifest for Someone else.' We all want to ensure we are healthy although we don't always eat, sleep and exercise the right amount. There are many reasons for the need for better health in this book, from genetic make up to being involved in an accident. Regardless of the reason for wanting a physical change to our body, believing you can get better is half the battle won.

There is no desire expressed in this book more closely aligned with the process of using the LOA than the desire for better health. Once someone acknowledges a physical issue and recognises the need for healing, they may seek medical advice - This is the Asking. Following the consultation, Belief comes into play, as the individual trusts that the prescribed medication or recommended action will help them heal or Receive a healthier body. Like with many blessings in life, once we receive better health, it's important that we maintain and care for it, less we risk losing it.

Being ill, under the weather, feeling sick or low, however you describe not feeling ones healthy self, has a bearing on how you present to the world around you. We see in the two parts of 'Negative Thoughts,' how people around you or your current circumstances can have a bearing on how you feel and can possibly, have you falling down a rabbit hole of doubt, frustration and down right low in your efforts to manifest.

Some of the enquirers had people around them that were naysayers, others had a 'friend' that complained everyday that they were "going to die or get cancer," there were others that were described as "allergic to good news," of course, there were people in some of the enquirers lives that were just out and out angry. Some were trying desperately to get away from them, and that would be the advise here. Keep them at arms length, this as we saw can be challenging, especially if you live with the person who is causing the ill feelings and having children to consider.

The question they all wanted answered is, how can you attempt to manifest with all this going on around them. Having sought out ways to distance yourself from the people who have decided to live in a woe is me bubble, one is to work on themselves and attempt to shake off, if you will, the cloak of doom and gloom. Working on ones self, in-order to rid themselves from negative thoughts can also be challenging.

These negative thoughts can come from trauma or mere doubt and fear. Some of the advise given was to seek medical attention if the negative thoughts intruded on their everyday activities to finding affirmations that is repeated every time a negative thought enters their head. Getting busy was also mentioned as a way of focusing their mind on other things.

Anger was also mentioned however, some enquirers felt that when they were angry, they appeared to manifest quickly! Enquirers and people they knew who equated Anger = Manifest Quickly was reminded that they all completed the basic steps of using the LOA in quick succession, thus ensuring a quick delivery of the wish made, which sometimes was not what they would have consciously desired.

In sticking with the use of LOA when feeling low or down, some enquirers complained of feeling stuck. They stated that they couldn't manifest or they could only manifest "the basics." After reminding the enquirers that we are always manifesting and one should be more aware of their speech regarding how they are currently feeling and what they would rather manifest. Having felt somewhat better or stronger, some enquirers begin to put the process of manifesting into practice only to find at times that everything begins to fall apart. This is what I call the breakdown or clearing out stage, one is to keep the faith and know that their wish is still on its way.

From time to time we may feel out of sorts or even low, it is at this time many of us want to heighten our vibration, some call it "getting into the feeling" or aligning with their want. Some wanted to know the degree they were vibrating on. The quickest way to align or get in the feeling of your want is to set about preparing or welcoming it, here your mind is focussed on your want, your vibration may become aligned with your want ushering it in to your reality.

Having manifested a want or two and proven the LOA, many attempt to manifest for a friend they feel may be struggling or they may want to make a wish come true for someone else. The issue with this, is we don't always know what that someone else truly wants. You may with all good intentions, believe that you will make another's life a little better or brighter, when the other person has deep rooted issues that require a medical professionals help or they just stated a want they felt you expected of them. There is also the fact that they don't really believe in the LOA, a factor to also consider when attempting to manifest for someone else.

It is important that both you and the person you intend to manifest for, want the same thing, believe and ask, failing this, manifesting for someone else can be challenging.

Now, I preach Law of Attraction, but I still get questions regarding 'Other Methods' to manifesting. I maintain that I feel that some other methods can be used or seen as an addition to use the LOA as I know whom grants the wishes, that is God and will not stray from that belief. The following chapter had enquirers 'Ask Me Anything,' and they do just that, from 'Is the LOA real' to 'How can I make someone prioritise me.' The questions really make for a good read!

As social beings, many of us naturally seek companionship and value the presence of others. It's common to want or need new friends, and building those connections often start with practical steps. Be the kind of person you'd like to meet and understand what you bring to the table in a new friendship.
Most people already have a clear idea of what they hope to gain from a friendship, but reflecting on what you offer helps create balanced, meaningful, and mutual relationships.

We then go from new friendships to ex's and how to get them back.
Much is written in this book about getting ones' ex back, and although many of us have been through this heart ache, it doesn't hurt any less when it happens again. Each heart break is a shock to the system. This chapter allows you to see the situations as it is presented to me, I do not mince words and after giving practical suggestions it always closes with 'Now it's time to care for you,' it is a time to grieve the relationship as well as the hopes and wishes that had been made in good faith, its a time to readjust your life without your ex partner in it. Some enquirers had children which also had to be factored in the grieving process as their lives had also erupted and a new 'norm' will have to be gently created.

Reading other people's woes, can sometimes allow you to appreciate your own life.

I hope everyone who reads this book learns something about themselves and discovers how to use the Law of Attraction to improve their lives, and positively impact those around them.

Hello Reader,

I am Dr. Angela Scott, I am passionate about helping those with mental health issues. Many people going through mental disorder just need someone to talk to. My work career has span over 30 years. I have been a psychologist for over 20 years, and the founder of Loveliveholistically which aims to offer that support . Based in the UK.

Many services close their phone lines at the end of the business day. Loveliveholistically aims to create a 24 hour phone line with qualified counsellors aiding callers with guidance and information. In order to keep this service running we need your help, as we are not funded by the government. Contact us to Donate.

The World Health Organization, state that One in four people in the world will be affected by mental or neurological disorders at some point in their lives. Around 450 million people currently suffer from such conditions, placing mental disorders among the leading causes of ill-health and disability worldwide. Contact us if you need to talk to someone today. Drscott@loveliveholistically.com

https://www.loveliveholistically.com/thoughts.php

NOTES:

196

NOTES:

NOTES:

198

NOTES:

www.ingramcontent.com/pod-product-compliance
Lightning Source LLC
Chambersburg PA
CBHW080018130626
46556CB00016B/3226